Eliminating Waste In Teaching

Timeless Lessons for Improving Teaching and Training

Insights from a Pioneering
Industrial Engineer

Dr. Lillian Moller Gilbreth
with
Dr. Bob Emiliani

Eliminating Waste In Teaching: Timeless Lessons for Improving Teaching and Training / Lillian Moller Gilbreth with Bob Emiliani

"Some Aspects of Eliminating Waste in Teaching," L.M. Gilbreth, Ph.D. dissertation, 1915 (OCLC 23524600), John Hay Library, Special Collections, Brown University, Providence, Rhode Island, USA. Copyright © Lillian Moller Gilbreth. Reproduced with the permission of the Carey family.

Cover art by Julia Emiliani.

Gilbreth Stopwatch reproduced with permission: Division of Work and Industry, National Museum of American History, Smithsonian Institution.

ISBN-13: 978-1-7320191-0-2

Library of Congress Control Number: 2019914414

1. Gilbreth, Lillian Moller (1879-1972) 2. Women Engineers
3. Teaching 4. Education 5. Training 6. Scientific Management
7. Lean Management

First Edition: October 2019 (09-20)

Published by Cubic LLC, South Kingstown, Rhode Island, USA

This publication provides accurate information with respect to the subject matter covered. It is sold with the understanding that it does not in any way represent legal, financial, business, consulting, or other professional service.

Lillian Evelyn Moller Gilbreth (1878-1972). Photo circa 1930.
Smithsonian Institution Archives, Accession 90-105, Image #SIA2008-1924

"[Scientific Management] will make the most progress in the shortest time in the school room when it is understood to be a result of an efficient social spirit."

– Lillian Moller Gilbreth

CONTENTS

Some Aspects of Eliminating Waste in Teaching

"…the proper understanding of and development of the human element is the great factor in efficient management, and that teaching is a most important element in establishing correlation between the industries and the schools."

– Lillian Moller Gilbreth

PREFACE

On a warm and sunny August morning, I drove from my home in southern Rhode Island to my alma mater, Brown University ('88 Ph.D.), to visit the John Hay Library in Providence. I had made a request to view Lillian Moller Gilbreth's 1915 doctoral dissertation, titled "Some Aspects of Eliminating Waste in Teaching," which, surprisingly, virtually nobody knows about. Unlike her other major works, Dr. Gilbreth's doctoral dissertation was unpublished. As I sat in the Special Collections section of the John Hay Library, I was amazed at what I read. Her doctoral dissertation was a penetrating analysis of teaching that remains relevant today. After thinking about it for a few days, I decided that I had to revive this important work and present it to today's audience.

The audience includes teachers (K-12 and higher education), educational administrators, education policy makers (local, state, and federal government), trainers (whether corporate or consultants), and even those are curious to know why they did not like school or why they did poorly in school. It also includes people who are interested in methods of waste elimination generally, and specifically the methods in use prior to the creation of Toyota's progressive management system, or its derivative, Lean management, and those interested in the history of Lillian Gilbreth and industrial engineering.

I have a personal connection to Dr. Gilbreth's work, and hence my great interest in it and to revive this work. I had the good fortune of being trained in Toyota's production system starting in 1994 when I was a business unit manager at Pratt and Whitney. What I learned from Shingijutsu consultants and from my participation in kaizen was both mind- and life-altering. I subsequently became a student of Toyota's management system and Lean. In Fall 1999 I left my employer and joined academia full-time as a professor.

In addition to establishing a research agenda in Lean leadership, I sought to apply what I learned in industry about waste elimination to teaching. I was motivated to do this because I was, overall, unhappy with how I was taught, and thought I could, and must, do better, because students deserve the best continuous effort to improve teaching that a teacher can offer.

To do this, I had to break with many traditions that form the mindset and methods of teaching. Fortunately, in U.S. higher education, faculty have great autonomy over the teaching methods used. That allowed me to experiment continuously such that my courses were never exactly the same from semester-to-semester. And I have been happy to make such changes, usually during the semester, to help assure improved student learning outcomes. The ability to freely experiment and make adjustments based upon both results and feedback, is, for me, one of the true joys of teaching.

Sadly, however, my enthusiasm for improving teaching is not widely shared. It seems most teachers prefer to teach the way they were taught, through observing their own teachers in the past or from feedback given by peer faculty after assessing their teaching. Dr. Gilbreth's doctoral dissertation may help overcome these archaic traditions. Readers will recognize her outstanding observation skills, penetrating insights, and simple recommendations for improvement that were the same as that found in companies that adopted Scientific Management in the early 1900s (Taylor, 1911; Cooke, 1913; Gilbreth, 1914; Gilbreth, 1914a).

Some people, perhaps many, will say, "The past is irrelevant" or "Best practices from the past have been incorporated into our present practice" Neither is true. Dr. Gilbreth's dissertation will quickly show that teaching problems which existed in 1915 remain with us today, and that many "best practices" from the past have not been incorporated into present practice. Instead, what we have in this and other important areas of human endeavor such as business, is the retention of archaic traditions that do not serve the needs of the people in the times in which they live. As Dr. Gilbreth would say, "It is an enormous waste."

The consequences of the continuation of archaic traditions can be severe, given that so much time, effort, and money have been put into educating people at all levels for the last 100 years. A poor education, or one which is so annoying that it shuts down learning after graduation, or one which results in high rates of incompletion, produces a poorly educated citizenry who will be unable to judiciously fulfill their varied roles and responsibilities in society. This introduces risks to society that will undoubtedly be much more costly than it would have been, then or now, to improve education in ways described by Dr. Gilbreth.

But, unfortunately, Dr. Gilbreth's doctoral dissertation went unpublished, and so her great work and improvement ideas gained no attention since 1915 – until now. It is my hope that this book acquires a following among improvement-minded people in teaching and related disciplines. I also hope that the traditionalists who read this book will comprehend its manifold opportunities for better educational methods and outcomes, as well as opportunities to reduce the costs of education and administration.

We are now at the start of digitizing myriad processes, including learning processes. It might seem that improving analog teaching is not something one should bother with. Yet, analog teaching will surely be with us for many decades to come – whether in K-12, undergraduate, or graduate education, corporate education, corporate training, or consulting – and so there is a need to be attentive to teaching problems so that improvements can be made.

When we talk of improvement, the timescale for making improvements is typically missing. People are then left to assume whatever time they think it might take to complete the process of making an improvement. Generally, they assume improvement takes a long time, and so people proceed very slowly in their efforts to make improvements. Yet conditions change daily, and therefore improvement must more-or-less keep pace with that. If it does not, then the great mismatch in time between changing conditions and improvement assures the status quo whether it is intended or not.

In all progressive forms of management – Scientific Management, Toyota management, and Lean management – improvements are made quickly. If you think an improvement will take a month, challenge yourself and your team to do it in three days. If you think an improvement will take a week, do it in four hours. In most cases, the actual time needed to make an improvement is a small fraction of the estimated time. But you will not know this if you choose to remain traditionbound. The point of improvement is to break with preconceptions and traditions, and do so decisively, to achieve results that are so much better that returning to the old way of doing things is undesirable.

Dr. Gilbreth's doctoral dissertation presents the facts and the sound logic of "change for the better." But facts and logic alone do not move people, especially leaders, to abandon their preconceptions and traditions. (Emiliani, 2018). It may be up to individuals at lower levels, the teachers, to engage in continuous improvement despite the many obstacles that administrators place in front of them. There are moral and ethical dimensions to teaching that transcend the need for the perpetuation of unnecessary and ineffective traditions in education.

The past is ever-present, helping to maintain the status quo, and yet the need for change is also ever-present. This constant tension is not easily resolved, but effort must be made to resolve it, and those efforts must produce strategies and tactics that lead to needed changes. Dr. Gilbreth's analyses and prescriptions are practical and doable. There is nothing in her work that one can characterize as theoretical in the sense that it is impractical or unproven.

I found Dr. Gilbreth's dissertation to be a wonderful and entertaining read, marvelling the depth of her insights and her unceremonious exposing of the truth. I found a deep alignment with her thinking and I know others will too. The question is, will you take concrete action to improve teaching, whether teacher, administrator, or policy maker? Will you succumb to the barriers or will you transcend them?

I hope you enjoy this book. Its production would not be possible without the help of many people. I would like to thank Karen Eberhart and Jennifer Betts of the John Hay Library, Special Collections, at Brown University for their assistance. I also thank Dr. Valerie Maier-Speredelozzi, Associate Professor of Industrial and Systems Engineering, and Karen Morse, archivist, both with the University of Rhode Island, and Kay Peterson of the Smithsonian Institution. Special thanks to Charles E. Carey Jr., grandson of Dr. Lillian Gilbreth, and the Carey family for permission to publish Dr. Gilbreth's doctoral dissertation. It is because of their generosity that we now have a new and fascinating avenue to learn even more about the brilliance of Dr. Lillian Moller Gilbreth.

Bob Emiliani, Ph.D.
South Kingstown, Rhode Island
October 2019

References

Cooke, M. (1913), "The Spirit and Social Significance of Scientific Management," *The Journal of Political Economy*, Vol. 21, No. 6, pp. 481-493, June

Emiliani, B. (2018), *The Triumph of Classical Management Over Lean Management: How Tradition Prevails and What to Do About It*, Cubic, LLC, South Kingstown, RI

Gilbreth, F.B. (1914), *Primer of Scientific Management*, D. Van Nostrand Co., New York, NY

Gilbreth, L.M. (1914a), *The Psychology of Management*, Sturgis and Walton Co., New York, NY

Taylor, F.W. (1911), *Principles of Scientific Management*, Harper and Brothers, New York, NY

FOREWORD

Dr. Lillian Gilbreth was a person of enormous achievement. She lived in a time when it was very difficult for women to do the things that she did. Yet she managed to overcome the many obstacles that came her way, and through it all she maintained a bright and positive outlook. Her life and work have been well documented elsewhere (Lancaster, 2004). What follows is a brief outline of her early life and time in Providence, Rhode Island, where she conducted the research for her doctoral dissertation while studying at Brown University.

Lillie (later, Lillian) Evelyn Moller was born on 24 May 1878, in Oakland California, the second of eleven children. She was home schooled until age nine and then entered the public school system. Upon completing high school, she enrolled in the University of California, Berkeley, and completed a Bachelor of Arts degree in English literature in 1900, followed by a Master of Arts degree in English literature, also from the University of California, Berkeley in 1902. She then enrolled in a Ph.D. program at the University of California, Berkeley, to study psychology in relation to management.

On 19 October 1904, she married Frank Bunker Gilbreth, then age 36, a former bricklayer and successful owner of a construction contracting company, which resulted in a relocation to New York and the start of childbearing. She had six children between the years 1905 to 1912. She completed her doctoral dissertation in psychology, and it was accepted by her dissertation advisors. But, because of relocation to New York, travel, her work on motion study, fatigue study, and Scientific Management in partnership with her husband Frank, and the children, she was unable to complete the final year of residency in Berkeley as was required for the Ph.D. program. The faculty would not grant her a waiver (Gilbreth, 1998), and so the university did not award the doctoral degree to her.

Most graduate students would have been crushed by this outcome and moved on from graduate studies to other interests. But apparently this was nothing more than a small setback for Lillian. Her dissertation was circulated among publishers and rejected because it was "ahead of its time" and "likely to interest only a few readers" (Gilbreth, 1926) – meaning, nobody would publish a book written by a woman (Gilbreth, 1998). Frank finally found a publisher and her dissertation was published in book form as *The Psychology of Management* (Gilbreth, 1914), but with only her first two initials so as not to make it apparent that a woman wrote the book (Gilbreth 1998). "This disturbed feminist Frank more than it did Lillian" (Gilbreth, 1998).

THE PSYCHOLOGY
OF
MANAGEMENT

The Function of the Mind in Determining,
Teaching and Installing Methods
of Least Waste

BY

L. M. GILBRETH, Ph.D.

Title page of Lillian Gilbreth's book, based on her University of California, Berkeley, doctoral dissertation.

Lillian moved forward with family, giving birth to six more children between the years 1914 and 1922, and her innovative work on Scientific Management. Lillian Gilbreth came to Providence, Rhode Island, in May 1912. Frank had started a management consulting business and was hired by the New England Butt Company as a consultant to improve efficiency (Lancaster, 1997, 2004). The company, located in the Elmwood section Providence, Rhode Island, was originally a maker of cast iron butt hinges, and transitioned to braiding machinery in the 1880s when cheaper stamped hinges came onto the market.

Frank Gilbreth was educated in a Boston technical high school, and, like many men of that era, became an engineer through the professional practice of technical work in the trades and allied fields. Both he and Lillian became prominent in the field of Scientific Management, having devised many methods for improving the efficiency of both office and manufacturing shop processes. Frank and Lillian worked together and had a particular focus on work simplification and motion and fatigue studies. Both were active members of the American Society of Mechanical Engineers, the professional organization that became the birthplace of modern progressive management (Towne, 1886; Taylor, 1895, 1903).

Both Frank and Lillian were pioneers of the emerging field of industrial engineering, known prior to 1911 as "industrial management." The shift to the term "industrial engineering" was fitting because of the technical nature of waste elimination, which required careful observation, measurement, and analysis, in addition to psychology and human relations which Lillian Gilbreth pioneered. The field of industrial engineering was soon formalized into undergraduate and graduate education in support of the growing needs of industry, though the focus of the curriculum would become more technical in nature after World War II.

The Gilbreth's detailed written descriptions of Scientific Management were among the best ever written (Gilbreth, 1914; Gilbreth, 1914a), and further humanized the quest for efficiency ("betterment" as it was also then referred to) in industry. Frederick Winslow Taylor's best description of Scientific Management came in 1912 in his testimony to Congress, which took place due to the controversies surrounding the improper "installation" of Scientific Management by company managers, for which Taylor has nothing to do with but was blamed for (Taylor, 1947). Taylor's colleague, Morris Cook, wrote a wonderful paper which helped people better understand the human element and social significance of Scientific Management (Cooke, 1913). These works show a clear lineage between Scientific Management and an innovation 60 years later, the Toyota production system, codified in 2001 as "The Toyota Way," whose two pillars are "Continuous Improvement" and "Respect for People" (Toyota, 2001). A Toyota consultant, Shigeo Shingo, admired the work of Frank and Lillian Gilbreth and began using their "tabletop improvement experiments" in his training course for Toyota engineers and shop workers from the mid-1950s through mid-1970s (Robinson and Robinson, 1994).

Frank Gilbreth's work at the New England Butt Company was successful. He was effective in engaging both workers and managers. His work to improve efficiency started with office work, which signaled to factory workers that they were not alone in the need to perform work more efficiently. Importantly, Gilbreth had respect for workers and their knowledge, which aided his recruiting workers for motion studies and his efforts to eliminate waste and improve efficiency throughout the company. The Gilbreth's more humanized approached to Scientific Management was an evolution from Taylor's view of workers, even though Taylor himself had started his career as a patternmaker and machinist (Copley, 1923).

The move to Providence proved to be beneficial to Frank, whose successful work at the New England Butt Company led to many other clients, and Lillian too, as she could "see [his] initial work from day to day" (Gilbreth, 1926). The family lived in half of a house on 71 Brown street, later moving to 77 Brown Street as the family grew larger (Gilbreth, 1998). Their home was a block or so away from Brown University "which, upon investigation, had proved cooperative in the plan of her taking the last year of attendance for her doctorate there and obtaining the necessary last word information on education and psychology" (Gilbreth, 1926). She began her studies in the fall of 1913 while pregnant with her seventh child, Lillian M. Gilbreth Jr.

Interestingly, the Gilbreths set up a laboratory in their home to develop new techniques in motion and micro-motion study using innovative new equipment designed by Frank, such as the stereo chronocyclegraph. Laboratories were also established in the companies where Frank did extensive management consulting work and asked workmen, whom he considered "investigators," to volunteer to participate in motion studies and help discover the "one best way" to do a task (Lancaster, 1997). The new equipment was also used to understand the motion of sports activities such as the golf (swing), track (running), baseball (pitch and batting), and football (throwing), as well as medical procedures (surgery), and work within the home (Gilbreth, 1998). It was a time of great discovery and learning. Frank and Lillian's work, appearing in books, technical journals, trade publications, and newspapers, soon became highly regarded in both America and abroad. Scientific Management was especially popular in Japan (Tsutsui, 1998; Lancaster, 2004).

Lillian was a Ph.D. candidate in the departments of education and psychology. She said she "spent there the happiest years" and exclaimed "And the days of visiting schools!" as work that she loved to do (Gilbreth, 1926). She clearly enjoyed the nexus of academic and industrial work in relation to the sciences of management and psychology. Lillian studied psychology under Dr. Edmund Delebarre, education with Professor Walter Jacobs, education psychology under Dr. Stephen Colvin, and mentored by Brown University President Dr. William Faunce and Dean Carl Barus in her academic work.

According to Lillian, "The work at Brown University progressed slowly, but satisfactorily, for the real purpose was not the 'Ph.D.' which was the ultimate result, but the constant feeding of new material – in the areas of psychology, education, and personnel – into the data to be used on the [management consulting] jobs" (Gilbreth, 1998). Her Ph.D. research, as is often the case, had a practical bent, as both

Frank and Lillian clearly recognized the critical importance of continuous education and training – continuous learning – in the successful "installation" of Scientific Management in industry. That is because progressive management goes against the voluminous, centuries-old traditions that define the ubiquitous classical management practice (Emiliani, 2018). So, in progressive management, education and training of managers and workers never ends due to continuous changes in business and the discovery of new ideas and improved methods. The need for continuous learning is well-recognized in both Toyota and Lean management practice.

To educate others about Scientific Management, the Gilbreth's found time to hold "Summer School in Scientific Management" at 26 Cabot Street in August for three years from 1915 to 1917. Attendees included academics (economists, psychologists, engineers), physicians (surgeons, pathologists, psychiatrists), and others where they learned the latest work in industrial management, motion studies, fatigue studies, and included visits to area companies where Frank had consulted – e.g. New England Butt Company (Gilbreth, 1926, 1998).

Lillian wrote her doctoral dissertation, "Some Aspects of Eliminating Waste in Teaching," from April to June 1915, which means the bulk of her research was conducted in 1914. In addition to that ambitious work, Lillian Gilbreth was also seeing to the publication of her University of California, Berkeley, dissertation as a book, *The Psychology of Management* (1914), as well the book *Primer of Scientific Management* (1914) authored by her husband Frank, but written mostly, if not entirely, by Lillian (see the note under the heading "Major Works by Frank Bunker Gilbreth and Lillian Gilbreth," page xxii). She was obviously extremely busy with work-related matters in the years 1912 and 1915. But that was not all. She also managed a household with six children, ages one to nine years, and was pregnant with her eighth child (who was stillborn on 13 September 1915). While Lillian had household help from relatives, college students, and others (Lancaster, 2004), it remains a most impressive example of work-life balance, organization, and efficiency in pursuit of a range of important life goals, as well as the betterment of industrial management practice – not just in the United States, but all over the world.

Lillian described the final stage of her Ph.D. studies as follows (Gilbreth, 1998): "The ordeal of the year was taking the oral examination for her Doctorate, after having had the thesis accepted, and no detail of the experience was ever forgotten. It was a rainy day; Frank was in Europe; she sat for long hours answering questions; was so nervous that her definition of psychology offended one of the examiners, who barked out, 'So you have become a behaviorist, have you?'; had no notion of how she was progressing, and when the committee filed out to discuss what she had done, and polled their votes, felt sure that she had failed. When kind Dean Barris [sic] led the procession back and said, 'I am pleased to announce,' she never heard the end of the sentence, for she was convinced that he would only have been pleased had she passed! She ran home happily through the rain to cable Frank, and tried to explain to the children why she was excited, and what a 'Ph.D.' meant."

The Gilbreths were among those at the very center of the Scientific Management movement and interacted with other movement leaders such as Frederick Winslow Taylor, Morris Cooke, Henry Gantt, Carl Barth, C. Bertrand Thompson, Horace Hathaway, and, of course, Harlow S. Person who worked tirelessly to keep the movement alive and thriving until his passing in 1955. Some friction developed between the Taylorites and the Gilbreths owing to differences in the methods of "installation" of Scientific Management in companies which resulted in the withholding of certain resources sought by Frank Gilbreth (Gilbreth, 1926, 1998; Lancaster, 1997). The Taylorites being, more rigid in their approach, had concerns about the

Gilbreth's more flexible approach to installation, which incorporated Lillian's work on human psychology and workers' welfare – "betterment" of workers' environment. Time would soon prove the Gilbreth's correct on this important point, as the subsequent system of progressive management created by Toyota would evolve to incorporate many of Lillian's ideas.

More importantly, their work resulted in interaction with leaders of hundreds of companies in industries ranging from manufacturing to healthcare, as well as with academics studying and teaching Scientific Management and industrial engineering, including Henry Farquhar, Dexter Kimball, Hugo Diemer, Ralph Barnes, Charles Going, and many others. Within a decade after its inception, the Scientific Management movement had such great influence that it gained a foothold in U.S. politics and federal government policy – a feat not replicated by Lean management.

The Gilbreths continued their work and raising their children. Frank was often away on travel consulting with dozens of prominent companies worldwide. As Lillian recounted, "Almost from the beginning of motion study the work of fatigue study had gone side by side with it, and it proved a most profitable one. It was welcome in the plant, for it was a noncontroversial work that enlisted the attention and cooperation of employer and employee alike, that undertook problems of common interest, in noncontroversial fields, and showed results profitable to everyone" (Gilbreth, 1926).

Frank suffered serious illnesses in 1918 while serving as a Major in the U.S. Army during World War I, but he recovered after a long period of convalescence. In 1920, the Gilbreths relocated to Montclair, New Jersey so that Frank could be closer to then-epicenter of engineering, New York City, and reduce his travel. Frank Gilbreth continued his work until on 14 June 1924, when he died unexpectedly at the age of

55. Lillian then took on the twin challenge of working full-time and continuing to raise her eleven children. At the end of her book about Frank's life and times, Lillian said (Gilbreth, 1926): "The proof of the value of the experiment [the quest of the one best way], the real outcome of such a Quest, will be its effect upon future generations."

The proof of the value of today's experiment, Lean management, will also be its effect on future generations. "The Quest goes on!"

In 1962, the University of Rhode Island in Kingston, Rhode Island, named its College of Engineering building "Gilbreth Hall" in honor of Frank and Lillian Gilbreth.

Dedication of Gilbreth Hall on 26 May 1962. Lillian Gilbreth with
T. Stephen Crawford (left), Dean of the College of Engineering, Dr. Lillian Gilbreth, and Dr. D. Edward Nichols, Chair of the Industrial Engineering department. Gilbreth Hall was torn down in 2017 to make room for the new and much larger Fascitelli Center for Advanced Engineering building.
Courtesy of the University Archives, University of Rhode Island Library.

Lillian Gilbreth worked until age 90. She passed away on 2 January 1972 in Phoenix, Arizona, at age 93, and was survived by 10 of her 12 children. The last of her surviving children, Frederick W. Gilbreth passed away in 2015 at age 99. Lillian Gilbreth's work in psychology, management, and engineering was widely recognized as groundbreaking. She was a member of more than two dozen technical organizations and received 23 honorary degrees and 26 medals and awards (Gilbreth, 1998). Her legacy includes the issuance of a stamp by the United States Postal Service on 24 February 1984, as part of the "Great Americans" series; The Institute of Industrial and Systems Engineers "highest and most esteemed honor," the Frank and Lillian Gilbreth Industrial Engineering Award; and the Society of Women Engineers' Lillian Moller Gilbreth Memorial Scholarship (established in 1958) for junior- and senior-level undergraduates.

Lillian Gilbreth honored in the United States Postal Service's "Great American" stamp series.

Dr. Lillian Moller Gilbreth was remarkable person whose remarkable work left a remarkable legacy that we must continue to learn from.

References

Cooke, M. (1913), "The Spirit and Social Significance of Scientific Management," The Journal of Political Economy, Vol. 21, No. 6, pp. 481-493, June

Copley, F. B. (1923), *Frederick W. Taylor: Father of Scientific Management*, Harper and Brothers, New York, NY

Emiliani, B. (2018), *The Triumph of Classical Management Over Lean Management: How Tradition Prevails and What to Do About It*, Cubic, LLC, South Kingstown, RI

Gilbreth, F.B. (1914), *Primer of Scientific Management*, D. Van Nostrand Co., New York, NY

Gilbreth, L.M. (1914a), *The Psychology of Management*, Sturgis and Walton Co., New York, NY

Gilbreth, L.M. (1926), *The Quest of the One Best Way: A Sketch of the Life of Frank Bunker Gilbreth*, Society of Women Engineers, New York, NY

Gilbreth, L.M. (1998), *As I Remember: An Autobiography by Lillian Gilbreth*, Engineering & Management Press, Norcross, GA

Lancaster, J. (1997), "Frank and Lillian Gilbreth Bring Order to Providence: The Introduction of Scientific Management at the New England Butt Company, 1912-1913," *Rhode Island History*, Vol. 55, No. 2, May, Rhode Island Historical Society, Providence, RI

Lancaster, J. (2004), *Making Time: Lillian Moller Gilbreth – A Life Beyond "Cheaper by the Dozen,"* Northeastern University Press, Lebanon, NH

Robinson, A. and Robinson, M. (1994), "On the Tabletop Improvement Experiments of Japan," *Production and Operations Management*, Vol. 3, No. 3, pp. 201-216

Taylor, F. W. (1895), "A Piece-Rate System," *ASME Transactions*, Vol. 16, pp. 856-903

Taylor, F.W. (1903), "Shop Management," *ASME Transactions*, Volume 24, pp. 1337-1480

Taylor, F. W. (1947), *Scientific Management: Comprising Shop Management, Scientific Management, Testimony Before the Special House Committee*, H. S. Person, Ed., Harper and Row Publishers, New York, NY (*Testimony* was originally published in 1912).

Towne, H. (1886), "The Engineer as an Economist," *ASME Transactions*, Vol. 7, pp. 428-432

Toyota (2001), "The Toyota Way 2001," Toyota Motor Corporation, internal document, Toyota City (Nagoya), Japan, April

Tsutsui, W. (1998), *Manufacturing Ideology: Scientific Management in Twentieth-Century Japan*, Princeton University Press, Princeton, NJ

Major Works by Frank Bunker Gilbreth and Lillian Gilbreth

According to Jane Lancaster in *Making Time* (pp. 164-165), Frank and Lillian always wrote in collaboration, but her name did not appear on the title page of Frank's books until after she earned her Ph.D. from Brown University.

Gilbreth, F.B. (1908), *Field System*, The Myron C. Clark Publishing Co., New York, NY

Gilbreth, F.B. (1908), *Concrete System*, The Engineering News Publishing Company, New York, NY

Gilbreth, F.B. (1909), *Bricklaying System*, The Myron C. Clark Publishing Co., New York, NY

Gilbreth, F.B. (1911), *Motion Study: A Method for Increasing the Efficiency of the Workman*, D. Van Nostrand Company, New York, NY

Gilbreth, F.B. (1912), *Primer of Scientific Management*, D. Van Nostrand Company, New York, NY

Gilbreth, L.M. (1914), *The Psychology of Management*, Sturgis and Walton Co., New York, NY

Gilbreth, F.B. and Gilbreth, L.M. (1916), *Fatigue Study: The Elimination of Humanity's Greatest Unnecessary Waste: A First Step in Motion Study*, Sturgis & Walton Company, New York, NY

Gilbreth, F.B. and Gilbreth, L.M. (1917), *Applied Motion Study: A Collection of Papers on the Efficient Method to Industrial Preparedness*, Sturgis & Walton Company, New York, NY

Gilbreth, F.B. and Gilbreth, L.M. (1920), *Motion Study for the Handicapped*, The MacMillan Company, New York, NY

Dr. Lillian Moller Gilbreth on YouTube

"Lillian Gilbreth: First Lady of Engineering," Purdue University Industrial Engineering, 16 March 2018, https://youtu.be/_9RlfBdLvE8

"Frank and Lillian Gilbreth Original Films," Axbom Innovation AB, 11 May 2014, https://www.youtube.com/watch?v=9fQJfap7SAQ

Audio of Lillian Gilbreth

"Interview with Dr. Lillian Gilbreth," WBAA Radio, Purdue University, 17 November 2011, https://www.wbaa.org/post/interview-dr-lillian-gilbreth#stream/0

INTRODUCTION

The subject of Dr. Gilbreth's dissertation is eliminating waste in the various processes associated with teaching students in a school classroom or laboratory setting. While the focus of Dr. Gilbreth's dissertation is primary school teaching, her observations, analyses, and recommendations are equally applicable to teaching in secondary schools and in higher education. Her findings are also applicable to teaching and training in industry, including coaching and mentoring. Lillian Gilbreth's work in fields of human psychology and Scientific Management emphasized individualism; to understand the person and their response to various human interactions, work assignments, and environmental conditions. From this, one could more clearly observe and understand reactions of the group. Scientifically understanding the individual and group through controlled experiments in teaching methods, one can then surmise students' sentiments, their attitudes and feelings, and measure learning outcomes for each student and the class.

In her dissertation, Dr. Gilbreth successfully bridges gaps between practices in industry and practices in teaching – managers' interactions with workers and teacher's interactions with students. She shows how the lessons learned from the "installation" of Scientific Management in industry (the "plants") to improve work productivity while reducing burdens on workers can be applied to teaching. This is a subject that has interested me for two decades, and, unknown to me until recently, I have been following in her footsteps. Upon leaving industry in 1999, I worked to develop a new teaching pedagogy in higher education based upon the principles and practices of Toyota's production system (Emiliani, 2004, 2005, 2015). It is called "Lean Teaching." Teachers in K-12 education who have read my work say they have the same problems, and the solutions I have identified will work for them as well. Dr. Gilbreth's work, as well as my recent work developing the Lean teaching pedagogy, show, beyond doubt, that eliminating waste in teaching produces better results for teachers and students compared to existing methods. The question is, will teachers, administrators, and policymakers challenge their preconceptions and abandon archaic traditions that have largely killed the spirit of discovery and learning for both them and for students?

For many years, people have been saying how public primary and secondary school education is in crisis, as is higher education (particularly the cost of tuition and learning outcomes). The focus of their attention is invariably things such as budgets, dollars spent per pupil, technology in the classroom, student focus, task discipline, testing students' knowledge, teacher and administrator accountability, and so on. However, there is never any discussion of teaching processes and how they can be improved to achieve better learning outcomes, higher quality, and lower costs to schools and society. In other words, how to improve the efficiency of teachers in instruction and students in learning.

I expect many people will balk at Dr. Gilbreth's comparisons of manufacturing plants in industry to schools – which are merely a different type of plant; a producer of educated human beings. Resistance will come most strongly from people who have made a career of working in education and have no experience or understanding of industry. In my case, I have experience in both and can attest to the fact that there are more similarities than differences.

Resistance will also come from those who say the profit motive in industry and methods used in service of the profit motive must not be adopted in education because education is for the common good and has no profit motive. To that I say, "We need to have a closer look this." Let's first separate industry practices that are zero-sum (win-lose) in service of the profit motive, and those that are non-zero-sum (win win). Cast aside the zero-sum practices – which don't work that well in industry because they produce an illusion of success and generate much antagonism – and carefully examine, with an open mind, the non-zero-sum practices that some in industry use. Progressive systems of management, beginning with early 20th century Scientific Management and evolving through to early 21st century Lean management have in mind the same thing: non-zero-sum outcomes. They have as their philosophical foundation the desire to produce better outcomes without doing harm to any stakeholder. This may seem like idealism to many who are unfamiliar with the mindset and methods of Scientific Management and Lean management. But it is not idealism because the fundamental feature of progressive management, whether it is applied to industry, healthcare, schools, or other organizations, is to eliminate waste, which is produced continuously and boundlessly by locally optimizing work and by zero-sum outcomes. That is what makes Scientific Management and Lean management progressive; they stop doing the things that harm people and make work easier.

It is important to recognize what win-win means in the so-called "real word." We characterize it as follows: one might not win as much as they would like, but they will not lose as much as they could. In progressive management practice, effort is made to avoid zero-sum outcomes. They are rare in occurrence, viewed as a mistake to avoid in the future, and trigger efforts to make amends; to restore balance in the relationship. Zero-sum outcomes are undesirable because they inhibit cooperation and teamwork – the "social spirit" as Dr. Gilbreth calls it – and consume greater amounts of all resources. It is thus undesirable. We would all be much happier at work and find our work more meaningful, easier to do, and produce better results if progressive management were the norm, but it is not.

Because progressive management is not the norm, we have to learn new things and think differently if we seek to create a better world in companies, schools, or any other organization. Our focus here, of course, is schools, and to experiment with new teaching methods based on progressive management thinking and practices, to make work less taxing for teachers and produce better outcomes for students. Teachers generally have students' best interests in mind, but their ability to make improvements in teaching methods may be constrained by education administrators, policies, state and federal laws, and so on. Some of those constrains can be quickly eliminated, while some cannot be eliminated at the present time. Traditions often stand in the way of progress. However, nothing will change unless effort is made to change policies, laws, etc., to allow needed progress to take place when it is needed, where it is needed, and in the amount needed. Anyone can cite a thousand barriers to change and the need to keep things as they are. But improvement does not come from the status quo. It comes from breaking the status quo. Dr. Gilbreth took pleasure in doing this, as do I, and so might you.

Why should we risk breaking the status quo? We are all former students. At any stage of our education – elementary school, middle school, high school, college, or graduate school – we have, in our individual judgment, encountered a few admirable teachers and many average and inferior teachers. Our regard for them in their work as teachers is almost entirely the result of the methods they used in teaching, the reasonableness or sensibility of the tasks assigned, their basic disposition towards students, their responsiveness, and their adaptability to class and individual student needs. Whether a teacher is admirable or not, these and many other aspects of teaching can be improved – and they must be improved as times change.

In her dissertation, Dr. Gilbreth often speaks the need for, and importance of, efficiency. Many people will not like the word "efficiency" in the context of education. I suggest it is a word that one should rank higher in preference than other words that are often used to describe teaching such as "difficult," "frustrating," or "stressful." You likely think efficiency means speeding people up, burning people out, de-skilling and dehumanizing people, and taking away one's knowledge and creativity. You may also think of it as "dull work" or a "drudgery." The image of a factory worker struggling to keep up the fast-moving assembly line likely comes to mind, and, worst of all, losing one's job due to the incessant drive for higher labor efficiency. Dr. Gilbreth's understanding of efficiency and meaning of efficiency are the opposite. She means "easier" and "pleasant," "exciting work" and "fun;" to experiment and try new things. No speeding up, no burning out. She means humanizing, up-skilling, allowing creative thinking to flourish in search of new ideas for improvement, and job security. She means making the work less of a struggle for both teacher and student, and much more effective.

It is never efficiency for efficiency's sake; it is never efficiency trading off against human well-being. It is always an improvement in efficiency with a concurrent improvement in the human condition and an elevation of the "social spirit." The foundational philosophy that enables improvement – continuous improvement in one's work – is "respect for people." It is a simple relationship, one that most managers and school administrators get wrong. They mistakenly believe that continuous improvement can occur in the absence of "respect for people." Unfortunately, the bad habit of managers in any organization engaged in the common management practice, classical management, is to disrespect people and dehumanize them and their work. People will not willingly participate in improvement of their work if it will cause them harm. Lillian Gilbreth's work was groundbreaking because she showed how to humanize efficiency and gain management and worker participation in process improvement. Progressive management must do no harm.

Improving work always means to simplify work and make it easier and less of a burden, and to complete the task in less time. However, simplifying work is not easy because work has been made very complicated, and made more complicated as time passes due to the addition of ever-expanding requirements. But with the new thinking and practices such as Dr. Gilbreth describes, and which exist today in the form of Lean management, there are wonderful processes that engage people and their creative capabilities to find ways to simplify the work. Done correctly, making the work easier also results in the production of a better product. In education, that means better teaching methods and students who have learned more and who can think and do more based on what they have learned.

This is the necessary background that readers need to understand Lillian Gilbreth's basic way of thinking as she studies teaching during her dissertation research and draws upon her knowledge of Scientific Management for ideas that will improve teaching. Interested readers are encouraged to learn more about Scientific Management by reading two other works by Frank and Lillian Gilbreth: *Primer of Scientific Management* (Gilbreth, 1912) and T*he Psychology of Management* (Gilbreth, 1914), as well as current-day progressive Lean management applied to teaching (Emiliani, 2015) and administration (Emiliani, 2015a).

What follows is a brief introduction to the two major sections of Dr. Gilbreth's doctoral dissertation. My goal is to prepare the reader and explain the relevance of each section, written in 1915, to the problems and needs of today. Please note that I made only two changes to the original document as it pertains to formatting: 1) paragraph indents have been eliminated and 2) line spacing was changed from double-space to a spacing of 1.15. Otherwise, I have preserved the formatting, syntax, grammar, and punctuation as they appear in the original document because it reflects the style of academic writing at the time. It includes a few misspellings as written, though not indicated by the usual "[sic]." This is consistent with my objective in reproducing her thesis, which is for readers to learn better ways of thinking about teaching and better methods of teaching – not to correct or critique Dr. Gilbreth's brilliant work. Despite being more than 100 years old, the dissertation is written in a very reader-friendly way that today's readers will surely enjoy and stimulate many new ideas.

A note of caution: People tend to judge work written long ago through the lens of the times in which they live. It is a mistake judge or criticize Lillian Gilbreth or her work for not thinking as we do today. Her work reflects the thinking and practices of the early 1900s, of which there is still much to learn from. Today, we think and do some things differently because we have different or better understanding of the problems or because times have changed. Alternatively, we think and do some things in old, inefficient, and ineffective ways because we are easily bound by tradition. The challenge for readers is to learn what was done then, compare it to now and in relation to the ever-present need to eliminate waste in teaching, and then apply the learning.

The Brown University Doctoral Dissertation

Preface

The overall purpose of Lillian Gilbreth's *second* doctoral dissertation was to analyze "the correlation between education in the industries and in the schools… and to work out a method by which successful practice in the industries might be applied in the schools." With her background in psychology learned while pursuing her *first* doctoral dissertation at the University of California, Berkeley, her personal observations of teaching while a student for 18 years, and as a result of the 12 years of work she did with Frank in industry, Lillian, more than all others, recognized the importance of teaching in relation to the successful installation and maintenance of Scientific Management. Scientific Management, being a different way of thinking and doing things, requires great emphasis on teaching as well as training. The old way of doing things was "rule of thumb" based on past experience (tradition) and thinking based on preconceptions. The new way of doing things was by careful measurement and analysis and thinking based on perception – the human senses. This means, going to the place where the work is actually performed observing, measuring, and interacting with the workers to co-discover new ways to perform the work better. In a nutshell, it is to make changes for the better based on facts, not opinions.

This is important because over time, management by opinion causes organizations and institutions suffer a loss of focus, experience internal discord, become less effective in their mission, undergo a loss of confidence among their clients, and must contend with unhappy or fleeing customers. Management by "rule of thumb" and opinion, rather than by facts is, sooner or later, fatal to organizations. Acceptance of the status quo leads to organization or institutional sclerosis and generates an environment that is both unpleasant and unhealthy to work in. And workers understandably fall into a pattern of only doing what the boss tells them to do to avoid friction with the boss. In such environments, workers ideas for improvement are quashed by managers and one will likely get into trouble for even articulating ideas. In this type of organization, the only thing of interest to managers is workers' labor. In Scientific Management, and todays' Lean management, managers are interested in workers minds as well as their labor. Management wants workers to think, recognize problems, generate ideas, and try them out to see if results in improvement, and then learn from it so that the learning can be applied to the next problem and the problems after that.

In addition to passionately advocating for progressive Scientific Management with a greater appreciation for human psychology, Dr. Gilbreth also saw the benefit of better teaching methods as these were instrumental in successfully establishing Scientific Management in companies. If the teaching methods used by industry in progressively managed organizations are successful, then could these same or similar methods be used in the schools to have happier, more engaged students who perform better in the classroom and execute their work with higher levels of capability and greater learning retention? Lillian Gilbreth's research shows that such results were possible in 1915. My work also shows that such results are possible today.

The path begins with challenging one's preconceptions, such as "Whatever comes from industry is of no use in education" and "Our work is highly regulated and there is nothing we can do about that." If we remain fixated on why we can't, then we must accept the status quo and stop complaining. But complaining is unlikely to cease, which indicates that we cannot, in fact, accept the status quo. Teachers know well that the problems are many and varied, and they will engage in improvement if the reasoning is sound, the methods for improvement are practical and produce results – and if administrators don't stand in the way. The latter is the greatest risk to progress, which can best be ameliorated by sustained public pressure.

Part I • General Principles of Waste Elimination

Dr. Gilbreth defines waste elimination as "cutting out needless time, money, material, or effort put into doing the work." Today, we define waste more specifically as overproduction, waiting, transportation, processing, inventory, motion, defects. These are the seven basic types of waste, but there are many more, and they exist in any type of productive work activity – that includes teaching.

Time is an extremely important factor in progressive management. It separates time into two basic categories: productive time and non-productive time (waste). Productive time is the time actually spent doing something productive. It is the work done in producing a product or service output. Non-productive time consists mostly of queue time – time where the work is waiting between steps in a process, or people waiting for some item that is needed in order for them to do their work. Non-productive time could include some small amount of time spent doing things that are not productive, but which are necessary under present conditions. Physical, material items can be idle, information can be idle, and people can be idle. Idleness prevents needed work from getting done and should be eliminated. Rest periods to prevent fatigue are not considered idle time.

Progressive management seeks to eliminate queue time so that the work can be completed sooner. If a work activity takes one hour to complete, then eight units of work can be completed in an eight-hour day. If 30 minutes per hour was idle time, and if the 30 minutes could be eliminated, then 16 units of work could be done per eight-hour day without speeding up the person(s) doing the work. However, a few less than 16 items would be produced because some rest breaks would be necessary to avoid fatigue and burn-out. Eliminating queue time is the basic idea behind progressive management, along with simplifying the productive work and eliminating unnecessary steps in the work.

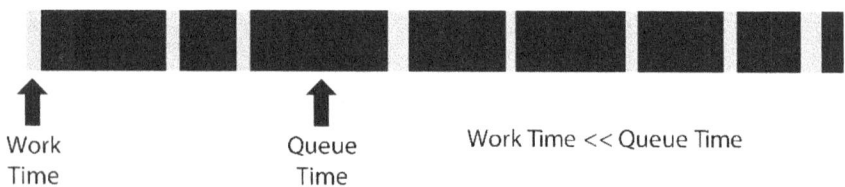

Work
Time

Queue
Time

Work Time << Queue Time

The above image illustrates the combination of work time and queue time that exists in a sequence of work resulting in the completion of a job. The work, shown in gray, is much less in total time than the sum of the queue time. If one eliminates the queue time, then the work is completed sooner without speeding anyone up. When greater attention is paid to the details of the work processes, quality is substantially improved. In addition, costs are also lowered and productive output, if more is needed, is increased.

To further understand the thinking behind progressive management and how work is performed, consider 5 individuals (or teams) doing the same type of work. Individual 1 does the work in 610 seconds, Individual 2 does the work in 540 seconds, Individual 3 does the work in 425 seconds, Individual 4 does the work in 980 seconds, and Individual 5 does the work in 705 seconds. All are capable individuals who produce the same high-quality work. But Individual 3 has found a method to do the work in 425 seconds. So why not carefully study that method to understand why it takes Individual 3 less time, and then teach that method to others so they too can do the work in less time and with less effort. Dr. Gilbreth refers to a scientific manager as a "waste eliminator." One can be a waste eliminator whether they are a manager or individual contributor. Preferably, process improvement is done in teams, so individuals 1 through 5 would work together to discover the least waste way of doing the work. By pooling their intelligence and creativity, together they may discover a method of doing the work in 315 seconds and make this the standard method that everyone uses. And, in achieving this brilliant outcome, they do no harm to the worker, co-workers, or other stakeholder.

The ever-present concern in progressive management is that good people are trapped in bad processes, and so management must take responsibility for this situation and lead efforts to improve processes – again and again. That is because the current improved process will soon need improvement due to changes in the work environment or other factors. In other words, a completed improvement is the beginning of the next improvement. Sometimes, perhaps most of the time, incentives play a role, and incentives can be non-monetary, monetary, or a combination of the two. Scientific management has been severely criticized for its reliance on monetary incentives to get workers and managers to learn and maintain new ways of doing things. Dr. Gilbreth describes how both monetary and non-monetary incentives can be used to engage people in both making and maintaining improvements.

Making the shift from the status quo ("rule of thumb," opinion, and tradition) to the thinking and practice of daily improvement "implies skilled teaching and efficient learning," according to Dr. Gilbreth. My own experiences as both a manager in industry and as a teacher in higher education confirms the truth of that statement. The manager (administrator) must be a skilled teacher and not merely an overseer of results. The latter simply generates disagreement and discord. It is true there are differences between a manager working in industry and a teacher working in schools. But there are also many similarities, which Dr. Gilbreth ably explains throughout her dissertation.

If teachers (and administrators) can think of themselves as managers in industry, then they will be more able to solve the persistent problems that plague teaching and education – problems that cannot be solved in any other way, because tradition and "rule of thumb" bind people to the same ways of thinking and the same small set of possible solutions. Breakthroughs occur when people see things from a different perspective.

Measurement of the right kind can help people to see things from a different perspective. Dr. Gilbreth writes that the whole of Scientific Management is based on measurement. Here again we can easily misinterpret her meaning based on our past experiences. For example, people mistakenly believe in the adage, "What gets measures gets managed." Managers, lacking productive work, believe in this adage and devise many measures for which to hold workers accountable. But we all know that just because something is measured does not mean it gets managed. People ignore measures they consider to be unimportant, they often game the measures, and they sometimes fake the measures. Predictably, we soon grow to dislike measures. We sense how they have been abused and how they impair our work.

Dr. Gilbreth's view and understanding of measurement is different. In Scientific Management, measurement is made to understand the work and improve the work, not measure the work to manage variation wherein reduction of variance is the sole indicator of improvement. In the latter case, workers and managers get good at gaming the metrics and thus make no actual headway in improving the work. In progressive management, the purpose of measurement is to improve the work: less time, less burden, less stress, safer, more interesting, better quality. If the metric does not help guide people's efforts to improve the work, then the metric should be eliminated or greatly deemphasized in decision-making.

Typically, teachers and administrators are responsible for too many processes and too many metrics. They are overburdened. Predictably, they pay attention only to the few processes and metrics that they are most comfortable with. The remedy in Scientific Management is "functionalization." Instead of an administrator doing many things poorly and just a few things well, divide the work of management into discrete functions, each best suited to the capability, learning, and temperament of the individual administrator so that the work each does is of much higher quality. Think of "functionalization" as giving someone the ability to specialize in a task, focus on doing the task well, learn continuously how to do the task better over time, and who becomes a resource to the teacher for improvement rather than an overseer of results.

In Lillian Gilbreth's day, functionalization was controversial among business leaders because it meant that instead of having a few managers doing many things, you had to hire more managers (overhead positions) to do fewer things. But the idea behind functionalization was to do those few things so well that the organization would perform better; it would be more productive and therefore be able to absorb the expense of hiring the additional managers. Business leaders who adopted Scientific Management in its full form found functionalization to be beneficial. Today we seem to have many more managers than workers, and the absence of focus that functionalization (or modern-day equivalent) can provide means that managers are of little help to workers. Managers constantly dwell on the need for higher productivity, lower costs, higher quality, etc., but do not understand their role in leading and helping workers achieve those outcomes, nor do they have the needed education and training. In sum, you can think of functionalization as a method or practice to help managers focus on doing a few things well rather than doing many things poorly. This means to eliminate work that is of no value, or work that can be assigned to a lower-paid person, or to someone who could benefit from doing the work as part of their training and individual development.

Functionalization is part of an overall effort to introduce standardization in an organization and to develop skills and capabilities that are best suited for each individual. In both Part I and Part II of Dr. Gilbreth's dissertation, she gives simple, practical recommendations for improvement. But you will notice that these recommendations must be applied in an exacting way, with no deviation, to achieve the desired result. This rigor applies to "standardization," which is a fundamental practice in Scientific Management. In addition to "standardization," there is repeated reference the "one best way." The latter was part of the early conception of Scientific Management in the late 1800s, and it remained through the 1920s. The idea was that through the careful study of how work was performed, one would discover the "one best way" to do the work. However, in Lillian Gilbreth's dissertation, reference is made to further improving the work after the "one best way" was discovered and put into practice. Frank Gilbreth eventually admitted that "the one best way" was a helpful business slogan and not something that was actually achievable (Lancaster, 2004).

As the theory and practice of Scientific Management evolved over time, it moved in the direction of "continuous improvement" and the realization that there is no end to improvement. The reason why there is no end to improvement is because circumstances change. The words "standard" and "standardization" soon became understood to mean the best-known way to do the work presently, until such time that people think of new and better ways to do the work. And because people think and are creative and innovative, one need not wait a long time until they come up with new ideas to improve the work, typically in days or a few weeks, but certainly not months or years. The standard, then becomes the point from which further improvement is made to improve efficiency. An improved process becomes the new standard from which further improvements are made, and so on.

You can think of a standard as the current record height in pole vaulting, and standardization as the current method by which pole vaulting is performed. Both change over time, as a result of careful study and practice, to produce better results.

Readers should therefore understand standards and standardization as something which evolves, not something that is static as the "one best way" suggests. It is understandable that workers, especially, are wary of standards and standardization because their job requires them to make adjustments as a result of the variation they encounter. In Scientific Management, and Lean management, the view is to understand and eliminate the sources of variation so that work can be standardized and then improved – continuously improved – for the benefit of all stakeholders.

Part II • Application of Waste Elimination to Teaching

About 35 percent of Dr. Gilbreth's dissertation explains the waste that exists in industrial work processes and the methods used to eliminate it. In Part II she shows the relevance of that work to teaching in the schools. A prerequisite to eliminating waste is to understand the current condition. Dr. Gilbreth refers to the preparation of various formal documents, called "surveys." These surveys are based on observation and measurement of the work and related conditions. The reason why such surveys are important is because we think we know the work that we do, yet we struggle to explain it when asked. We have difficulty describing it accurately and in detail, and therefore likely do not know, specifically, what needs improvement. And we may not truly understand how to improve or what constitutes an actual improvement. Hence, the need for a skilled observer to document the work as it is performed under real working conditions.

One hundred years ago, under the rules of Scientific Management, the surveys were extensive and somewhat complicated. This required the separation of planning (observation and analysis) from performing (working). Someone skilled in planning would, through observation and measurement, determine how best to do the job and teach it to the worker. Under the rules of current-day Lean management, the collection of information pertaining to the current state has been greatly simplified and consists of a few one-page charts that graphically depict the work. Often, however, a skilled observer may be needed, or unskilled observers can be given the task of observing the work to develop their observation skills.

Part II of Dr. Gilbreth's dissertation recounts her skilled observations of teachers, students, equipment, materials, and so on, and her recommendations for improvement. Teachers will surely recognize these inefficiencies, and, as former students, we will too. The question is, do teachers simply accept the waste as "That's just the way things are."? Or, is action taken to eliminate waste and make an improvement? It is likely that in most cases, teachers are satisfied making the initial improvement and stop there. That may have been good enough in the early 1900s, but the thinking and practice of improvement has changed from one-time improvement to continuous improvement. What is now common practice was a newly developing practice in 1915.

Some of Dr. Gilbreth's recommendations may seem odd or extreme, but they should not be dismissed. Instead, try it and see what happens. Perhaps you will find it beneficial, perhaps not. The important point is to try. Too often people think though an improvement idea in their head and judge it to be unhelpful or unlikely to produce a good result without having tried it. They talk themselves out of taking action. But in truth, you don't actually know if it is a bad idea (or a good idea) unless you try it. Along with trying an idea, no matter how wild it may seem, comes learning, and the learning results in the creation of additional improvement ideas. It is mostly through the creative process of trial-and-error that continuous improvement is achieved.

In reading Part II of the dissertation, it will become apparent that teaching children and young adults in grades K-12 is an excellent place to teach efficiency and efficient methods through the examples of how teaching and related activities are managed in the classroom and in the school. If teachers can explain the reasoning behind the efficient methods used in the classroom and elsewhere in the school, then some of that will be remembered later in life and used at work and at home. Business, despite its appearance of great efficiency, is actually very inefficient. The same is true of not-for-profit organizations, non-governmental organizations (NGOs), and government at any level. Perhaps in time, students who learn about waste elimination will someday lead organizations more efficiently and in ways that do no harm to stakeholders.

Dr. Gilbreth's observations and recommendations are keenly insightful and occasionally humorous to those of us experienced in continuous improvement. Often, she speaks of equipment layout; the desks and chairs for both teacher and students, the blackboards, and so on. The layout of these are inefficient and most often determined by tradition, rather than by careful scientific study – observation, rational thought, and analysis. Again, note that the words "careful scientific study" suggest that both study and related solutions will take a long time. This is no longer the case; careful scientific study can be done in 30 minutes to a few hours to perhaps several hours – but not days, weeks, months, or years as many will assume.

She also notes the difficulty that teachers, like any other worker, have with change. One example pertains to the classroom clock on the wall (p. 135):

> "It is customary for the writer in suggesting possible changes in equipment always to mention early the proper placing of the clock. It is surprising the number of objections to moving it which are encountered... The clock incident might be considered a test case, that will show early and clearly the teacher's attitude towards actual physical changes involved in waste elimination."

Waste elimination often involves physical changes in the placement of equipment and people. Resistance is common at first, as people will cite the many reasons for things being as they are. Yet, once physical changes are made, people can see its benefit though in improvement in the flow of work and reduced effort and stress.

In another passage, she notes the resistance (p. 141):

> "It should be, to say the least, not tactful to enumerate the contents of the average teacher's desk. We find 'How about standardizing your own desk?' a fighting question. However, we recommend such standardization not only as furnishing a model to the pupils, but as furnishing an admirable instruction to the teacher in search of a method of standardization."

Resistance to improvement, indifference to improvement, dislike of improvement, etc., are understandable. Teachers have found ways of thinking about things, ways of arranging equipment, ways of doing things, ways of interacting with students, and so on, that they find to be acceptable because they seem to work well. Indeed, they do. The question is, however, can these be made to work better in ways that benefit both pupil and teacher? Specifically, less work for the teacher, less struggle for students, and learning for both. A closed mind is the enemy of improvement. This is just one of many barriers that make needed improvement more difficult to achieve than it ought to be.

There are remedies, however. One remedy is to make improvement fun. If improvement is made fun, then teachers will flock to it. If improvement is instead forced upon teachers, as administrators are prone to do, them improvement efforts will, at best, muddle along as dull and tedious work, and will soon die. Engagement in continuous improvement can be characterized as something akin to jury duty in which everyone must eventually participate. If improvement is made to be a fun activity, then people will enjoy their "jury duty" and willingly participate in future improvement activities.

One way to make improvement fun is to have people participate in finding solutions to common problems that affect all teachers. Dr.

Gilbreth cites examples in which workers were asked to design ladies work clothes ("frocks") that were suited to the job, and to design a more efficient pencil rack (p. 142):

> "The pencil rack in the plant has been a source of arousing great interest in motion study. It is customary in every plant to ask all interested to design pencil racks that will require the least motions possible to deposit or pick up a pencil, and that will, at the same time, maintain the pencils in the best condition possible. The result is not only a rack that is efficient, but also a greatly increased interest in the subject of motion economy."

There are a thousand ways to make improvement fun.

Throughout her dissertation, Dr. Gilbreth makes recommendations that are either no cost or low cost. This is an important point because people invariably want to spend money to solve problems – usually, a lot of money. As it is practiced today, continuous improvement has a basic rule that people should "spend ideas, not money." When people are challenged in this way, they are compelled to think creativity and use their imagination to solve difficult problems. In business, many "nos" are established to set boundary conditions for improvement activities. Examples of some "nos" from industry include (Emiliani *et al*, 2015b):

No money
No people
No space
No cranes
No conveyors
No set-up time
No warehouse

No band aids / rework
No batches
No adjustments
No extra machines
No piling up
No shared resources
No status quo
No sacred cows

There are many more "nos" as they relate to production in a manufacturing setting. At first it may seem impossible to make improvements with so many constraints. Yet, every time, people use their ideas and creativity to discover many practical ways to improve. And in doing so, they develop higher-order thinking skills that can be applied to other problems. The "nos" challenge people to think creatively and that helps make continuous improvement fun. It also strengthens people's confidence in their creative capabilities and problem-solving skills.

We can also establish "nos" for improving teaching processes. My own "nos" for improvement presently number 59 (Emiliani, 2017):

No unprepared
No batching
No too fast
No too slow
No delays
No ignoring students
No ignoring feedback or complaints
No ignoring abnormal conditions
No indifference
No unresponsiveness
No games

No tricks
No confusion
No unclear expectations
No re-work
No overloading
No over-processing
No busy-work
No "me" (teacher) focus
No complacency
No complex grading
No status quo
No mid-term exam
No final exam
No term paper
No pontificating
No going off topic
No large PowerPoint slide decks
No reading PowerPoint slides
No unavailable
No haughtiness
No jokes
No deviation (without explanation)
No rambling
No theory-only
No lecture-only
No repeating the book
No disorganization
No unnecessary materials
No irrelevant materials
No obsolete materials
No expensive materials
No insults or put-downs
No unfairness

No bad experiences
No dishonesty
No bad communication
No miscommunication
No laziness
No begin class late
No end class late
No teach x and test y
No boring
No not allowing questions
No unreasonableness
No unhelpfulness
No hostility
No stress
No disrespect

One must think creatively to develop efficient teaching processes under these constraints. But the job is never done, as one must reflect on the improvement made and then think about how improvements can be made again and again. Fortunately, teachers have some latitude to experiment in their work and, importantly, the feedback they get from students is often immediate and so corrections can be made swiftly.

In her dissertation, Dr. Gilbreth often recounts asking teachers why they do what they do. Most of the responses are some form of "That's the way we have always done it." It reflects an acceptance of the status quo, which is understandable because it avoids many potentially difficult or unpleasant things, such as having to think, interact with administrators (guardians of the status quo), petition the school board for policy changes, gain the support of local and state legislators, etc. So to improve processes, people need a bit of a push from a progressive-minded leader, under the steadfast rule of "do no harm," a personal dislike of the status quo, and an interest in working with one's colleagues to make teaching better for themselves and learning better for students. They may also need help from someone who is experienced in process improvement methods – a facilitator or consultant – though this is optional. Continuous improvement can certainly be a do-it-yourself effort, whether individually or in teams.

Today there are many resources available from which to learn about the processes that are used to improve work. These include books, videos, webinars, conferences, training, and so on. To newcomers, the difficult part will be sorting the good resources from the not so good and bad resources. There are good learning resources that come from manufacturing and service companies. The former should not be ignored merely because it seems to be so distant from the job of teaching. As Dr. Gilbreth's dissertations shows, much that has been done in manufacturing to improve processes can be applied to improving teaching. Service industry examples will be helpful, as will papers and books on improving teaching and administrative processes in education (Ziskovsky and Ziskovsky, 2007; Balzer, 2010; LeMahieu *et al.*, 2017).

I am sure you will find "Some Aspects of Eliminating Waste in Teaching" to be remarkably readable for a doctoral dissertation. Don't forget, Dr. Gilbreth's bachelor's and master's degrees were in English literature, so good writing is to be expected. I am also certain that you will find the dissertation interesting and stimulating in terms of reflecting on your own work teaching and will be inspired to think of new ideas for improving your teaching.

A Note on Unfamiliar Terms

Dr. Gilbreth uses some terms that may be unfamiliar to readers, as they originated from the practice of Scientific Management in industry. An "elasticity station," today called a "buffer," is a small surplus supply teaching material to assure that the teacher does not run out. Running out of material is to be avoided because it would delay the class and delay learning. She refers to "packets" and the "packet principle," today called "kitting," which means to supply a worker with a kit containing all the material that they will need to do their work. An example being, all the parts needed to assemble a flashlight neatly organized in the sequence in which it is assembled. A similar idea may apply to students working in certain classes or for some kinds of projects. She also refers to the "replenishment system," which today is called "kanban system" It is a system that visually signals, at a glance, the need for additional material when supplies run low or run out. Dr. Gilbreth defines other terms that readers may be unfamiliar with in her dissertation.

References

Balzer, W.K. (2010), *Lean Higher Education: Increasing the Value and Performance of University Processes*, Routledge, New York, NY

Emiliani, M.L. (2004), "Improving Business School Courses by Applying Lean Principles and Practices," *Quality Assurance in Education*, Vol. 12, No. 4, pp. 175-187

Emiliani, M.L. (2005), "Using Kaizen to Improve Graduate Business School Degree Programs," *Quality Assurance in Education*, Vol. 13, No. 1, pp. 37-52

Emiliani, B. (2015), *Lean Teaching: A Guide to Becoming a Better Teacher*, The CLBM, LLC, Wethersfield, Conn.

Emiliani, B. (2015a), *Lean University: A Guide to Renewal and Prosperity*, The CLBM, LLC, Wethersfield, Conn.

Emiliani, B., Yoshino, K., and Go, R. (2015b), *Kaizen Forever: The Teachings of Chihiro Nakao*, The CLBM, LLC, Wethersfield, Conn.

Emiliani, B. (2017), "Professor Emiliani's 'Nos' for Teaching," https://bobemiliani.com/professor-emilianis-nos-for-teaching/, accessed 21 September 2019

Gilbreth, F.B. (1912), *Primer of Scientific Management*, D. Van Nostrand Company, New York, NY

Gilbreth, L.M. (1914), *The Psychology of Management*, Sturgis and Walton Co., New York, NY

Goldsmith, S. (2017), "Bringing the Power of Lean to Education," *Governing the States and Localities*, Folsom, Calif., https://www.governing.com/commentary/col-lean-continuous-improvement-education-des-moines-schools.html, accessed 21 September 2019

Lancaster, J. (2004), *Making Time: Lillian Moller Gilbreth – A Life Beyond "Cheaper by the Dozen,"* Northeastern University Press, Lebanon, NH

LeMahieu, P., Nordstrum, L., and Greco, P. (2017), "Lean for Education," *Quality Assurance in Education*, Vol. 25 No. 1, pp. 74-90.

Ziskovsky, B. and Ziskovsky, J. (2007), "Doing More With Less: Applying Process Improvement to K-12 Education," https://www.lean.org/Search/Documents/398.pdf, Lean Enterprise Education, Inc., Shoreview, Minn. accessed 21 September 2019

Dr. Lillian Moller Gilbreth's Doctoral Dissertation

SOME ASPECTS OF ELIMINATING WASTE IN TEACHING

A thesis presented in partial fulfillment

of the requirement for the degree

of Doctor of Philosophy

at Brown University

By

Lillian Moller Gilbreth

PREFACE

The materials embodied in this thesis were prepared in the following manner:-

The writer received a training in the theory and practice of education in the University of California, under Prof. Elmer Brown, now president of New York University; Prof. Bailey, whose great interest was child psychology; Prof. Dressler, the writer on school hygiene and related topics; and the faculty of the department of psychology, which included Prof. Stratton. This training included observation of class room methods.

The training in California was supplemented by some months' study in Columbia University, which made possible observation in the Horace Mann, School and in other model New York schools, although the actual class room work done there was, directly, not along educational lines.

The past ten years, spent in the study and practice of scientific management, made clear the importance of teaching in the industries. The writer has been actually engaged in such teaching in the industries, and has, whenever possible, observed actual school room practice, in order to transfer successful methods of teaching in the class room to the industries.

Since the fall of 1913, the writer has been engaged in study and investigation under the direction of the departments of education and psychology in Brown University, with the view of analyzing more efficiently the correlation between education in the industries and in the schools. In the fall of 1914, Prof. Colvin suggested that the writer supplement her study of such correlation by an intensive study of schoolroom practice in and about Providence, in order to note resemblances between school practice and industrial practice, and to work out a method by which successful practice in the industries might be applied in the schools. The writer applied at once to the Superintendent of Public Schools, and received permission to visit the schools, and an introduction to the principals of the various schools. She was urged, however, not to visit one class oftener than once or twice, in order that the schoolroom practice might not be disturbed, and also not to inform the teacher, whose class she was visiting, as to the purpose of the visit. It was felt that, if her purpose were known, she might be suspected of a critical attitude, which might antagonize the teacher, or which might so change the regular class procedure that she would be unable to make observations as to regular every-day practice.

With these restrictions in mind, the writer visited various class rooms in and about Providence on an average of two mornings a week for five months.

She also, thru the courtesy of the Director of The Music School, spent one entire day each week and several hours on another afternoon observing class work at The Music School. This work offered an admirable opportunity for intensive study. Six classes were under observation. Five of these were taught by a visiting teacher. She came from a distance, and was at the school only one day a week. Therefore, it was possible to observe her procedure during her entire teaching time at the school. All of these classes were classes in harmony. The first class consisted of older students; the second class, of teachers; the third class, of high school girls who had had one year's training in harmony; the fourth class, of high school girls who had had no training in harmony; the fifth class, of girls from eight to twelve years old, who had had one year's training in harmony; and the sixth class, which met on the other afternoon, and was taught by the Director of the school, consisted of younger children who had had no training in harmony.

In the case of the visiting harmony teacher, as in the cases of the various classes visited in the public and private schools, nothing was said by the writer as to the purpose of visiting the work. The Director of The Music School did, however, know of the purpose, but was careful, also, to say nothing of it to the visiting teacher.

The only teachers in the school who were informed of the purpose of the investigations were those who were attending the same college classes as was the writer. Of these, one, Miss Wentworth, offered to cooperate in any way possible, not only by allowing the writer to visit her class, but also by endeavoring to install, under the writer's directions, any methods of eliminating waste in the industries that might seem to the writer applicable to the particular problem of that class room.

Miss Wentworth, the teacher who kindly cooperated in a waste eliminating experiment, had become interested in scientific management. The writer had prepared for Miss Wentworth a copy of the functional chart, under which scientific management operates, also a description of these various functions, and some notes on the sequence of the installation of waste-eliminating methods.

The writer also visited Miss Wentworth's room at the school for several days in succession, observing the practice. During these visits several things became apparent. The first was that it was impossible to visit the particular class room frequently without arousing the curiosity of the other teachers in the building as to the purpose of the visits. It had been an express condition of permission to visit the schools that such curiosity should not be aroused. The second thing that became apparent was that the class was more or less distracted by the constant presence of the visitor. The third thing that became apparent was that, while the teacher cooperating had every desire to do everything possible to further the investigation, she had neither time, opportunity, nor the specialized training in scientific management to make radical changes such as the writer advocated. The fourth thing was that the teacher would take more interest in making the changes if the entire matter were left to her direct supervision. The fifth thing was that no complicated change could be attempted, if accurate records of performance were to be obtained.

For these reasons, and at the suggestion of Prof. Colvin, a very definite and simple problem in waste elimination was suggested, and a solution was outlined. Miss Wentworth, as her own account of the experiment shows, followed out the experiment exactly as planned, and made careful records of the processes and the results. These are stated in her own words in Appendix E.

After outlining the method of attack for Miss Wentworth, the writer did not again visit her class room, as it was felt that visits during the process of the experiment might add another variable that might in some way affect or detract from the value of the results.

Because of the restrictions under which the writer worked, it was not possible to make notes while making observations in the various other class rooms.

The practice was to select a school or class to be visited and to find out in advance as much about the school as possible,- any particularly good teachers or successful methods to be seen there, or any bad practice which had been reported to the writer. By this means it was possible to have in mind definite things which should be observed.

In addition to this the writer had in mind the working rules for making a survey of an industrial plant. These are embodied in the thesis in substance for making a survey. These furnished a list of things to be observed. The plan was to observe, as does the trained survey maker, typified by Dr. Ayres in the Springfield, Illinois, survey, first, existing practice, and, second, possible changes for the better that might be made.

When a morning had been spent visiting classes, the afternoon or the next day was spent in writing up the observations. At first the observations were written out at length as descriptions of what actually occurred during a certain period of time; but, as the investigations went on, it seemed advisable to record them under the principles that they exemplified, rather than to group them under time and place headings. Slips of paper were prepared, and after each day's observation, the various things noted were recorded on these slips. At the head of each slip was a title, such as, "incentive," "socializing work," "handling materials," etc.,- the division of class room practice under which the observation fell. Under this was noted the specific example that had been observed. Under this was placed a note as to whether the practice was judged to be good or bad, as to the reason for this, and a possible remedy if it were a bad practice. The latter two statements were not written in full in most cases, as a series of symbols relating to the general plan indicated to the writer at a glance the exact rating of the example and the method by which it could be handled.

Typical observations are appended to various chapters. These observations have been written up from the slips on which they were recorded, - the symbols placed upon the slips being here interpreted in full form. In each case a statement is made of the condition observed, and also a comment upon this condition and its relation to waste elimination.

The observations are grouped as they relate themselves to efficient methods of waste elimination common in the industries and the schools. Each observation must be considered as typical of a class. Where many examples of the same class were noted, while these have each been recorded by the observer upon a separate slip, in writing up these slips, duplication has been, as far as possible, avoided. However, the record slips, as they stand, would make it a task involving time of transcription only to multiply these illustrations indefinitely.

The observations on the harmony classes were made by a different method. Full notes of the practice were made during the class hours, along with comments on the practice and any suggestions that occurred to the writer as to methods of bettering this practice. This was possible because the members of the classes were constantly taking notes, and the writer was not conspicuous when taking notes also.

At the end of the six months spent in actually visiting class rooms, the writer reviewed the data accumulated, and attempted to classify the results and combine the findings, with the material already accumulated, into a thesis. It was her impression from this review that all of her observations and investigations went to prove:

1. That there was much waste in existing class room practice.
2. That waste eliminating methods that had proved successful in the industries might be used with profit in the schools.
3. That actual application of such methods could best be made by the teaching force.
4. That, in order to make the teaching force realize the possibility of applying industrial methods, it was necessary to state the practice in the industry and its application to the schoolroom.
5. That, while it was necessary to use the specific examples of waste observed in school methods, and to cite successful

examples of waste elimination in the schools, it was the wisest to state all these in general rather than in specific terms; this for several reasons:-

A. The writer had been admitted as a guest to the classes visited and must observe the obligations binding a guest.
B. The writer had not been able to state to the teacher visited the purpose of the observations, therefore felt bound not to specify time, place, or persons commented upon.
C. While a detailed, concrete description of a specific instance might make more clear the definite nature of the problems; on the other hand, the more general statement would be just as accurate, and would not arouse a feeling of antagonism towards the writer.

The writer, therefore, as shown by the thesis, developed this plan in detail. The specific examples contained in the observations were put in general terms, and introduced into the body of the thesis.

The practice of scientific management as recorded in the thesis is the actual practice that exists in the organization to which the writer belongs. This organization was the first to realize the importance of teaching, in scientific management. The writer endeavored to emphasize, in her book on "The Psychology of Management," the fact that the proper understanding of and development of the human element is the great factor in efficient management, and that teaching is a most important element in establishing correlation between the industries and the schools.

On the completion of the body of the thesis, the writer reviewed the accepted standard literature of management and also much of the literature of psychology and education, in order to include the references that serve as a confirmation of the various statements made.

It is believed that this thesis, based as it is upon actual, intensive, personal observation, extending over eighteen years in the schools and twelve years in the industries, furnishes an accurate description of conditions existing in these institutions. It is hoped that the outline of a possible correlation between efficient practice in the industries and the schools, which, so far as the writer knows, has never been attempted before by any one with experience in scientific management, may serve as a contribution to the field of education that will stimulate to extended investigations and experimentation along the lines outlined.

Part I

General Principles of Waste Elimination

CHAPTER I
Waste Elimination in Scientific Management

Examples of Waste Elimination.

A group of young people in a factory were wasting their own time, as well as that of their employers, by working at a pace so slow that they accomplished little, and were not interested in their work. Raising their pay if they did more work had little effect upon them, because they were accustomed to turn their pay envelopes over to their parents. A new method of management was tried, and the work was completed in about half the time. The workers became interested in it, and they and the company were better satisfied with the results.[1*]

A number of girls in a textile factory were engaged in folding cotton cloth. They had used the same method for years, and had been turning out the same amount of work. A change of method was made. Using this, they folded four hundred dozen pieces of cloth where they folded one hundred and fifty dozen before, and were no more tired at the end of the day's work.[2]

Bricklayers in many parts of the country were laying one hundred and twenty bricks an hour. The way of doing the work was changed, and now the same men lay three hundred and fifty bricks an hour, with no decrease in the quality of the work, and with no more fatigue.[3]

A girl at an exposition in England was putting papers on boxes of shoe polish. She was a star worker, and she worked at top speed. Her methods were changed only slightly, and, where she had been doing twenty-four boxes in forty seconds, at the second try with the new method she did twenty-four in twenty seconds, exactly half the time, and with less effort.[4]

---

* Numbers in the text refer to references at the close of the chapters.

A surgeon had been operating in a modern, well-equipped hospital with the usual set of instruments, arranged in the usual manner. His method of doing the work had not been changed, but the arrangement of his material had been bettered. He did not attempt to take less time for performing an operation, but he found that with the new methods the handling time of the instruments was cut down, and he had much more time to think over what he was doing.[5]

The men in a New England factory, engaged in making certain pieces of machinery, had been all pretty much of the well-known type of New England mechanic. A number of them had done the same kind of work, and with the same proportion of success. A study was made of their capacities and abilities, and at the end of one year a machinist had become an inspector; a probation messenger had become assistant in the purchasing department; another machinist had become a chart maker; a messenger had become the head of an information bureau; a foreman had become a superintendent; a draftsman had been advanced to take charge of the discipline of the entire plant; and a skilled laborer had become a machine shop foreman.

In the same plant the material, which used to travel from one place to another by a maze-like path, now goes thru the shortest path which could be made, and, as a result, much more work is turned out.[6]

All of these examples- illustrate one point, that is, that there is an enormous amount of waste all thru our usual way of doing things, and that even a short study of any problem will bring out a better, because a shorter or cheaper or less tiring, way of doing the work.

Definition of Waste Elimination.

This is the problem of waste elimination. It is cutting out needless time, money, material, or effort put into doing the work. Given the work to be done, the question is how to do this work at the least cost of material and of human strength or effort possible.

History of Waste Elimination.

This waste elimination is no new thing. As far back as we have thinkers at all, men have been putting their minds on planning out better and easier ways of doing the things that they recognized had to be done. The type of the thinker and the ideas of the people among whom he lived determined, more or less, whether he should feel that it was more important to spare material or to spare men. We have only to turn back to the end of the eighteenth and the beginning of the nineteenth century, to find Babbage[7] and Adam Smith[8] laying great emphasis on the need of making work count for as much as possible. We may not agree always with the ways or methods which they prescribed for getting more work done, but we must feel that their underlying ideas of making everything count, and wasting as little as possible, were valuable. About ten years ago the great emphasis seemed to be on cutting down waste of <u>material</u> things.[9] There was much talk, and splendid talk, and necessary talk, about saying our natural resources, saving forests, going slow on the use of coal, keeping certain scenic spots for the good of the nation, and even cutting down on the use of Christmas trees; but it is really only within the last few years that the great emphasis has swung over towards saving human effort. We are coming to realize that in every place where there are people working, there is an enormous amount of waste.[10]

Waste Elimination in the Industries.

Because they have had an excellent training in the necessity for measuring things carefully, the engineers have been prominent in taking up the study and the practice of cutting out waste. Because they have worked chiefly in industrial plants, they have applied the methods which they have devised to the industries, and have worked out, now, a complete system of discovering, and solving, the problems of eliminating unnecessary elements of every kind. In their work, too, it was at first a question mainly of saving material or money, either by handling the material better, or by finding out better methods of doing the work. Gradually, however, the general subject of study has come to be the <u>person</u> doing the work, and the chief gains to-day are being made by saving the workers.[11]

Specific Application of These Derived Methods to Teaching.

With the emphasis on the human element, has come a clearer realization that these methods of waste elimination developed in the industries have a special application to teaching.[12] They apply to all activities where human efficiency is the problem, but are most significant where transference of skill, or teaching, is the important point. It will be the purpose of the following pages to treat the art of teaching from the standpoint of the principles and practice that has been brought out in the work of the scientific manager, or waste eliminator. stated more definitely, the discussion which follows is to be the consideration of the problems of eliminating waste in the class room.

Methods of Waste Elimination.

The method by which waste is eliminated is by measuring the work that is to be done, and the workers. When one has as exact a knowledge as is possible of the work and of the worker, the two are fitted together in the best way available.[13] From the measurement, then, is worked out the best method of doing each part, or element, of the work. The results of the measurement are taken as standards, that is to say, the work is done every time in the best way that is known. The worker who is best able to do any particular kind of work is allowed to do that work, and is not forced to do work for which he is not fitted.[14] This system of management,- which consists simply of measuring what is done, and then using such methods as the measurement determined to be best, has been called "Efficiency," or "Scientific Management," and is the best method of cutting out waste to-day.

Field of Scientific Management and Problems of Scientific Management.

The field in which it may be used is not limited[15]. Wherever people of any type are working at any work it is possible to measure them, and what they are doing. It is then possible to see that each one is given what he is best able to do, in such amount as he is able to do it, do it well, and continue to do it. His continuance must be for his own good and the good of every one,- which means that he must keep in good health, and that he must like the work; that is, that he and the work must fit well together.[16] In order that he shall like the work, he must be taught to do it well, and he must be adequately paid for doing it.[17] To measure him, and to fit him to the work that he can do and do well, are comparatively easy problems. To teach him, and to see that he is happy in his work and gets the most he can out of it, are more difficult problems.

Illustrations of Methods of Solution.

Let us return a moment to our illustrations, and see how the problems were solved there. Take the children who were working at a slow pace. The chief trouble there was, that they had no reason for working any faster. Of course, in order to see exactly how fast they should work, it was necessary to study them, and to study the work; to measure them in their work. In order to make sure that they could get thru the amount of work that was then set, it was necessary to teach them. But in their case the final thing that made them enjoy their work, and get thru the amount set, was letting them have a holiday as soon as the work was finished.[18] It was what might be called "providing the fitting incentive."

Take the girls folding the cotton cloth. There were various things that had to be done for them. In the first place, the materials and equipment with which they worked were not the best possible. The girls had to be studied, and the work had to be studied, in order that the best possible equipment, general surroundings, and apparatus might be determined and provided. In the second place the workers got needlessly tired from doing the work. They had been working, sitting at low tables, on chairs many of which were too law for them,- and they had worked continuously throughout a long day. The fatigue problem was studied. As a result, they were given high work tables, where they could stand part of the day and sit part of the day in high chairs with footstools. The chair was on casters, so that the girl using it could push it back, or pull it forward without looking at it, simply by putting a foot back thru one rung. Then, the day was divided into work periods and rest periods. There were ten periods in every hour. For the first four the girl sat; for the next two she stood; for the seventh, eighth and ninth she sat or stood as she pleased; at the end of the ninth period she stopped work; and during the tenth she walked about, chatted with the other girls, or amused herself as she pleased.

There were slight modifications made in the period that came before noon, and in the last period at night, but, in the main, this was the plan. Finally, the worker's mental attitude towards her work was changed. She was not only taught to do her work with less motions, but she was shown just <u>why</u> the new motions were easier than the old motions, and accomplished more. Gradually she came to think in good methods of doing work, or "to think in elementary motions," as it is phrased.[19] In this way she not only got more work done, but a new element of interest was added. Thru a combination of all these methods of changing her work, she got thru much more work in the working time, and also enjoyed the work more. The people for whom she did the work were able to pay her higher wages, because of the increased production. Finally, because the work was done with her cooperation, she became accustomed to working with others, and realized the benefit of a social spirit.

Take the bricklayers. They were working according to tradition, following exactly the methods which they had learned from imitating others, and using equipment which was centuries old. First, their motions were studied. This motion study brought out the fact that a much better type of working tools and equipment could be used for the work.[20] Then those things, for which the need was felt, were invented. Next, the workers were taught better methods. It so happens that the work of bricklaying has been divided from earliest times among different kinds of workers. This accepted division was retained, but the men laying the brick were so separated by the better, newly devised equipment, from the men bringing the material, that each type of worker was able to do his work more efficiently. As a result, here too, as with the girls folding, there grew up a change in the mental attitude of the worker and an added interest in his work. This, joined with the better teaching and the larger amount of pay which he was able to get, made of him an efficient and a happy member of the community.

Take the girl putting papers on boxes of shoe polish. It was only a minute's work of one trained in cutting out waste, to rearrange her material, and to show her that by making a different kind of motion she could accomplish more with less effort.[21]

Take the surgeon. He had been trained to think in an orderly manner, but had not been trained to realize that the arrangement of the materials with which he worked had an effect not only upon the speed with which he could do his work, but upon the amount of time which he could safely allow himself for planning detailed procedure during an operation.[22] For the first time, he was called upon to decide <u>before starting to operate</u> exactly where and how he desired each instrument to be placed, in order that there might be no time lost in looking for it, or fumbling for it. This arrangement put the relation between planning and performing in a new light. The orderly and habitual arrangement of the instruments helped to develop an orderly and habitual method of performing the operation. It reduced much of the mechanical work to habit, thus giving the surgeon mental and physical freedom to handle critical situations in the operation.

Take the men working in the New England factory. They had done the same work so many years that there had come into their minds, and into the minds of the manager, the idea that they were in fixed positions. There was no desire on any one's part to keep them from advancing. It was simply that it was no one's duty to make a study of their capabilities, and to see that, while each one was <u>required</u> to do a set amount of excellent work, he was <u>allowed</u> to do that work which he could do best, and which he enjoyed most. An elementary study of the qualifications and aspirations of the various men soon showed possibilities for transfers and advancements.[23] Tests and measurements then determined what should be done to adjust the men better to the work. The actual changes were then made, by teaching the men to fill the positions Which they were best able to fill.

The result was that an enormous amount of power that lay dormant in these men, and that had been wasted for years, was developed and put to use.

The paths by which the material travelled were straightened out as follows: A plan of each floor of the building was made. Colored strings, fastened by pins, were then put up. Each string showed the path by which one special type of material travelled. A study of these path strings made it possible to shorten the paths by cutting out unnecessary winding and doubling. In this way the material was enabled to move faster; the men got the material that was needed quicker; and time that had been wasted in waiting for material could now be put into accomplishing actual work.

Principles that Underlie the Solution.

Such are typical solutions by Scientific Management of the problem of waste elimination that arises in the industries. Let us state them in the most general terms.

Problem I.   A young person working at, what is apparently too slow a pace. Cause: Little interest in the work because no incentive. Remedy: A sufficient incentive.

Problem II.   A girl accomplishing too little for the amount of effort expended. Cause: A poor method of work, unnecessary fatigue, insufficient incentive. Remedy: Better equipment and method, proper rest from fatigue, improved incentive.

Problem III.   A man apparently doing less work than he is capable of doing. Cause: Antiquated method and equipment. Remedy: Improved method and equipment.

Problem IV.   A girl working hard, but accomplishing little. Cause: Poor arrangement of equipment and consequently poor methods. Remedy: Improved arrangement of equipment, which remains unchanged, and more efficient method.

Problem V.   A worker whose handling time of tools is long in comparison with the amount of work actually done with them. Cause: Unstandardized arrangement of the tools with consequent lack of habit in handling them. Remedy: Standardized arrangement of tools, resulting in habits of motions in using them.

Problem VI.   An entire group working at an unnecessarily slow pace. Cause: Work not properly assigned to individual workers, and material not handled in such an orderly fashion as to be available to the workers when they need it. Remedy: Better assignment of work and better routing, or moving, of materials.

Common Elements in Shop and
School Waste Elimination.

If, instead of the individual terms used in the specific illustrations, or the general terms used in the summary, these examples be thought of in terms of the school room, the common elements in shop and school waste elimination will become most apparent. We may think of the worker as the student, of the equipment as consisting of books, pens, paper, desks, chairs, etc., instead of the tools, work bench, and work place of the individual worker. We may think of methods as methods of working problems, of making a drawing, instead of folding a piece of cotton cloth, or laying a brick. In any case, the waste comes thru equipment that is itself poor, ill-adapted to the work, or poorly handled; thru necessary fatigue, or fatigue not properly handled; thru poor teaching, or poor learning; thru insufficient incentive; or thru same other common, ordinary, usual cause. These are the problems of waste that actually arise in the industries, and have been solved in the industries; but it is apparent that they are not problems that are peculiar to shops. They are problems that arise from the relations of people to one another, and to the work that is to be done.[24] They are problems that arise in any place where people are gathered together to do anything. They are, then, problems of the school as well as of the shop. Many of them, such as the problems of teaching, are, _primarily_, problems of the school and only secondarily problems of the shop.[25] To show just how, and to what extent, the problems and the solutions in the school and in the shop are related, is the work of the next chapter.

References
1. Taylor, F. W., "Shop Management," Harper Edition, p. 73.
2. Gilbreth, F. B. and L. M., "Fatigue Study," Ch. VII.
3. Gilbreth, F. B., "Bricklaying System," Ch. XIV.
   Gilbreth, F. B., "Motion Study," Ch. II.
4. Gilbreth, F. B., "Motion Study," Introduction, Letter by H. L. Gantt.
5. Gilbreth, F. B., "Motion Study in Surgery." Paper read before the American Medical Association, Atlantic City, June 25, 1914.
6. Gilbreth, F. B. and L. M., "Sociology of Management," Ch. IV.
7. Babbage, Charles, "Economy of Manufactures," Preface, p. 5, page 172, sec. 224-225.
8. Smith, Adam, "Wealth of Nations," p. 2, also Book I., Ch. I., p. 4.
9. Shaler, N. S., "Man and the Earth." Proceedings of a Conference of Governors in the White House, Washington, D. C., May 13-15, 1908.
10. Gilbreth, F. B., "Motion Study," Ch. I.
11. Hartness, James, "The Human Factor in Works Management," Ch. I.
12. Gilbreth, L. M., "The Psychology of Management," Ch. VIII.
13. Cooke, M. L., Bulletin No.5, Carnegie Foundation for the Advancement of Teaching, p. 15.
14. Gillette and Dana, "Cost Keeping and Management Engineering," p. 1.
15. Gilbreth, L. M., "The Psychology of Management," p. 6.
16. Colvin, S. S., "Human Behavior," Pages 90, 74, 154.
17. Gantt, H. L., "Work, Wages, and Profits," 2nd Edition, p. 48.
18. Gilbreth, L. M., "The Psychology of Management," p. 284.
19. Gilbreth, F. B.
20. Gilbreth, F. B., "Bricklaying System," Pages 6-7.
21. Gilbreth, F. B., "Motion Study," Ch. IV.
22. Gilbreth, F. B., "Hospital Efficiency from the Standpoint of the Efficiency Expert." Paper read before the Boston Medical Society, January, 1915.

23. Gilbreth, F. B. and L. M., "The Sociology of Management,"
    Ch. III.
24. Gilbreth, F. B., "Primer of Scientific Management," Ch., III.
25. Gilbreth, L. M., "The Psychology of Management," Ch. VIII.

CHAPTER II
The Relation Between Education
and Scientific Management

Teaching: the Important Common Element.

We have shown that the school and the shop alike have to deal with problems of human relationship and of accomplishing work. The most important element. Both in the school and in the scientifically managed shop the teaching element.[1] This is only true, however, of the scientifically managed shop. In the old type of shop the emphasis was laid upon getting the work done, with little recognition of the fact that the way in which the workers were taught was the most important element in the amount of work they accomplished.[2] In the newer type or management, as will be shown at length later, it is recognized that the transference of skill,- that is, the teaching of the man who does not know by the man who does know, is the point to be emphasized. To be specific, take a girl folding cloth according to an old method. Her equipment, chair, and working conditions can be put in standard condition in a few moments. An ordinary inspection now and then will provide that these conditions are maintained. The important thing is that she be taught the new set of motions which the new method includes. This means breaking down old habits, and building up new ones. It means a detailed and repeated demonstration or the new method which she must be taught to think most efficient, as well as to follow with her hands.[3]

Teaching is not only an important element of a change made by Scientific Management, as this illustration shows, but it is a fundamental element of every change made by Scientific Management that involves the human element. This being the case, a comparison between teaching in the schools and teaching in the shops run by Scientific Management must yield valuable results. In order to make this comparison, we must first understand what teaching means in education, and what teaching means in management.

What Teaching Is.

The term "teaching" is, at first sight, one of the simplest words in the language. Yet it is a most difficult word to define, for within the idea as to what constitutes teaching may lie the entire theory of education.[4] Is teaching showing the child how to develop the powers that are in him?[5] Or is teaching giving the child something to imitate, or a copy, and showing how to make himself like this thing?[6] Or is teaching acting as a model oneself, and trusting to a belief in the child's inborn capacity-to-imitate to make it sure that he will be like the model?[7] Or, again, is teaching simply giving the child a desire to learn, and an idea where the things to learn are to be found?[8] Or is teaching laying emphasis on forming associations,[9] and providing the subject matter to be associated only secondarily?

It is for each teacher to formulate his own definition of teaching. However, it maybe said, perhaps, that the average teacher has elements of all these different ideas of teaching in his own ideal as to what teaching should be. He thinks

1. That the child should be taught to develop himself;
2. That the development has two parts,-
    a.   The things which are presented to the child,
    b.   The way in which the child responds to these things;
3. That the teacher's duty is to put things of value before the child, to show him not only everything possible that is worth knowing, but also to show him where such things are to be found.[10]

Further, the teacher believes that he, himself, should act as a model in every respect; and, finally, that he should help the child to act upon the things that the child sees and thinks about, and aid the child to group what he gets into usable knowledge.

We might summarize the teacher's duties, then, into providing available knowledge, and seeing that the pupil acquires and uses it in the most efficient manner possible. The relation between acquiring and using is very close. Many people doubt whether any knowledge is really acquired until it is in such shape that it can be directly and easily used.[11] On the other hand, it is really more important during the learning period that the child learns how to learn, than that he uses what he is getting in an immediate, definite, and concrete way. On the relations between the two depends in large part the conflict between vocational training and so-called "cultural" training.[12] There is at the present time little thought, in any of the lower schools, given to teaching the learner how to teach. If the teacher succeeds in stimulating his pupils to learn, and to use what they learn, his teaching is rated as successful.

Teaching and Scientific Management.

A manager is one who determines who shall do certain work, and who provides that the work can be done. A scientific manager, in addition to this, determines how the work shall be done, and provides that his directions be and are accurately carried out.[13] This provision for accurate fulfillment of assigned work implies skilled teaching and efficient learning. The results are tested far more accurately than they are in the school, by the quantity and the quality of the output, and by the accurate measurement of the worker, or learner, during and after the work. The worker must learn, and he must to it immediately. He must also, in every case, learn to teach as well as to do, for it is a part of the plan that he transfer the skill, after he has acquired it, to those who are next in line for the work.[14]

Likenesses Between the Work of the Teacher and the Manager.

The teacher and the manager are each put in charge of a group of people, and are, to a certain extent, responsible for them. Each is put in the position of being over those he is directing, that is to say, of having the right to say what is to be done, who is to do it, how much is to be done, and what the doer is to get for doing it. Each has the same problem of seeing that each one in his group does that work which it is best that he does, that he does the amount which is best for his health and for the general good, that he is interested in what he does, and that he learns something, or improves in some way by doing it.

Differences Between the Work of the Teacher and the Manager.

The type of responsibility differs. The teacher has, in most cases, young children who are in their formative years, and who are entrusted to him for a certain amount of time, during which he takes the place of the parent or guardian in addition to his function as a teacher. The average manager has adults, or at least people of responsible age, under him, and, under present social conditions, he is simply supposed to provide safe and decent working conditions, a proper wage for the work done, with, at best, an opportunity to learn and progress.

In the second place there is a difference in training. The teacher of to-day is a specialist in teaching. He has received not only general training, which insures that he is an educated member of the community, but special training in subjects which he is to teach and in the methods by which he is to teach them. Before he starts to teach he has decided what group of children he wishes to teach. His training has fitted him to understand the mental and physical conditions, development and type of training needed for his particular group of pupils. He has been told of the various problems which will arise. He knows the difficulties of discipline. He has had a training in psychology, and often in child psychology. He knows what he is likely to find in the minds of his pupils.

The average manager has had little or no systematic training for his position. Only within the last few years have courses for management in various industries been attempted.[15] The manager is apt to be in one of several situations. He may have come "up from the ranks," in which case there is a decided probability that he has had no training even in elementary psychology, that he does not understand either teaching or discipline, and, in many cases, that he has had no training in the broad underlying economic and industrial principles which are at the base of his particular trade, or his little specialized branch of the trade. Or, he may not have come "up from the ranks," and has not, in all probability, had any first-hand experience with those whom he is trying to manage, knows little or nothing of their problems and their physical or mental capacity, and is working more or less in the dark when he tries to work with them. If he is a college graduate, and technically trained for the line of industry which he is managing, nine chances in ten, or better nine hundred and ninety-nine chances in a thousand, and this is stating it mildly, he has had no training in psychology or education, and little or no training in the actual hand processes of the work that he is doing. If he <u>has</u> had the psychological training and the educational training and even the theoretical training in the industrial work, he has not had the practical shop training which makes him "finger wise" in the work and able to follow with his hands and his mind the worker's processes.

Advantages of the Teacher Work.

The teacher's work is, then, like the manager's in many respects. Where there are differences, the advantage is on the side of the teacher. He has not only the general and specific training for his work. He has also, in every case, been, first, a pupil, knowing the difficulties; of the pupil, and, second, a teacher, specially trained to overcome those difficulties. The economic pressure which drives the manager is removed from the teacher. He does not have to turn out work, or output, which is for sale, and upon whose sale depends his bread and butter, as is, the case in the plant. True, if his pupils do not "make good," he may lose his position, but, under ordinary conditions, whether times are good or bad, if he does faithful work, he gets his salary, and, if his pupils are able to pass their examinations and advance in their grades, his work is judged satisfactory.[16] Again, the teacher is relieved of much of the responsibility for the planning which is a part of the work of the manager. As for the human relationship, the children with whom he works are, in spite of individual relations, all fairly of an age, and have all fairly the same amount of preparation. They are plastic, many of them having even no idea of what they wish to do and become.[17] This gives the teacher an opportunity for an enormous amount of influence. In case things do not work smoothly, and discipline is needed, the teacher can receive help, if he requires it, and, in many cases, can pass all serious discipline cases over to some one who is responsible for handling them. All of these things that we have called "advantages" of teaching might, from one standpoint, be looked upon as restrictions upon the teacher. It is only when we compare conditions in the school and in the shop that we realize that, rather than being restricted, the teacher is relieved of many pressing and, often, harrowing responsibilities.

On the other hand, the average manager has not an adequate training, and has almost unlimited responsibility. He must decide what work is to be done, and how much work is to be done. He must provide the material and equipment. He has often to deal with workers differing widely in age, race, and training. He often has to deal with those who have never been taught to have right aims, or whom life has handled so badly that the work they are doing is in no wise related to the work that they aim to do, would like to do, or are fit to do. He must provide the teaching and be responsible for all the discipline. He must provide the incentive, or inducements, for workers to stay with him and work for him. Finally, he must manage in such a way that he can do all of these things, and yet make enough to live on himself, and also to pay and satisfy the people from whom he must borrow the money to "run the business." The work of the most modern manager in the most scientifically managed plant might, for scope and responsibility, better be compared with the work of an old-fashioned minister in a country church than with that of the present day teacher in the modern city school.

To sum up, the <u>extent</u> of the teacher's problem is limited when compared with the extent of the manager's, but the <u>content</u> of the teacher's problem is no less important, in that, as has been well said, "It is a more refined and subtle problem in that it deals more largely with the subjective aspects of efficiency, and has to do with immature and developing minds."[18]

Aims of the Teacher and the Scientific Manager.

If we compare the aims of the teacher and of the manager, we find that we can state them so that they seem very similar or very different. Both aim to turn out the best type of product possible. with the least expenditure of waste. The product of the teacher is a trained pupil. The actual work that that pupil does is usually potential, something that he <u>may</u> do, and <u>is fit</u> to do, and <u>should be ready</u> to do. The products of the factory or the industry should be two. They are, if the manager is a scientific manager. They are, first, the material thing produced, which has a market value, and, second, the trained worker produced, who not only has the potentialities of the school child, but who is actually making worth-while things.

Debts of Scientific Management to Education.

The debt which the scientific manager owes to education is a large one, and one which the scientific manager is only too glad to acknowledge. As soon as the manager realizes that successful management is largely a matter of transference of skill, or of teaching, the science of psychology and the art of teaching becomes available, and are being gradually, though it must be admitted slowly, used. The pioneer workers in the field of management are more than ready to acknowledge that they are using, and must constantly use, the data accumulated by the profession of education. Managers are not only reading the literature of education, but are going into the schools and colleges for actual object lessons in how to teach. They are studying methods and their results. More than this, they are cutting out waste in the learning process by applying actual and accurate tests to the method and their results. The great contribution of the science of management is in the derivation of accurate tests. It is these tests of efficiency which management can offer to education as some compensation for the aid she is ready and glad to own.

Need of Comparative Study of Education and Management.

We can see, then, there must be great value in a comparative study of education and management, and, especially, of methods of teaching in the two fields. We have attempted to show the likenesses between the fields and the differences in order to make clear the possibility and the need for cooperation. We have shown that ideas have been transferred successfully from the teaching field to the field of management. Wen now advocate a similar transference of successful methods from the field of management to the field of education. One of the greatest wastes that exists everywhere is the lack of using work already done. It is only too common practice to begin at the beginning instead of beginning where the last accurate worker left off. Every teacher acknowledged that there is waste in teaching, and that it is possible that some of this waste shall be eliminated. Now it is perfectly conceivable that one should start in eliminating this waste without leaving the teaching field, and that one should do excellent work; but surely this is not good practice. If waste elimination has been done in another field, and if this field has been shown to be closely related enough to the teaching field to have the methods transferable, surely the most efficient practice is to inspect the sister field thoroughly, and to adopt whatever is usable before doing first-hand work. We advocate, then, that the teaching profession review carefully the work done by the managers in the industries with the idea of carrying over any methods which may prove of value, and testing them in the teaching field for themselves. It must be emphasized here that the industrial field certainly exhibits methods of testing efficiency, which can be learned and used with profit by anyone.[19] Even if the teacher should find little or nothing concrete that he can use, he will certainly get stimulus to new work in his own line. An understanding on the part of the teacher of the most important methods and accomplishments of Scientific Management will be profitable and interesting to his own work. He will look at this work with what is called a "new slant."

It will not detract from the real human element to think of the school room for a time as a plant producing a product, and as subject to all the tests for efficiency to which such a plant must submit. The resemblances, as we have seen, are many. No matter what our opinion of the work of each, we must realize that, as a matter of fact, the finished work of the school, widely different as the word "finished" must be interpreted in various cases, goes into the industries. There has been, as far back as our knowledge goes, a gap between the two, and a gap which has tended to grow larger rather than smaller, certainly up to within the last few years. The one thing that can bridge this gap, in fact, the solution of all problems, is education, or training, and who is to furnish such education as will be broad enough and useful enough to bridge the gap if not the teacher?

The first step in coming to a common understanding is to establish a common vocabulary.[20] It will be necessary for the manager to learn the teacher's vocabulary. It is difficult to persuade, any man or woman that he has a vocabulary that, more or less, shuts him off from communication with people in other lines of work. It is even more difficult to convince anyone that he uses words without a very definite idea of their meaning, and yet nine-tenths of the disputes could be settled, if those disputing would start by defining their terms. Now the managers must learn the teaching vocabulary, and they will learn it as soon as they realize the importance of it to them, but it would be a gracious act on the part of the teachers to go more than half way, that is to say, not only to understand the vocabulary of scientific, or measured, management, but to translate the art of teaching into that vocabulary. As soon as we get the common vocabulary, the two lines of activity can be closely related. It is a great temptation to outline the outcome of such a Utopian plan. The great work of measurement and standardization that must be done can then be divided, with the result that much more rapid progress can be made. The question of vocational guidance will be practically solved. The whole twin apprentice plan, and similar methods of training will be either adopted as they stand, or so reconstructed and elaborated that there will be no gap between the school and the industry. There will be no period in the boy's or girl's life when he will feel ill at ease, or ill prepared for what is expected of him. With the close relationship of the school and the industries, will come a unifying effect upon all the activities, of society. The two will have demonstrated the possibility of different activities working together. There appears to be a straight road towards that millenium of which we all dream.

It is too early in the day, however, to indulge in daydreams as to ultimate outcomes. The first step for the teacher of to-day is to take the time and make the effort to examine and test what has been done in the industries, and to see how' far results there can be used in the work of teaching in the schools. The answer to these questions can be given by the teachers, and by them only. It is for those who have had the experience in the industries, and who know what has been done there, to present the results there in as nearly aa possible such form as will be most interesting to the teachers, and to suggest any possible places where industrial methods and tests could be used in the schools, leaving it to the teacher, who is acquainted with the conditions of the specific problem, actually to test out the methods advocated, and to give the results of his tests to the waiting educational and industrial world.

References
1. Gantt, H. L., Paper 928, A. S. M. E., p. 372.
2. Gilbreth, L. M., "The Psychology of Management," p. 208-210.
3. James, W., "Briefer Course," p. 134.
   James, W., "Advanced Course," p. 134.
   Colvin, S. S., "Human Behavior," p. 165.
   Calkins, M. W., "A First Book in Psychology," p. 354.
   Read, M. S., "An Introductory Psychology," p. 179-194.
4. Monroe, Paul, "Cyclopedia of Education."
5. Graves, F. P., "History of Education," p.123.
   Monroe, Paul, "Source Book of History of Education," p, 131.
   Monroe, Paul, "Cyclopedia of Education," 'Pestallozi,"
      "Senaca," "Rousseau."
6. Bolton, F. E., "Principles of Education," Ch, 16.
   Graves, F. P., "History of Education," p. 16, 38, 71, 87,-
      "Descriptions of Ancient Education."
7. Monroe, Paul, "Cyclopedia of Education," p. 325,- Plutarch.
8. Thorndike, E. L., "Principles of Teaching," Ch. V.
   Pillsbury, W. B., "Attention," Ch. IV.
   Bolton, F. E., "Principles of Education," p. 669.
9. Monroe, Paul, "Cyclopedia of Education,"- Herbart.
   Bolton, F. E., "Principles of Education," Ch. XIV.
10. Bagley, W. C., "The Educative Process," p. 38.
11. O'Shea, M. V., "Education as Adjustment," p. 141.
    Thorndike, E. L., "Principles of Teaching," Ch. 13, p. 206.
12. Snedden, "Problems of Educational Adjustment."
    Carlton, F. T., "Education and Industrial Evolution," Ch. IV.
13. Taylor, Frederick W., "Shop Management," Harper Edition, p. 70.
14. Gantt, H. L., "Work, Wages, and Profits," Second Edition, Ch. VI.

15. Papers presented at the Efficiency Session of the Twentieth Annual Convention of the Society for the Promoting of Engineering Education held at Boston, Mass., June 26-29, 1912.
16. Journal of the National Education Association of the United States. Paper by William M. Davidson, p. 286.
17. Bagley, W. C., "The Educative Process," Pages 30-31.
18. Colvin, S. S.
19. Taylor, Frederick W., "The Principles of Scientific Management," Ch. I.
    Gilbreth, F. B., "Motion Study," Ch. I.
    Gilbreth, L. M., "The Psychology of Management," p. 16.
20. Dartmouth College Conferences. First Tuck School Conference on Scientific Management, p. 356.

CHAPTER III
What Scientific Management Is

The Theory and Practice of Scientific Management.

It will be the aim of the next three chapters to present Scientific Management. The ideal method by which one can get some idea of the science of management in a short space of time is,-

1. By reading the literature of the subject.
2. By actually visiting some plant in which Scientific Management is in operation.
3. By talking with those who have actually installed the science, in order to learn how the changes were made, and how the new better conditions were maintained.

It will be the aim, here, to come as near to this ideal condition as possible; to state in this chapter the laws, or principles, that underlie the science of management in a more concise form than they are set forth in the available literature; to present in the chapter that follows the actual practice in a scientifically managed plant, and the tests by which such practice may be known to be scientific; and to describe in the third chapter the process of making the installation, and of maintaining what has been installed.

Scientific Management is a new subject. Its real development has come within the experience of those now living. Because of this, a non-partisan and complete history of it has not yet been written. The literature lies mostly in books, pamphlets, and current publications, for the industries and in the vocabulary of the industries. The actual applications, as yet, are, many of them, in machine shops or other industrial plants, where the type of work being done in itself makes it difficult for those not actually in industrial work to follow the management easily. There are, therefore, some advantages in becoming acquainted with Scientific Management thru a non-technical summary, rather than thru the first-hand study of literature in plants.

Definition of Scientific Management.

Scientific Management is such management as is based upon a science, that is to say, upon measurement.[1] It differs from other management,- which is based upon guesswork, or tradition, or experience. A science is a body of facts which are the result of accurate measurement of the data studied. Scientific Management, then, is the result of submitting ordinary management to measurement, and of deriving from the measurement a new type of management, which has actual facts as its foundations.[2]

History of Such Management.

It is not easy to trace the early history of the science of management. Adam Smith[3], Coulomb[4], and Babbage[5] were pioneers in advocating a systematic study of work, and as far back as Leonardo Da Vinci we can find traces of the feeling of the necessity for investigating what was done, in order that it might be done better.[6]

This study was put on a really scientific basis, when it was recognized that the subject studied must be divided into the smallest practicable elements, and that element must be accurately measured and tested.[7] As soon as this idea became thoroughly recognized, experts in various lines became interested in the problem, and took up the measurement along various lines. The most successful practice existing was carefully observed in order to discover the causes of the success. In other words, the most successful practice was made the standard.[8] This was then carefully measured. The causes for the success were found to be in some cases what had been expected, and in others what had not been expected. This was a matter of secondary importance, as the investigators learned as much from the things that. turned out differently from what they expected, as from the things that turned out exactly as they expected.

Underlying the success, and demonstrated as the causes of it, were eight fundamental laws, which Doctor Taylor formulated as the "eight principles" that underlie good management.[9] The laws have been stated by Taylor in terms of industrial relationships, and have since been summarized by an educator, who realizes their application to the school, as well as the shop, in general terms.

The First Law.

The first law reads, "Measure your product." Accept nothing as worthy to be made a standard until it has actually been tested by applying accurate measurement to it. In the industries the practice is as follows:

Among various workers engaged in the same type of work one is observed who seems to accomplish more work in a given time, or to work with greater ease, or to accumulate less fatigue, or to have, very apparently, some better method of working, than his fellows. This method is divided into as small elements as possible, and an accurate record is made of the method by which the work is done, the amount of time that is taken, and every attending circumstance.[10] The methods of other workers doing the same work, are then also recorded, as some element in a method, which, as a whole, is not so good, may be better than a single element in the best method. It has been noted that the ideal method of doing a piece of work seldom lies in the consecutive acts of one worker. From the elements, as recorded, is built up a standard method of doing the work, which consists of the most efficient performance of each element. Changes may be made, as equipment is bettered, as materials change, or as a worker better suited to the work is put at it, but such changes must submit to the same accurate measurement.

It was in exactly this fashion that the efficient method of laying brick was derived. The method of that bricklayer who laid the most brick with the least effort was recorded. Then, records were made of other bricklayers who made large output with little effort, and from the data gathered the standard method was derived. A close study of the motions resulted in the invention of new equipment which made a later better method possible, but the inventions were the result of the measurement, and the efficient method by which the larger number of brick can now be laid is attributed to the measurement as a direct cause, rather than to the inventions, which were a by-product.[11]

In the same way, actual measurement might be applied to methods in the school room. A finishes ten problems during the time that the average member of the class finishes five, and appears no more exhausted. Just what are the elements that enter into the work that he does? Are there other elements in the work of others, who are close to his performance, which are different from the elements in his work? If so, these also must be recorded. When all the different elements that enter into success in the work of various pupils have been measured and recorded, a standard method of doing the examples may be adopted, which will be, at least, "a point to start from."

The Second Law.

The second law reads, "Divide your responsibility." In the shop the responsibility is divided between the management and the workmen, that is, there is a recognition by both management and worker that each has a part and an interest in the work, and that, in order that the best results may take place, the work must be divided. That part is assigned to the manager that he is best fitted to do, and that part assigned to the worker that he is best fitted to do. The division is called "equal" in the sense that the work of each is of equal importance, and the responsibility of one is the same as the responsibility of the other.[12] Any work done is a partnership between manager and worker, with all the mutual responsibilities and duties of a partnership.

This is done in the industries by separating the planning from the performing. The management force does the planning, the workers the performing. The interresponsibility is maintained by having the planners teach the performers exactly how the work is to be done, and by making it a duty of the performers to obtain this teaching from the planners, to come to them personally, and see that the necessary instruction is received. The division of work and responsibility is, in addition, secured by dividing the planning of the work among various planners who are specially trained for the different types of work, and by dividing the performing among different workers, who are, also, specially trained and fitted to do exactly what is assigned them to do. The work, then, as it comes in, is divided among various people, each of whom is responsible for doing a part of it, and who are all responsible to one another that it is done. This will be brought out more in detail in the chapter on the sequence of installation, where we must show exactly how this division of work is carried on.

In the school room such division of work has long existed, in that practically all planning has been done by the teacher, and all performing by the pupils. The danger has been exactly the opposite to that in the industries. In the industries too much responsibility has lain with the worker. In the school too much responsibility has been placed upon the teacher. The pupils too often feel that they are responsible for nothing except regular attendance, and a greater or less amount of passive attention.[13] Examples of excellent division of responsibility have been noted in the evening schools. Here, in one instance, the writer has noted that the teacher has planned the work, and has made the pupils understand that he is ready to give the instruction. They are old enough and experienced enough to realize that it is to their advantage to receive this instruction. They have accepted the responsibility of getting what they need, and come to the teacher for this teaching, when they feel that being taught would be an advantage to them. It is more difficult to make younger children feel responsible for the work that they do, to understand the divided responsibility between themselves and their teacher. This is because the child so seldom understands the benefits that he gets from any work that he does at school. The moment that the incentive changes, and that he realizes that he does get actual benefit, it is possible, although he be much younger than the typical evening school pupil, to make him take some responsibility for what he learns. A study of the incentive in the industries may be of help here.

The Third Law.

The third law reads, "Define and circumscribe your task." The task is simply the amount of work that any member of the organization is expected to do.[14] It is not necessarily any more than he has done, nor is it necessarily work done after a different fashion than he has done it. It is simply applying measurement to the work of everybody in the organization, in order to find out what the, or she, is able to do. For, after all, the doer, and not what is done, is the final element in deciding what the doer is to do. To say that the task is "defined" simply means that, when the work is finally in such shape that the worker can best do it, accurate measurement has decided <u>what</u> the work is that the worker is to do, <u>where</u> he is to do it, <u>when</u> he is to do it, <u>how much</u> he is to do in a given amount of time, <u>how</u> he is to do it, and <u>how much</u> he is to get for doing it. The task is "circumscribed" in the sense that it is set aside from other work which the man may do, or from other work which others may do; that is to say, we have to consider the man's task not only as related to him, but to the other members of the organization, to look at it in an individual, and also in a social, light.

A task in the industries states that worker $\underline{A}$ is expected to do task $\underline{B}$ according to method $\underline{C}$. He is allowed a certain amount of time for doing it. He is prescribed certain rest periods and he is paid a fixed amount for accomplishing the fixed task of the required quality within the fixed time.[15]

Now what is the case in the school? The average teacher will say at once that the class task is something with which he has little, or nothing, to do. The requirements for the year, or the half year, perhaps even for the month, the week, or the day, are made by some supervising authority. His daily program may even be laid out, at least, as to the amount of time that shall be devoted each day to each subject in the course of study. Yet even within these fixed limits there is much that could be done. Radical improvements in daily schedules and in standards must probably come, and will come, from the supervising authorities themselves. Splendid work in measuring and standardizing tasks is being done in the field of education.[16*] The results of such work will be given to the teacher by the educators doing it direct, without passing thru the industrial, or any other, medium. The teacher should use these as far and as fast as he can. In the meantime, he should test his assigned tasks for himself. How much time do you allow for doing ten examples in arithmetic? How many pupils actually accomplish the ten? What percent do the others accomplish? What is the nature of the errors? What are the methods used by the most successful pupils? Could they accomplish twelve, or fifteen, or more in the same time, and with the same quality of work? What is the

---

* See Appendix A.

incentive to complete as much work as possible in the time? How much fatigue seems to be accumulated? All of these questions are involved in properly setting the task. The assignment of the proper task depends on accurate measurement, but there is no excuse for not defining and circumscribing the task from the start. The worker in the scientifically managed plant knows exactly <u>what</u> he is expected to do, and <u>how</u> he is expected to do it. This makes concentration possible. Is it always equally possible in the schoolroom?

The Fourth Law.

The fourth law reads, "Provide favorable conditions." This implies so arranging the work that it can be done, and that it can always be done. The management sees that the worker is provided with all materials needed to do the work at the <u>time</u> that he needs them, in the <u>place</u> that he needs them, in the <u>order</u> that he needs them, and exactly of such <u>amount</u> as he needs, that he may neither lack anything, nor be encumbered by superfluous supplies. Every element, from the material side, is at hand and in an obvious sequence, that is to say, the worker does not need to think of material and equipment. They have been put in place before he starts, and are in such position that he uses one piece after another, as it is easiest for him to pick it up and put it in place. As for his mental condition, the management has provided such teaching that be is in no doubt as to the method he is to use. The only decision he must make is as to whether he is willing to work or not. He is able to work since he is prepared.

The average teacher has an excellent record for seeing that the prescribed task can actually be done. In almost any school room one can see the teacher watching the class with the greatest care, to make sure they have everything they need for their work, sufficient time in which to do it, and an understanding of the method by which the work is to be done. But has the possible waste here been measured?

Sometimes "time for getting ready," "time for doing the work," and "time for cleaning up" are not separated. John may lose time during the arithmetic test by having to go to the supply closet for a sheet of paper, or Mary by having to stop to sharpen a pencil. The question may be worded in such a way that time must be taken from the test period to explain the method to be used, which should have been stated in formulating the question.[17] Or, if the test come from an outside source, actual time spent working the problems may be stated, and time in laying out and putting materials in order may be thoughtlessly included by the teacher Or again, one method of distributing supplies may be included in the time for doing a test one day. A different and shorter method may be used a second day, yet no allowance be made when the papers are all corrected at some later time, because the teacher has made no note as to the method used and the time taken. These are all small things, but upon them rests the possibility of accomplishing the task in the assigned time, if the time has been at all carefully assigned. The important thing at the start is not so much that the task be properly assigned, as that identical conditions for performing it be constantly present, that some sort of standard be adopted. How widely these standards differ from efficient standards can be determined later.

The Fifth Law.

The fifth law reads, "Reward efficiency." This implies furnishing a sufficient incentive to induce the worker to do the work of the quantity and quality desired in the assigned time, and according to the assigned method. It has been discovered in the industries, that the amount of incentive must differ with type of work done.[18] If the work demands simply bodily exertion, a certain incentive is needed. If it demands close application and thinking, a higher incentive is needed. If it demands thinking and application and also bodily effort, a far higher incentive is needed to make the worker willing to keep at it. If

Sufficient incentive is not offered, the worker will immediately slow down to a more easy pace, even if he gets much less for doing the work.

In the school, the amount and nature of the reward offered has never been accurately determined.[19] In the school there has always been a feeling that efficiency should be rewarded, but a reward that would be satisfactory to both teacher and pupil is not always available. Perhaps this lack of reward accounts to some extent for the lack of efficiency, which, it is acknowledged, exists. Just what does the teacher get for efficient work? Just what does the pupil get? Is the reward in each case high enough to insure that enough work is done, that the work is of high grade, and it is done with some degree of pleasure? Is the reward, perhaps, too great? What is the best type of reward? Some may, perhaps, object to the word "reward" entirely. In that case we will use "return." There must be returns in some form. In the industry the test is that the reward must be sufficient to induce the worker to <u>do</u> the work, to <u>continue</u> to do it, and to <u>enjoy</u> doing it. Would not this be an excellent test for the reward in the school? If not, what better test can we offer?

The Sixth Law.

The sixth law reads, "Punish failure." Such punishment under Scientific Management is constructive, in that its aim is to induce the worker not to abandon the work, but to go at it in such a fashion that he can accomplish it.[20] To be specific, $\underline{A}$ turns out a less amount of work than is required by the task. The foreman notes this in the record, and at once inquires into the cause. If $\underline{A}$ does not understand the method, he is taught. If there is some mistake in the set-up, the man who prepares the equipment is brought to terms. If there is a flaw in material, the man responsible is notified, and the material for the next day is most carefully inspected. If $\underline{A}$ has "slowed down," his physical condition, and any reasons for this, within or without the plant, are inquired into. If the work does not fit A, he is transferred to another type of work. Only in case his failure to make the task can be attributed plainly to unwillingness to make it is something that might be called "punishment" resorted to.

This sixth law, as applied to the teaching field, brings up many problems.[21] There is the problem of retardation, or repeating. There is the problem of pupils leaving school, and the question as to what becomes of them. There is the problem of handling the unsuccessful teacher, or the teacher, who, while getting good results with his pupils, feels that teaching is a failure as regards his own happiness and self development. There is the problem of dealing with the lazy child, and the stupid child, and the abnormal child, and any other child who, for any reason, does not do the work successfully. Here comes in the large question of punishment. What is it for? What kind is it? How does it turn out? Then there is discipline. Can it be defined as punishment? Should it ever be punishment? Is it not always adjustment? Should it not always be constructive? Who should give it? All of these are questions having a close relationship to teaching. Have we ever applied measurement here? If so, where are the standards?

The Seventh Law.

The seventh law reads, "Suit the work to the worker." This provides for the scientific selection, training, teaching, and developing of the worker. This takes up the matter entirely from the human side. We have first made the environment as perfect as possible. We are here concerned with showing the worker how best to adapt himself, and fit into the improved environment.

The teacher's problem differs from that of the manager in that the manager must fit the work to an individual, who, if not in his final position, is, at least, from the manager's standpoint, in his final stage of development. The teacher is teaching a child in his training stage, in his period of development. The teacher must, therefore, make more constant adjustment of the work to the worker. The question here is whether the work is being properly adapted to the stage in the development. Suppose <u>A</u> is solving a problem. Is he using the material and methods that best fit his age and development? Or, is he, perhaps, handling his material according to a method that was excellent in the lower grades, or, perhaps, attempting to use a method that would be excellent in the higher grades, but that is not most efficient with him? We find sometimes in asking the teacher, "Why do you do it so?" the answer, "That is the way they have done it ever since the first grade." Now it is just possible that the method was excellent for the first grade, but is it most efficient for the fourth, or the sixth, or the eighth? Or again, the answer might be, "That is the method they will use in the eighth grade." But may it not be that the method used now should be a preparation rather than a duplicate of the method then to be used? The question is not so much, "Is the method right?" as "Have you ever considered whether it is right or not, or is it simply traditional to use it?"

The Eighth Law.

The eighth law reads, "Secure cooperation." This takes up the underlying ideal, or aim, that must be established, if the new kind of management is to live. It might be possible, but it would be extremely difficult, to install management based on a science without cooperation. It would be absolutely impossible to maintain it. This cooperation is obtained in the shops thru the division of work and responsibility, and thru the recognition that the cooperation of all is essential to success.

As for cooperation in the school, room, how can we make the class cooperate not only with the teacher, but with one another? A number of admirable solutions of this problem exist.

One successful teacher has aroused and maintained a social spirit in her class, room by allowing the pupils to help in the teaching by making them feel that they are all members of a social group who help one another. She is successful in this, in that she really feels this herself, and succeeds in imparting this feeling to each pupil in her room.

Another type of successful teacher uses as an incentive for excellent work the privilege of becoming class teacher. The responsibility and prestige of this position are an effective appeal.

Another type of successful teacher has induced cooperation by cultivating the spirit of class rivalry, this particular class against all other classes in the building.

Still another type has gained class cooperation by making a first year class in a commercial high school see the close relationship of their school work to success in their life work. She is arrayed with them against the entire industrial world. She is helping them to prepare themselves for success in the world's work.

Another type has turned his English class into a self-governing organization to which every member of the class is proud to belong, and for whose success he feels responsible.

Still another has inspired his history class to make of the recitation hour a class product. Each one undertakes some specific phase of the subject in hand, and knows that, unless he contributes his share, the whole which the class hour was intended to present to the class group will be incomplete. Suppose the subject is "England at the time of Elizabeth." One has "the wars;" another, "the diplomatic relations;" a third, the geographic conditions;" a fourth, "the poets;" a fifth, "the prose writers;" a sixth, "dramatic activities." At the end of the hour the class knows that it is expected to have a definite, well-proportioned picture of the time, and each one does his share towards making the picture possible.

All of these are effective methods. Perhaps the ideal method of gaining cooperation will include elements of them all, but many a class room has no such element. The teacher is arrayed against the pupils. The teacher may, even, be considered a natural enemy of the pupils. There is no feeling of confidence. This is well exemplified by the difficulty with which many pupils can be made to understand that a written test is not a means of making the teacher think that one knows a great deal, or that one knows more than one really does know, but is rather an opportunity for the teacher to discover just what he has made clear, and what he has failed to make clear, in order that he may better cooperate with the pupils in overcoming difficulties. The writer has seen a class of girls nine to twelve years old astounded to hear that the purpose of a test was to help the teacher to teach better. "Do you want me to tell you what I _don't_ know?" said the youngest member of the class. "Certainly," said the teacher. "Well, I can do that," said the small child, and went to work with a will. In contrast to this we may cite the example of the boy passing a college entrance rhetoric examination, who rejoiced to catch the instructor asking, "Can you cite five rules for the use of the comma?" and calmly answered, "I can," waiting with an air of defiance to see what would happen.

Measurement Fundamental.

These are, then, the laws that underlie Scientific Management, and the last seven laws are all derived from the first, which is "Measure everything that you do, and abide by the results of your measurement." <u>How</u> you measure, <u>when</u> you measure, <u>whom</u> you measure, <u>where</u> you measure, <u>how much</u> you measure, these are details to be settled. If you know <u>why</u> you measure, if you determine that you will measure, you have taken the important step. If the literature of Scientific Management, as read at length in its original sources, or as summarized in its underlying ideas here, convinces one that measurement is necessary, and that the results of the measurement are helpful, it has done all that it could hope to do.

References
1. Gilbreth, F. B., "Primer of Scientific Management," p. 1.
2. Towne, H. R., Introduction to "Principles of Scientific Management," p, 7.
3. "Wealth of Nations"- 1776.
4. Charles Augustin de Coulomb. 1773-1806.
5. "On the Economy of Machinery and Manufactures"- 1832.
6. 1452-1519. Note Books. Book III.
7. Taylor, F. W., A. S. M. E., Paper 647, "A Piece Rate System," 1895.
8. Cooke, M. L., "Academic and Industrial Education," Carnegie Foundation Bulletin No.5, p. 6.
9. Taylor, F. W., "Shop Management," Harper Edition, Pages 63-64.
    Taylor, F. W., "The Principles of Scientific Management," Pages 36-37.
10. Taylor, F. W., "Shop Management," Harper Edition, Pages 171, 180-182.
    Gilbreth, F. B., "Motion study," p. 107.
11. Gilbreth, F. B., "Bricklaying System," Ch, VII. Paper for American Academy of Political and Social Science.
12. Taylor, F. W., "The Principles of Scientific Management," p. 37.
13. King, Irving, "Social Aspects of Education," Ch. XVI.
14. Gilbreth, F. B., "Primer of Scientific Management," p. 9.
15. Gantt, H. L., "Work, Wages, and Profits," Second Edition, Ch. VIII., "The Task Idea."
16. Ayres, L. P., "A Scale for Measuring the Quality of Handwriting in School Children"- Russell Sage Foundation, New York City, No. 113.
    Ayres, L. P., "The Measurement of Educational Processes and Products"- Russell Sage Foundation, No. 116.
    Bagley, W. C., "Class Room Management." Ch, XV.

Baker, J. H., "Economy of Time in Education," U. S. Bulletin of Education, 1913, No. 38.

Buckingham, B. R., "Spelling Ability, Its Measurement and Distribution."

Cook and O'Shea, "The Child and His Spelling."

Courtis, S. A., "Teachers' Manual."

    "   " " "Bulletins of Courtis Standard Tests."

    "   " " "Manual of Instruction for Giving and Scoring the Courtis Standard Tests in the Three R's.

Courtis , S. A., "Educational Diagnosis."

Hillegas, M. B., "A Scale for the Measurement of Quality in English Composition by Young People," Teachers College Record, Sept., 1912.

Starch, D., "The Measurement of Handwriting," Journal of Educational Psychology, Oct., 1913.

Starch, D. and Elliott, E. C., "Reliability of Grading Work in English," School Review, Vol. XX., 442-457

Starch, D. and Elliott, E. C., "Reliability of Grading Work in History," School Review, Dec., 1913.

Starch, D. and Elliott, E. C., "Reliability of Grading Work in Mathematics," School Review, April, 1913.

Stone, C. W., "Arithmetical Abilities and Some Factors Determining Them."

Strayer and Thorndike, "Educational Administration," Sec. 18, 19.

Thorndike, E. L., "Education," Pages 212-228.

    "   " " "Principles of Teaching," Pages 257-273.

Thorndike, E. L., "Handwriting," Teachers College Record, Vol. II., No. 2, March, 1910.

Thorndike, E. L., "The Measurement of Achievement in Drawing," Teachers College Record, Nov., 1913.

Wallin, J. E. W., "Spelling Efficiency in Relation to Age, Grade, and Sex, and the Question of Transfer."

Yerkes, "The Importance of Social Status as Indicated by the Results of the Point Scale Method of Measuring Mental Capacity," Journal of Educational Psychology, March, 1915.

17. Bagley, W. C., "The Educative Process," Pages 324-326.
De Garmo, C., "Interest and Education," p. 181.
Stevens, R., "The Question as a Measure of Efficiency in Instruction: A Critical study of Class Room Practice."

18. Taylor, F. W., "Shop Management," Harper Edition, p. 26.

19. O'Shea, M. V., "Education as Adjustment," p. 151.

20. Dodge, James M., "The Spirit in Which Scientific Management Should Be Approached." Conference on Scientific Management at Dartmouth College, Oct., 1911.

21. Strayer and Thorndike, "Educational Administration," Sec. 6.

Observations Illustrating the Possible
Application of Laws of Management

I.

Observation

A class in 6 A arithmetic. Written work. A page of problems in the text book assigned. The average pupil in the class completes five examples in the time set, ten minutes. A completes ten with apparently no extra effort or fatigue. The teacher says that A has had the same training as the others, and that she is unable to state why he should complete more in the time set. From all appearances he uses the same methods in working the examples as the others, perhaps attends a little more closely to work than the average pupil. His work does not, as might perhaps be expected, present a poorer appearance than does the work of the average pupil; neither is it so exceptionally neat that it would attract particular attention.

Comment

There must be some reason for A's superior performance. An investigation of this might enable the teacher to cause all members of the class to use the same method. This illustrates the need for the application of the first law of management, "Measure the product."

II.

Observation.

An ungraded class in an evening school. This class is doing the work of the higher grammar grades in all Subjects. There are but ten members. As practically each of these is at a different place, much individual instruction is necessary. The teacher assigns work to each pupil. The pupil then goes ahead until he feels the need of instruction. During a typical, class hour one Polish girl received help in the greatest common multiple, one man came up for instruction in interest, two young Irishmen asked help for pronunciation of difficult words in the reading lesson.

Comment.

There was a strong feeling of divided responsibility. The pupils had been made to feel that the teacher was ready and glad to be of service, but that they were responsible for getting any teaching or help that they actually needed. This responsibility was assumed with the result that no time was wasted by the teacher's volunteering help where it was not needed, or neglecting to give help where it was needed. This falls under the second law, "Divide your responsibility," and illustrates the possibility of applying this law in the school room.

III.

Observation.

A harmony class of children around ten. Home work is being assigned. The teacher assigns somewhat as follows: "Take Section I, B, No. 2; B, Section II, No.1, etc. Also review previous work, and especially bring in any assignment of last time that I have not called for this time." The pupils appear slightly confused in taking down the lesson, but say nothing. At the next meeting of the class the confusion that really took place become s apparent. Some have prepared the sections really assigned. Others have taken the assignment to be Section I, B, No.1 and Section I, B, No. 2, etc. As to the other work required, some have brought little; some a great deal; some, apparently discouraged, have brought none at all.

Comment.

The trouble here is very evidently a failure to make plain to the pupils exactly what is required. This falls clearly under the third law, "Define and circumscribe the task."

IV.

Observation.

A class in first year commercial arithmetic in the commercial department of a high school. The teacher follows what is evidently a plan prepared beforehand, as she never pauses to plan an assignment. The assignment is, say, "Take page 20, examples 1-10; page 22, examples 1-5; page 23, examples 4-6, etc." She gives the assignment but once. There are no questions and the pupils note down the assignment with speed and precision.

Comment.

Here is evidently a habit of giving a task on the part of the teacher and a habit of recording such an assignment on the part of the class. The least possible amount of time is taken by the assigning process. There are no questions as to what is meant, but the speed with which the class note tile assignment, collect their books, and prepare to leave the room shows not only that they understand what they are to do, but that they are accustomed to the orderly procedure observed. This illustrates the advantage of circumscribing and defining the task, and also falls under the third law.

V.

Observation.

A fifth year spelling class. A certain amount of time each day was set aside for spelling. The class was observed twice. One day the blank slips of paper were distributed by the teacher, who was meantime talking to the writer, saying that she was trying out different methods of distributing paper in order to see which was the best. The next day the paper was distributed by monitors sitting in the front seats. The same number of words was given out by the teacher each day, that is, twenty words. The writing was done with ink. The first day all had sufficient ink. The second day several pupils complained of lacking ink, and the inkwells were filled by the teacher. As a result of these variations the time which the pupils actually had to devote to the spelling of the words differed for the two days. The teacher was swift motioned, and, so far as could be observed without accurate timing, succeeded in distributing the papers more rapidly than they were distributed by the monitors. This gave added time the second day, as did the fact that there was no pause to supply ink. The time for the spelling lesson each day included the time for giving out the paper, seeing that all supplies were at hand, collecting the papers, etc. So far as could be noted the teacher made no allowance for this "Get ready" and "Clean up" time, and no other notes as to the time actually devoted to the spelling of the words.

Comment.

It is impossible to judge fairly of a task unless the "Get ready" and "Clean up" time is separated from the actual working time. Neither is it possible to get excellent work if unnecessary deviations and interruptions are allowed to occur. This falls under the fourth law, "Provide favorable conditions."

VI.

Observation.

Class in first year commercial arithmetic in the commercial department of the high school. Teacher decides suddenly to have the answer to a problem which is being worked mentally written and handed in. She simply says, "Write answer." Each pupil has a pencil and a block of paper in a fixed position on the desk. The pad and pencil are immediately drawn into position, and the name of the pupil, date, and answer are recorded at top speed, and the papers are collected by monitors in the back seats, all this without any word of direction except the "Write answer."

Comment.

Here not only have the most favorable conditions for performing the work been provided, but the whole process has become so standardized that it has become a habit. The response to the teacher's direction is made with the least amount of time and effort possible. This illustrates admirably the advantages of the fourth law, "Provide favorable conditions."

VII.

Observation.

A class in harmony. Children from eight to twelve. The assignment is to bring in a simple melody to the nursery rhyme "Hey diddle, diddle", No reward is offered. At the next session of the class about two out of the eight bring in no melodies at all. Of those brought in some are poor in melody, some untidy, only one or two passable. The assignment for the next lesson is a similar nursery rhyme. The teacher says, when making the assignment, "I shall, have the best melody copied into my own book, and shall take it back to New York with me to show my class there." At the next session the melodies are handed in. There is found to be one from every pupil in the class, and both in melody and form the work has improved greatly.

Comment.

We see here the benefit of the reward that is promised ahead, and that is definite and personal. The pupil evidently enjoy the idea of copying out their work to be admired, presumably by others, even though this copying involves extra effort for which they get no particular credit. This falls under the fifth law, "Reward efficiency," as does also what happened when no reward for effort was offered, and the resulting melodies, such as were handed in, were of not particularly good quality.

VIII.

Observation.

A principal's office in a grammar school. A boy of perhaps twelve sent up to be admonished for lack of attention and for "playing in the school room". The principal punished the boy by recounting his past history in his presence to the writer and a friend, and by sending him, finally, to the ungraded room. The boy seemed greatly embarrassed by being taken to task in the presence of visitors. It seemed doubtful whether he considered himself the hero of exploits worthy to be recounted, or a sinner who had violated every section of the school code. He certainly did not seem to feel inclined to any different behavior at the end of the admonition than at the beginning, and it seemed doubtful whether he, any more than the visitors, understood why he was assigned to the ungraded room, since a desire to play rather than an unwillingness to do the work of his room seemed to be at the basis of the trouble.

Comment.

The punishment here administered was evidently in no sense constructive, as neither the immediate remedy, the admonition, nor the ultimate remedy, the ungraded room, seemed likely to make the boy understand that his fault was lack of cooperation and hindering the progress of the social group. This comes under the sixth law, "Punish failure," meaning by this furnishing such adjustment that the one who fails may be able to learn to succeed.

IX.

Observation.

A harmony class of girls of high school age. The teacher is endeavoring to explain the relation of the tones of the scale to one another. She speaks of the tonic as the home tone, and of the various notes as sisters and brothers, who no matter where they wander always return home, of the dominant as grandmother's house, etc. The class look decidedly bored.

Comment.

This same method of presenting the tones in their relation to one another was used with excellent success with a class of younger children, who appreciated the personifying of the notes, and seemed to take a sympathetic interest in them, but these older children evidently felt that they were being treated as babies, and assumed the bored, grownup air fitting the situation. The same method of presenting the subject when used with the teachers proved very successful. They evidently appreciated at once the attraction that this presentation would have for small children, and thought of it in terms of their own teaching. The subject was presented in practically the same way to the five classes observed, and in every case the teacher s and younger children welcomed it, while the older girls evidently found it distasteful. This illustrates the seventh law, "Suit the work to the worker."

X.
Observation.

A 6 B grade. Problems in addition being done at the board. Half the pupils act as pupils, the other half as teachers. When half the arithmetic period is over, the teams change places. Those who have been teachers become pupils, and the pupils teachers.

Comment.

From thus socializing the work an excellent social spirit is created in the class room. This is evidently fostered by the fact that the teacher feels this spirit herself, and imparts it consciously, or unconsciously, to the class. This illustrates the eighth law, "Secure cooperation."

XI.
Observation.

A sixth grade in arithmetic in a private school. The pupils are girls from nine to twelve. A new principle in arithmetic was being explained. At the end of the explanation an example was given out, and the first girl to solve it accurately was allowed to become teacher, and to explain the method by which she worked to the remainder of the class. The pupil teacher entered into the spirit of the thing at once, stepped. Gravely to the front of the room, and explained the example with great "manner". The others seemed envious of her, and greatly desirous of becoming teachers in their turn.

Comment.

The explanation given by the pupil teacher was really no different from the ordinary explanation given by any member of the class called upon to explain how a problem was solved. The honor of being called "teacher" add standing in the teacher's position seemed to be the real incentive. The noteworthy thing was the manner with which the teacher and all the pupils cooperated to make the experiment a success. This again illustrates the eighth law, "Secure cooperation."

XII.
Observation.

A class in commercial arithmetic. A first year class, therefore, composed of pupils from many grammar schools, and, presumably, not having acquired, as yet, a great deal of class or school spirit. The teacher says continually, "This is a first year class in this work, but I believe they can do as good work as any first or second year class in the building." Again, "This, you know, is a class in commercial arithmetic, and we are all busy together, getting ready to show the business men of this town what a real preparation in commercial arithmetic is."

Comment.

The class feels that they, as individuals and as a group, are lined up with the teacher against every other class and against the industrial world, and are working as a unit to place themselves at the head of any competition in which they may enter. This again illustrates the benefits of the eighth law, "Secure cooperation."

XIII.

Observation.

A class in fifth grade arithmetic. This class during the session observed was doing drill work on the fundamental operations. It was very evident that the pupils took little interest in the work. The teacher handed the recitation excellently, but the pupils were slow to respond, and evidently very much disgruntled at something. At the close of the recitation hour the pupils were heard to say, as they passed to another class, "Put us back to baby work." "That is what they are doing in the first grade," etc. The teacher was asked what was the reason for the drill and for the behavior of the class. She replied that the class had had very poor training in the fundamentals, and that, while they were supposed to be doing regular fifth year arithmetic, it was necessary to have them get a complete mastery of the fundamentals before proceeding with the other work. The writer urged that the teacher explain this to the class, and endeavor to get them to cooperate to finish the drill work quickly and get at the more interesting and advanced arithmetic. This the teacher, who was extremely desirous of handling the situation in the most efficient manner possible, was delighted to do. The report of the next day's work brought home to the writer by one of the pupils who said, "Oh mother, we had a wonderful time in arithmetic to-day. You know we have never learned to multiply and do those things as fast as we should, but we are going to practice on that a lot now, and, as soon as we learn to do it fast, we can just race thru the whole term's work. I wish you could have heard us do it this morning."

Comment

Here again we find an illustration of the eighth law, "Secure cooperation." The moment the pupils understood. the situation, they lined up with the teacher, instead of against her, to overcome the obstacle.

CHAPTER IV
The Practice of Scientific Management and Its Tests

Visiting a Scientifically Managed Plant.

Reading a description of a scientifically managed plant is in some ways more satisfactory than actually visiting one. No matter how well the practice of the plant is standardized, there will be more or less deviation from the standard, and the visitor well informed on the theory must note, here and there, lapses from the high standard that he expects to see in operation. In a description of such a plant it is possible to present it at its high water mark, with all parts of the system actually in operation.

The visitor to the scientifically managed plant will receive a very different impression, if he has seen plants run under the old type of management, than if he has not. If he is unacquainted with industrial plants, he is really not properly prepared to appreciate a scientifically managed plant. It is necessary, to understand what is going on, to visit many industrial plants of older types, doing different kinds of work, and to understand the conditions existing there and the problems involved. One must note the atmosphere, which is apt to denote either hurry, or a leisure which is unproductive. One must note the percentage of men engaged in book work of various types to those actually at work on machines, or on making the product in some way. One must see how stores are handled, and where tools are kept, and must trace the material from the time it enters the building, during the time it is worked upon, and until it leaves the plant a finished product. One must study the workers, their expressions, the amount and type of work that they have to do, and the method by which they do it. It is unfair, as well as difficult, to describe such an old-time plant, for there are so many differences between the different examples that it is almost impossible to give a fair typical description. One plant handles the human element excellently, but is inefficient in handling materials. Another plant has worked up the material side to a point of comparative efficiency, but has made little progress with the human element. Some amount of training in the observation of such plants is necessary before one can make an estimate worth anything at all.

The visitor to a scientifically managed plant, who is unacquainted with the older type of plant, is, then, at some disadvantage. On the other hand, he has a decided advantage by not being hampered by traditional views. The proportion of mental work to physical work does not trouble him in the least. The sight of chairs for working and chairs for resting is no unnatural one. The fact that strenuous activity and efficient are not synonyms is easily accepted. He is not troubled by memories of "the way we have always done it." He can judge what he sees at its face value.

If you walk into a scientifically managed plant, you will find one part of it set aside as the planning department.[1] You will find here gathered together a large number of workers, in proportion to the total number in the organization, whose entire business it is to layout what is to be done in the minutest detail. You will find the work of these men, or women, going out into the performing part of the plant in the form of instruction cards. You will find that each performer has a definite program, and that each piece of work, as he does it, takes him to a definite work place, where all materials for doing the specific piece of work are ready for him, and where the instruction card, giving the method in detail, is placed where he can use it most conveniently. You will walk thru the stores department and the tool department, and find that all the stores are in one place, all the tools in another, that the departments are in charge of specially trained men, who keep the working equipment in proper order, and see that the proper amount is sent out to the work place at the proper times. You will note the atmosphere of order throughout the entire establishment, and the atmosphere of certainty.[2] Nothing seems to be done by chance. Everything is provided for and adjusted. You will note the lack of bustle and confusion, everything and every person being in a definite place at a definite time. The workers are characterized by a contented expression, by attention to what they are doing, and by a readiness to assist one another, and evident willingness to cooperate.

Likenesses, to the Well-run School Room.

If you are a teacher, you will notice at once the likeness to a well-directed and well-ordered school room. There is the same lack of hurry and bustle, yet evident progress and activity. There is the same air of definiteness, of a well thought out plan that is operating smoothly There is the same feeling of perfect adjustment. There is the same individual freedom existing under social restraint.

Tests of Operating Efficiency.

A close study of various types of plants, operating under the older, as well as the new, type of management, has resulted in the formulation of nine tests that may be applied to management, and that management must pass, if it can maintain its claim to being scientific.[3] These tests any visitor , no matter how inexperienced, may apply to the plant, with, at least, some hope of rating its efficiency. In describing these tests we aim not only to point out their application to the industrial plant, but at the same time their possible application to the school room. Perhaps, by so doing, we may carry over the likenesses and differences more easily.

The First Test, Individuality.

The properly managed plant must conserve and foster individuality.[4] The school room must also do this, but in a very different way. The plant must give every one working in it a chance to become a specialist in the highest sense of that word, a chance to do that work that he can do best, and that he likes to do most, and to be relieved of work that he dislikes and cannot do well. For example, the man who likes to plan must be put in the planning department. The man who hates to plan must be put in some place in the performing department where decisions are made as few as possible, and where his work is prepared for him in great detail. If he has a fondness for seeing things grow under his hands, he might well be put at assembling. If he is fond of keeping things in good running order, he will be put at maintenance. This problem of placement is made easy in many cases by the fact that the worker has a particular desire to do some type of work, that can be considered and gratified. In the case of young workers the problem becomes more complicated, but in the case of the adult worker, even in a plant whose line of work is not complicated, the problem of developing individuality is comparatively simple.

The problem is much more complicated in the school. It is distinctly not the duty of the elementary, or even of the secondary school to make specialists. In fact one great danger of some modern types of training is that these schools will make specialists. It would be more exact to say that the danger is that these schools will offer specialized training. There can be no doubt that the trend to-day is towards specializing, towards having every adult become an expert in a small field. However, the success of the expert depends not only upon his special, but upon his general training, and, because of the specializing tendency of the age, it is the duty of the elementary and secondary schools to supply that general training that the specialist needs. To be efficient, the teacher in these schools must study the individuality of the pupils in order to understand the needs of the individual pupils, but, the stronger the tendency to specialize in the child, the more necessary that he be given in his formative years those things which his training would otherwise lack. The child is no judge as to what he needs. Very often he knows little about what his own aptitudes are. We are constantly surprised, in the industries, to find new aptitudes in adult workers, who have had no idea of these aptitudes themselves.[5] How much more must there lie concealed in the child aptitudes of Which he has no knowledge, and that nothing but a general training can bring out. A child's likes and dislikes are influenced by so many variables, by so many different elements., that any rough classification of him as of a "certain type" to be supplied with certain specialized training is harmful rather than helpful. Demand consideration of individuality? Yes, but afford the opportunity for a well-balanced, well-rounded individual to manifest himself.

The Second Test, Functionalization.

Work must be so divided and planned that individuality has a chance to develop. The scientifically managed plant not only separates the planning from the performing, but separates every piece of work to be done into parts which demand certain qualities, such as will be found in certain types of individuals.[6] Not only this, but the work is so set up as to suit individuals in certain phases of their development, or training.[7] For example, in assembly work the parts of the machine to be put together are put in order, and in the best position for the assembler to handle, by the learner. This not only relieves the assembler from doing work of a lower type than he is fitted to do and likes to do, but affords a training for that learner that prepares him constructively for doing his later work. Every position in the organization is designed not only as an ultimate position, or a final position, for some worker whose capabilities it exactly fits, but as a training position, where this satisfied and efficient worker puts all who need such training thru a set training period that is part of their necessary industrial education.

This test of functionalization applies equally to the school. It is the other aspect of developing individuality. It is the arrangement of the work done in the school room in such a way that it is of most benefit to the individuals comprising the class. <u>A</u> needs history, because he wants to be a writer, and will actually use it every day, if he is. <u>B</u> needs history, because he wants to be a mechanic and will go from the elementary into a trade school. His one opportunity for getting history, therefore, is in the elementary school. <u>C</u> needs history, because he apparently takes a narrow and intensive view of everything, and needs the broad, general outlines that history gives. But the method by which history is presented to these three must be suited to their individual needs. There is a strange misunderstanding on the part of many teachers as to the attitude of the managers in the industries on what the school training of the boys and girls who are to come to them should be. "What shall I do?" says the distracted teacher. "The man in the plant wants an apprentice already partially trained in the trade, a young boy or girl with a special training." But the progressive manager of to-day wants no such thing. He wants some one who has some idea of what he can do, who knows how to go to work to do a thing, who is at home in the learning process. He wants an educated learner. Again and again, these managers say, "We are willing to teach them, but they must know how to learn." The school must so functionalize its methods as to prepare each individual to recognize his method of attack, his way of getting at a subject. It must teach him to fit into the complicated, specialized, social inter-relation which is our modern industrial life.

The Third Test, Measurement.

The scientifically managed plant must show that it is operating in accordance with the results of accurate measurement.[8] It will show this not only in the orderliness of its procedure, but also in the fact that somewhere in the plant measurements are actually being taken in order that standards may be improved.

These measurements may be going on where commercial work is actually being done, or in a laboratory, or betterment room, specially set aside for the purpose. It has become recognized that the laboratory is the ideal place for making measurements. When the work is commercially performed ultimately, the working conditions and methods must conform to, and equal, the laboratory practice. In this laboratory, or wherever the measurement is being done, three branches of work must be considered.

1.   The proper <u>unit of measurement</u>, that is, exactly what unit is to be measured, must be determined.[9] The importance of selecting the proper unit may be illustrated by attempting to measure the output of a concrete gang. If you count the empty cement boxes for output, there is an incentive to use more cement than is necessary. If you count the batches of concrete dumped out of a mixer, you provide an incentive for spilling the concrete, and using too much stone in proportion to the sand and cement. The proper thing to measure is the cubic feet of forms filled, testing the quality and quantity constantly by your specifications. The unit measured must always be that one which would provide the strongest incentive for doing the work rapidly.

2. The <u>method of measurement</u> to be used must be determined. The importance of the work measured and the amount of it being done determines how accurately and extensively a measure can be used. Luckily, the most accurate methods of measurement, micromotion[10] and the cyclegraph method, have been so reduced in cost that they are available in practically all cases at present.*

3. The <u>devices</u> to be used must be selected. The use to be made of the measurement is here the determining factor. In the laboratory of the plant one visits one will find being measured some process where a chance for a large saving is thought to exist. Such may be the assembly of the product of the factory, the means of transportation, etc.

The question of measurement is of equal importance in the school room. The work done in this line by education itself has already been referred to.[11] The methods and devices invented in the industries, are just beginning to be applied. The problems to be investigated at first are extremely simple ones. The following might illustrate. Suppose ten examples in mental arithmetic are to be done. The old method means laying down the pen in a ridge at the front of the desk between the examples, and folding the hands in the lap. The new method suggested is retaining the pen in the hand, moving the hand to the line where the next answer is to be written before the next problem is stated. What is the amount of time saved? The importance of such a measurement as this, as must be frequently emphasized, is not so much the amount of time saved, as the training in thinking in terms of saving time and of working efficiently.

---

* See Appendix B.

The Fourth Test, Analysis and Synthesis.

To be efficient, the methods used in the industrial plant must be constructive. Whatever is changed must be first analyzed, or divided, then tested.[12] Then, the useless, or wasteful, elements must be eliminated, and the useful elements combined, or synthesized, into new, or better, wholes.[13] The substitution of new methods, or equipment, or material, without such testing is wasteful. The new may be better, as a whole, than the old, but efficient elements of the old, which do not exist in the new, may be discarded and permanently lost.

This same constructive method is necessary in the school room. Before doing away with an old practice it must be carefully analyzed, and the analyzed elements compared with the elements of the proposed innovation. In this way there can be no "inventing downwards" in whole, or in parts. Suppose the teacher, who has been giving mental arithmetic tests according to the older method outlined a few minutes ago, decides upon reading of the newer method that it will undoubtedly occupy less time, and, therefore, that he will install it immediately. He may fail to consider that there are other elements besides the time element involved. There must be some reason why the older method was installed in the first place. Some say that it was to prevent the children from cheating. Some say that returning to the standard position for attention makes it easier for the child to attend, and to solve the problems.[14] Some say that changing the position to "attention," to "reaching for the pen," etc., is a necessary rest. There might be still other defenses for the old method. There may be, and probably is in this particular case, no valid excuse for the extra time involved in the old method, but nothing but a careful analysis into elements, and a constructive building up of the new method will take all of these elements into fitting account.

The Fifth Test, Standardization.

The results of the measurement must be formulated into a standard which must be adopted, followed, and maintained, until an improved standard is introduced.[15] When the standard is made it must be used, and used constantly. The importance of habit formation lies at the basis of this. If the standard is not maintained, if exceptions in the habitual manner of performing the work are allowed, the full value of the measurement will not be attained.[16] A standard method of running a drill press has been devised. The equipment has been placed so that the shortest and easiest motions possible are used. The operator is then required to use these motions, and to use them every time. If he is tired, he not only <u>may</u> stop and rest, but he <u>must</u> stop and rest. He cannot "rest himself" by varying the method.

In the same way, in the school room, if a standard is established it must be maintained. The fatigue element should be considered in making the standards, and rest allowed for. There is not only loss, but positive harm in failing to maintain standards. The writer remembers clearly having been trained, as a child, to stand, upon completion of a test. On one occasion, having received some new pedagogical idea, the teacher decided not to have the pupils stand, but to have them raise their hands. Evidently with some idea of marking the change decisively, she announced at the beginning of the test that any one who stood at the close would receive demerits. At the close of the test, as might have been expected, practically all in the class who were concentrating upon the work stood. The demerits were given, and the class rebelled loudly. The teacher tried the new method for perhaps a week or two. She then decided that the older standing method was more satisfactory, and directed the class to return to it. She was astounded that for weeks it seemed impossible to make the class follow a uniform practice. By this time the constantly distributed demerits had lost all significance to the class, and discipline became a serious problem. There was a disastrous effect upon all concerted class action. Nothing but most careful records would demonstrate how far-reaching was the bad effect upon that class of arbitrarily changing standards.

The Sixth Test, Records and programs.

The scientifically managed plant must show records of what has happened, and programs of what is happening and what is to happen.[17] The complete and detailed records make accurate programs possible, and the detailed programs make keeping of accurate records easy. For example, the chart department records amount of performance each day, relation between actual performance and expected performance, delays, etc. When a new program being made these charts furnish accurate data as to what may reasonably be expected. More than this, they furnish what are called the exceptions. By referring to charts, those in control and responsible can see not only where successes and failures occur, but can also find out where to look for the reasons for these. This is part of what is called the "exception principle."[18]

Such records and programs are also a necessary element of the efficient school life. The records of what has happened must include as far as possible why it has happened, in order that the program, which is a prediction, may have some good chance of fulfillment. The exception principle will here, also, prove to be a great time saver, as it is in the industries.

The Seventh Test, Teaching.

In the scientifically managed industrial plant teaching must be going on constantly,[19] and must be, in some form or another, a part of the work of most members of the organization. The plan of promotion demands this, in that each man is expected to train some one for his position before he advances to the position above. Every man is, therefore, at the same time a teacher and a learner. For example, the information bureau in the plant is that place in which is kept all information which should be available to any one. Many members of the organization are supposed to work for some time in this information bureau as a part of their training. There are various positions in the bureau, according to the size and needs of the plant. The head of this bureau never is promoted until he has trained some one under him to be the head. The next man trains the man below him. The last man in the information bureau is training one, or more, members in still more elementary positions in the organization to be fit to take his task. This insures maintenance of the information bureau, and at the same time adequate training in its work for a large number of people.

The teaching element, which is a new thing in management, is the oldest and most fundamental part of school life. However, there has not been as yet a general appreciation of the benefits in having each member of the school organization a teacher as well as a learner. We all recognize as a general principle that the best way to know a thing is to try to teach it, but we are not always careful to afford this opportunity to the learner. The reason for this, undoubtedly, is that we wish to afford each pupil the very best teaching possible, and that we hesitate to allow another pupil, who perhaps is not adequately informed, to instruct him. This danger is over-rated. We realize in play and in all other relations of child life that one child learns from another. If we simply emphasize the fact that the child who teaches, also learns, and apply this in the school room, we may not only add to the teaching and learning, but to the social spirit. Successful attempts at doing this have been already cited. One teacher frequently divides her class into pairs, sending them then to the board. A in each pair works the example on the board, while B acts as critic and teacher.

When several examples have been done in this fashion, <u>B</u> becomes pupil and <u>A</u> teacher. The teammates are shifted each time this plan is tried, and the results certainly are, to all appearances, eminently satisfactory. Even such an elementary idea of the theory and practice of teaching as can be given in the younger years becomes of added value to-day, from the very fact that workers in the industries under the new system of management are expected to be teachers. This will be another bridge over the gap between the schools and the industries.

The Eighth Test, Incentives.

The incentives in a scientifically managed plant must be adequate in every sense of that term. The reward must provide for progress, and the punishment must provide for maintenance. The rewards have been characterized as:

1. Positive.
2. Pre-determined.
3. Personal.
4. Fixed.
5. Assured.
6. Prompt.

They are positive in the sense that the man actually gets them. They are pre-determined, because they are fixed. Before the man starts in to do the work he knows just what he is going to get. They are personal, in that they are given directly to the individual himself.[20] They are fixed, in that they are not changed. They are assured, in that there is no doubt in the worker's mind that he will certainly get them. The reputation of the organization stands back of the reward. They are prompt, in that they are received so soon after the work is completed that the man's attention is held.[21]

The punishment is always an adjustment. It is realized that any other type of punishment is wasteful.[22] The aim of the punishment is to put things back to smooth running pace, to get the attitude of all concerned right as quickly as possible. Punishments are in the hands of a disinterested person, who is recognized as an adjustor.

The same type of incentive might be required in the school, There is nothing concerning which opinions differ more widely than as to incentives in the school. It is far easier to criticise than it is to do constructive work in this field. It is easy to say that, if John completes ten examples in less time than the rest of the class, and of perfect quality, his immediate reward consists of sitting idle until the others have finished. The question is, "What is the remedy?" The answer here seems to be, "Let John turn to his other lessons, or to some pleasurable task." The objection at once arises, "This will be an incentive to the others to hurry thru their work. The result may be poor work." However, we must remember that the result may not be poor work, and that if it is, it will be fairly simple to say the next day, "Your work must be of good quality before you can take out your readers." The entire subject of incentives must be discussed at length later. It will be of help, perhaps, to remember that an industrial reward must please, to be adequate.

As for punishment in the school, certainly any punishment which is not an adjustment is most wasteful.[23] Child and teacher alike become physically and mentally exhausted, with a resulting negative attitude that is fatal to doing any good work.

The Ninth Test, Welfare.

A plant must provide for welfare, physical, mental, and moral. It must provide for the welfare of the group as well as of the individual, and mean welfare that is worked for rather than given. In other words, welfare must imply cooperation. The knowledge of sanitation and hygiene that has been accumulated is all taken into account, as is the excellent work done under so-called "welfare workers." The newer idea, however, is not that the ideal working conditions are a gift to the worker, but rather that they are his right, and that the duty lies upon worker and manager alike to maintain them.

Welfare in the school has received much longer and more careful attention than in the industries. The modern schoolhouse is a far better work place than the modern factory. Educators are pioneer workers in the welfare field. Group hygiene, personal hygiene, equipment, fatigue, are all considered in the schools. The only suggestion we might receive here is as to the necessity of the pupils cooperating in all this work, which too often is considered as something done <u>for</u> them, rather than as something <u>with</u> them. The settlements have well solved this problem, by training the children who attend them to carry out the welfare work in their homes. Something of this sort might well be done with the children in the schools.[24]

The Practice and the Results.

The scientifically managed plant should, then, be so practicing management as to pass these nine tests favorably. It should present working examples, which demonstrate that the principles of Scientific Management are in operation. As a result two things are to be noted.

1. A larger amount of output should be leaving the plant than it is possible under the old type of management, the output being of the same, or better, quality.
2. The working force should be advancing individually and cooperating socially.

Can we not look. for the same results in the scientifically managed school?

References
1. Going, C. B., "Principles of Industrial Engineering," p. 48.
2. Parkhurst, F. A., "Applied Methods of Scientific Management," Ch. V., VI.
3. Gilbreth, L. M., "The Psychology of Management," p. 16.
4. Munsterberg, H., "American Problems," p. 34.
   Sully, J., "Teacher's Handbook of Psychology," p. 14.
5. Gantt, H. L., Paper 928, A. S. M. E., para. 6.
   Gilbreth, F. B., "Cost Reducing System."
   Taylor, F. W., "Shop Management," Harper Edition, p. 33.
6. Cooke, M. L., Bulletin No.5, Carnegie Foundation for the Advancement of Teaching, p. 15.
   Gillette and Dana, "Cost Keeping and Management Engineering," p. 1.
7. Gantt, H. L., "Work, Wages, and Profits," p. 120.
8. Gantt, H. L., "Work, Wages, and Profits," p. 15.
9. Dana, R. T., For Construction Service Co., "Handbook of Steam Shovel Work," p. 161.
   Munsterberg, H., "American Problems," p. 37.
   Stratton, G. M., "Experimental Psychology and Culture," p. 59.
   Taylor, F. Vol. XXVIII., A. S. M. E., Paper 1119, para. 68.
10. Industrial Engineering, Jan., 1913.
11. Chapter III.
12. Taylor and Thompson, "Concrete, Plain and Reinforced," p. 193.
13. Gantt, H. L., "Work, Wages, and Profits," p. 35.
    Le Chatelier, H., Discussion of Paper 1119, A. S. M. E., p. 303.
14. Bagley, W. C., "Class Room Management," p. 38.
15. Cooke, M. L., Bulletin No.5, Carnegie Foundation for the Advancement of Teaching, p. 6.
    Metcalfe, Capt., "Cost of Manufactures."
16. Bagley, W. C., "Class Room Management," p. 16.
    Colvin, S. S., "The Learning Process," p. 65.

James, W., "Psychology," Ch. IV.

17. Gantt, H. L., "Work, Wages, and Profits," Pages 186, 200, 203.
18. Gilbreth, L. M., "The Psychology of Management,"
    Pages 187-188.
19. Gantt, H. L., Paper 928, A. S. M. E., p. 372.
20. Gillette, H. P., "Cost Analysis Engineering."
21. Taylor, F. W., Paper 647, A. S. M. E., para. 33, 59.
22. Dodge, J. M., "The Spirit in Which Scientific Management
    Should be Approached," Tuck School Conference on Scientific
    Management, p. 142 ff.
23. Bagley, W. C., "Class Room Management," Ch. VIII.
24. King, I., "Social Aspects of Education," Ch. IV.

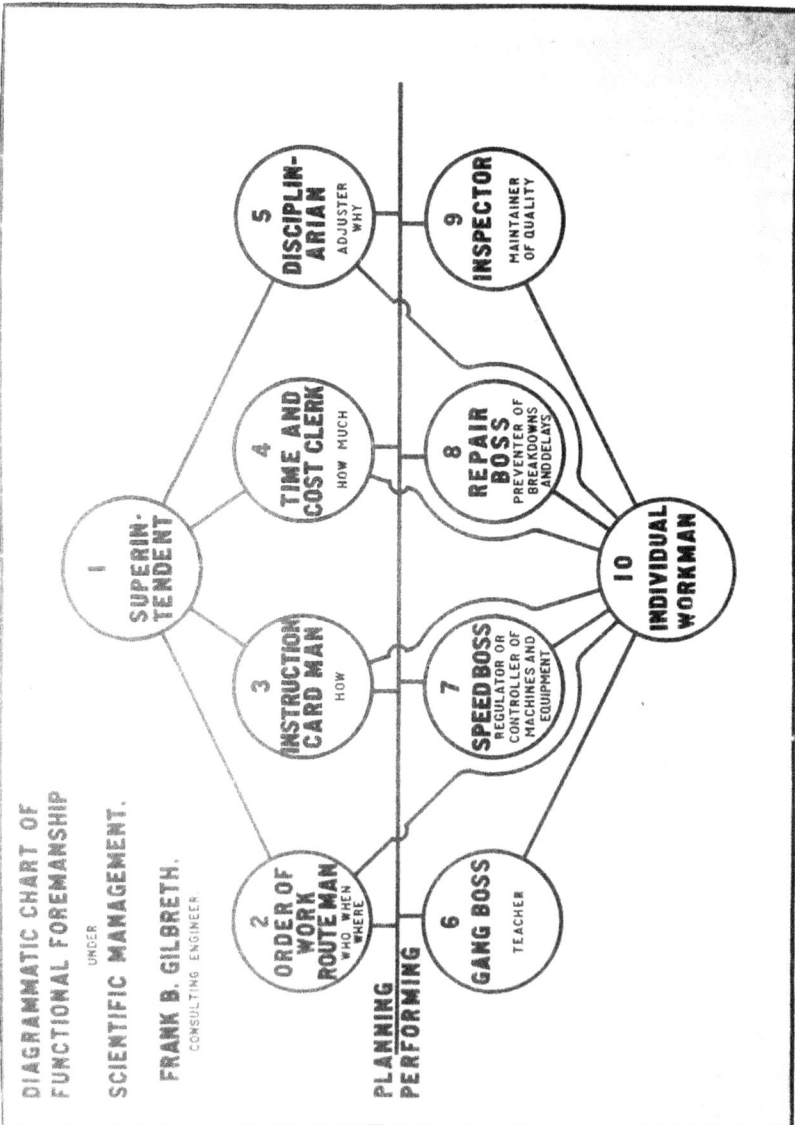

DIAGRAMMATIC CHART OF FUNCTIONAL FOREMANSHIP UNDER SCIENTIFIC MANAGEMENT.

FRANK B. GILBRETH, CONSULTING ENGINEER

PLANNING
PERFORMING

1 SUPERINTENDENT

2 ORDER OF WORK ROUTE MAN — WHO WHEN WHERE

3 INSTRUCTION CARD MAN — HOW

4 TIME AND COST CLERK — HOW MUCH

5 DISCIPLINARIAN — ADJUSTER WHY

6 GANG BOSS — TEACHER

7 SPEED BOSS — REGULATOR OR CONTROLLER OF MACHINES AND EQUIPMENT

8 REPAIR BOSS — PREVENTER OF BREAKDOWNS AND DELAYS

9 INSPECTOR — MAINTAINER OF QUALITY

10 INDIVIDUAL WORKMAN

CHAPTER V
Installing and Maintaining Scientific Management

The Relation Between Installation and Maintenance.

If one talks with anyone who is engaged in introducing Scientific Management into industrial plants, he will tell one that his work divides itself into the problem of installation and the problem of maintenance, and that the two problems are closely related. We must have in mind constantly how the new system is to be put in, and how it is to be kept in.

The Sequence of Installation.

The order in which the various elements of the science are installed is determined by the ease with which the various elements can be maintained.[1] It is a fundamental rule that no change is to be made until one can be sure that the change will be accepted, and the new method followed; and the changes are to be made no faster than they can be successfully maintained. The installer of Scientific Management must have in mind, then,

1.   An outline of the proposed changes.
2.   The order, or program, in which changes are to be made, this being based upon a measured knowledge as to which changes it is easiest to make.

The Outline of Changes to be Made.

No one recognizes more clearly than the teacher the advantage of a definite plan in bringing about desired changes. The teacher will naturally, then, be in sympathy with the manager in following such a plan, and will desire to examine the plan most carefully to see whether it shows itself definite, adequate, and likely to enlist the cooperation and interest of all those whom it affects.

The changes that are made in Scientific Management affect the materials that are handled, and the men who comprise the organization. This is true, in the plant, of workers, equipment, and tools. It will be true also in the school room of teachers, pupils, and materials used. The changes in the human element are the more important, and control the changes in the material. For example, it is in order that more efficient methods of work may be followed that the arrangement of tools and stores is standardized, and that material is routed. These important human changes that control all other changes are represented in the functional chart, which is a diagram that illustrates the methods of the science of management.[2] This chart, as will be noted, consists of ten circles connected with one another, the upper five of which are divided from the lower five by a horizontal line. As has been previously stated, the work to be done is functionalized, and the responsibility for doing it is functionalized, or divided, into different typical groups of activities.[3] The ten circles of the diagram represent the ten functions into which work is divided, and among which responsibility is divided. The horizontal line, which represents the separation of the planning from the performing, divides the ten functions into five planning functions and five performing functions.

This separation of planning from performing is the fundamental functionalization of the work. In the industrial plants. it has been found most successful not only to separate planning from performing in point of time, but also to have most of the planning done by a different set of people than those who do the perfroming.[4] This does not mean that any member of the organization does. either all planning, or all performing. The division between planning and performing in the industries implies that the planner does the brain, pen, pencil, and paper work on the article that is to be manufactured, while the performer does the brain and manual work, using the actual materials which are to be transformed into the product. For example, if a machine is to be made, the planning department does everything, except the work, with the actual materials of constructing the machine. It makes all decisions that it is possible to make in advance. It is more important that the time of the planning be separated from the time of the performing than that the two should be done by different persons. It is possible, and it often actually happens in small organizations, that the same man will first plan a piece of work to be done, and will later, as a member of the performing department, do the work. For example, he may spend half his time planning, and the other half in the shop; or, if times are dull and a piece of work has been planned, he may work in the shop on the planned work for days or weeks, until times become better. The separation in time is fundamental.

This same separation, in time, of planning from performing takes place in efficient teaching. The good teacher starts the term with a plan that covers the general management of his class. He even plans his lessons in advance of the session. There is nothing either in the plant or the shop to prevent a plan being set aside in case of an emergency; but the general plan exists, and is immediately put into effect as soon as the emergency has been met.

An enormous amount of waste has been eliminated by this insistence on the separation of planning from performing. Decision time has been cut down. It is not necessary to stop so often to consider what is best to do, and to decide which alternative to choose. This means more output, when output is desired, and more time for making important decisions, when these are the vital things. As a case in point for the output:- in assembling a certain type of machine it was found that a packet, that is, a wooden easel constructed of what looks like ordinary lattice work, placed near the work table of the person putting the machine together, would greatly cut down the time that it took to handle the material. The wooden strips that make up the easel are four inches apart. Where they cross one another, different length nails and hooks are inserted. On these hooks and nails the different parts of the machine that is to be put together are hung, in just that order that they are to be used by the worker. The first hook that he reaches towards contains the material that he uses first; the second hook, that which he uses second; etc. If eight small parts are to be used at one time, these are placed on a nail which will just hold the eight, and no more. This loaded packet absolutely eliminates the necessity of making decisions as to the number of parts that shall be handled at one time, and the order in which the various groups of parts must be put on the machine.

How the time gained may be utilized for making really important decisions has been illustrated before by citing the surgeon, who is enabled, thru having his tools properly placed and routed, to devote extra time to decisions as to how, when, and where he desires to operate next.

The plan must be elastic enough to provide for an emergency. This is done in the plants, as must be shown later at greater length, by the elasticity station. To refer again to the man assembling a machine, there is a table and a packet for each man. There are also extra tables and packets, so that, if any part of the material proves defective, the worker can move at once to another "set up" without loss of time. Such elasticity stations might well exist in the school, where a lack of, or defect in, some piece of working equipment often slows down not only an individual, but a whole class.

In the school it is more necessary than in the plant that each individual become a planner as well as a performer, but it is perfectly possible to separate the planning periods from the performing periods. The simplest divisions into "time to get ready," "time to do the work," and "time to clean up" will provide for this.

Functionalizing the Plant and the School Room.

In considering the functional chart, we note that the ten functions are usually occupied in a plant by ten different people, that is, we note that there are ten different titles. Of these ten nine are in charge of, or teaching the tenth, who is the individual worker. In a very small plant these nine teaching functions may be represented by but one man, who would divide his work into nine parts, and consider himself as exercising nine different functions. In a very large plant there may be many more than one man under each function, with a chief of the function in charge of each group.

In the school, the nine teaching functions will be performed by the teacher himself, who will think of himself in the nine different aspects illustrated. Each function represents a different type of work, which must be separated from the other types in order to get the best results. The advantage of separating the work into various types of work is that one realizes how many different types of work are involved in successful management, and that one is enabled to give the proper attention to each, and to see that none is left out.

The First Function, The Superintendent.

It is the duty of the superintendent to see that the entire organization is running efficiently. He must see that all functions are in proper operation. He must compare the work of the organization in which he is interested with that of other organizations, and he must examine the work of his own plant constantly, on the exception principle. It is the superintendent's duty to preserve a balance in the organization. This he does by making sure that each one of the other functions is being properly handled. He insures that sufficient amount of progress is being made in the plant by taking time to visit other plants doing similar work, and other plants doing different work, and comparing them with his own plant. We have described before the work of the chart department. The superintendent keeps in constant touch with the charts. He notes where the exceptionally good work is being done, and where the exceptionally bad work is being done, and the reasons for these conditions.

The teacher, as a superintendent, has the same duties. He must see that he himself is devoting sufficient attention to each element of his work, and that the class is receiving the proper teaching, and is responding in the proper fashion. He should insure progress by spending enough time visiting other class rooms and other lines of work to get the new ideas that he will desire to use in his own work. He should also constantly keep in touch with his teaching and the pupils' learning by the use of the exception principle. This he will do by consulting his various types of records. One useful type of record is the typical class test. If, when such a test is given, the teacher makes a careful record of the attending circumstances, and if, when the test is corrected, the teacher notes the number and nature of the errors, valuable information is sure to appear. If the notes show that all pupils work under the same conditions, and if, in spite of this fact, $\underline{A}$ did ten examples and had one hundred percent correct, while the average in the class did from five to eight with sixty to eighty percent correct, and if $\underline{B}$ managed to do only four, with fifty percent correct, the reasons Why $\underline{A}$ succeeded, and $\underline{B}$ failed absolutely, will bear careful investigation. Much has been done in the field of education on the tabulation and study of errors, but the average individual teacher has not felt his responsibility to make such studies for himself. In the industries, the workers gladly cooperate towards having the causes of their high or low scores recorded, because they are only too anxious to get the high pay that the high output brings. If the worker with a good score knows what enables him to get it, he will immediately ask that the favorable conditions be made standard. If he knows why he failed, he will insist that the impediment towards rapid or accurate work be removed. In the same way the pupils may cooperate by being allowed time at the end of a test period, and space at the end of a test paper, to write why they think they have done successful, or unsuccessful, work. There does not exist the incentive for the pupil that does exist for the worker. However, the average child is ready and glad to tell why he succeeded or failed, if he is encouraged to do so. The average mother is at present receiving information which might also be of use to the teacher.

The exception principle is of great value in enabling one to "attack the big problems" first. It is the "thing that is very bad" that one wants to remedy quickly, the "thing that is very good" that one wants to recognize and make standard as soon as possible.

The Second Function, The Order of Work or Route Man.

This function is responsible for planning <u>who</u> is to do any work, <u>when</u> it is to be done, and <u>where</u> it is to be done.[5] It issues two series of programs. One is the program of the individual worker, telling him <u>what</u> he is to do, <u>when</u> he is to do it, and <u>where</u> he is to do it. The other is the program of the piece of work, directing <u>who</u> shall work on it, <u>when</u>, and <u>where</u>. The program of the individual is most like the program in the school room. John Jones comes to work in the morning. He finds ready for him a program for that entire day. He comes at eight, or eight-thirty, or nine, to a particular work place, and there he finds a particular piece of work ready for him to do. When he has finished this, he goes to another stipulated work place, and there finds his work ready, and so it is thru the entire day. The planning is elastic enough so that he is never delayed, though others work at a slower pace, and he at the pace, or faster, than might be expected. Neither is he ever out of work, although he completes more than he is expected to complete in the time set.

In the same way every pupil in the class room should have a definite program, which will provide for his being occupied constantly, with no delays caused by lack of equipment, or by waiting for others. This involves, in the school, the difficult problem of individual versus class work.[6] The amount of class work that is at present generally considered necessary makes it difficult to allow individual pupils to progress at that pace to which they are best suited, but there is no excuse for delays thru lack of equipment, or for failure to provide some type of related profitable work for those who can finish an assigned task in less than the class time. It is the duty of the teacher, as the order of work and route man, to see that such regular work and supplies are provided for each and every member of the class.

The Third Function, The Instruction Card Man.

The instruction card department has charge of method.[7] It determines how any and every piece of work in the organization is to be performed. It does this in no haphazard fashion. As rapidly as possible the method outlined and given to the worker is made one that is the result of accurate measurement. Even before a time allowance for the individual worker can be accurately set, the method to be used can be described in detail.[8] The worker receives an instruction card in writing. The language is simple and plain. Where necessary, the work to be done is illustrated with drawings, or photographs, or in any other way that will make the method clear. There is no opening for confusion as to what is meant, hence the least amount of time possible is wasted learning what is to be done. If the work is new work, the instruction is detailed. If it is old work, the instruction card may become a summary, but at any time a detailed instruction card is available to the worker, that he may review exactly what is to be done, and have it clearly in mind before he starts to work.

It is the duty of the teacher, as the instruction card man, to see that he has clearly in mind methods by which work is to be done. The value of the written instruction card for all cases may be questioned. There can be no question, however, as to the necessity of absolute clearness as to the method to be used. There is much waste in the average school room, especially when a new class is being trained, in teaching and learning the methods to be used. A "System" of class room methods might eliminate all of this. As an example of waste elimination in office work, take the typical Office System. This is a simple manual, containing, in the fewest words possible, rules as to office procedure, how each piece of work in the office is to be handled, and the reason for the method used.[9] This is used as the final authority, even before scientifically derived instruction cards are made, and is never entirely discarded, as its statement of the reasons for doing things is often helpful in gaining cooperation. The average child is far more willing to do things when he understands the reason for doing them, than is generally believed. To cite a concrete illustration, a new teacher found upon taking over a class in fifth year arithmetic that their preparation had been so poor that it was necessary to put them back to a drill on fundamental operations, lasting for weeks. The class rebelled, in school and at home, over the degradation of being given "babies' work." When speed in the fundamental operations was shown to be a stepping-stone towards rapid mastering of more complicated work, the class attacked the work with energy, and a spirit of cooperation that carried them forward at a surprising rate of speed. The close relationship between methods and reasons for their use must never be forgotten.

The Fourth Function, The Time and Cost Clerk.

It is the duty of the time and cost clerk to record what has been done, how much time it has taken to do it, and what it has cost, thus furnishing valuable data for the work on records and programs. He has charge of the "how much," the relation between outlay and return.[10]

The experienced teacher, unconsciously many times, gives attention to this function of his work. He acquires "judgment" as to how much he can expect to do in a set amount of time, as to the wear and tear on the class of doing the work, and as to the inducements that he must offer in order to accomplish what he sets out to do. However, unless this judgment is based on some type of accurate record, there is no assurance that it is worth a great deal, and even the most experienced teacher will acknowledge considerable loss of time, while "guaging" a new class. The inexperienced teacher, having no such judgment, is absolutely at sea. We have spoken previously of the task, and the necessity for measured records upon which to base it. Such a standardized task, when it does come, will by no means deprive the teacher of the chance to exercise initiative, for the individual element must always be reckoned with, and the teacher must always provide the percent of variation from standard that her own particular class group requires. It is cheering news to hear that the problem of the standard task is being attacked scientifically by a prominent educator, the results of whose work will be formulated into standards, which, because of his standing, will be unquestioned. No teacher, however, can afford to wait for recognized standards before attacking the time and cost problem. One cannot appreciate or use the results without some work in the field one's self.

The Fifth Function, The Disciplinarian.

The fifth function is that of discipline, of adjustment.[11] The disciplinarian may be said to have charge of the "why" in the organization, for the reason that he is conversant with all aspects of the situation. It is his duty to present this broader view to each member of the organization, and thus to convince each individual that his own welfare, as well as the welfare of the group, demands that he fit into the organization plan. The disciplinarian is supposed to be a preventer of trouble in the first place, and an adjustor only in case his preventive measures do not prove all that he hopes for. In the plant the disciplinarian is not in direct charge of the work of any member of the organization except of the few in his own function. He is a member of the employment staff, in order that he may become acquainted with the home conditions, training, etc., of the members of the organization. He also has a voice in changing wages, or reassignment of duties, and thus keeps in touch with the plant history of each individual. He is absolutely unprejudiced and unbiased. Any member of the organization may appeal to the disciplinarian upon any matter whatever.

The teacher, as a disciplinarian, has an advantage in that discipline in the schools has never been in the hands of those mentally but little superior to the disciplined. The teacher is, from the nature of his position, apt to be fair and unbiased in all cases involving disputes between individual pupils. One solution of school room difficulties that might be adopted from the industries is the considering of all offences as primarily against the social group, the teacher being regarded as the representative of the best social spirit.[12] This removes the personal elements, and helps the teacher to be more impartial. If the teacher will consider social spirit as the real disciplinarian, and himself but the agent, and if he will explain the reason for punishing infringements against the social spirit, adjustments will often become much simplified. Certain school groups have tried putting the discipline in the hands of the pupils themselves, and with some apparent success. However, such a group is seldom likely to explain the reason for the penalty inflicted, and the fundamental principle of functionalization seems to demand that the adjusting element shall be functionalized in the teacher, who shall be recognized as the embodiment of the social spirit as acting in an adjusting capacity.

The Sixth Function, The Gang Boss.

The gang boss in the plant is the teacher whose work it is to interpret the directions of the planning department to the worker.[13] While the worker may come into direct touch with every function of the planning department, this would mean a great waste of time. For this reason a man actually acquainted with the work, and usually one who has done it many times himself, and who is at the same time in close touch with those who plan the work, teaches the individual. Thru interrelation of pay and responsibility he is so interested in the result that he never gives up teaching until the worker is successful, or is transferred to a different type of job.

In the school room almost the entire time of the teacher is given up to this "gang boss" work, that is, is spent by him in seeing that the pupils actually do their work, learning as he has planned they shall learn it. The chief problem here, then, is to determine just what percent of the time shall be spent in such teaching. The industry has simply the suggestion to offer here that functionalizing the work, that is, putting the planning of it in other than the teaching period, gives the teacher, during the teaching period, an unhampered mind to devote to the matter of actual instruction.[14]

The Seventh Function, The Speed Boss.

The speed boss is responsible that all things with which the worker works are set at a proper speed.[15] In a machine shop his specific duty is to see that the machinery runs at the prescribed rate of speed. In other types of industry his duty is to have charge of all things in motion.

The teacher has little need to be a speed boss, if he has planned properly. In laboratory work he must see that moving equipment is working at the proper speed. He must also see that any direction for speed can be carried out.

The Eighth Function, The Repair Boss.

The repair boss is responsible for the condition of all working equipment. His work is primarily preventive. He is supposed to see that no accidents happen. He must be able, in an emergency, to put things back in the proper shape in the shortest amount of time possible.[16]

The teacher has important duties as a repair boss, especially on the preventive side. It is most important, especially with young children, that they are enabled as often as possible to do as they are required to do. There is actually tune saved by preventing breakdowns, either physical or mental, and by breakdowns are meant not serious disturbances, but unnecessary delays in the progress of the work. It takes so little to distract a child's attention from his work: Going to the cupboard for a new sheet of paper, stopping to sharpen a pencil, getting a new pen, these all mean taking the attention from the problem in hand, and a loss of time while getting back into the working attitude. In the same way, a complication or distraction while solving a problem will take the attention from the work. There is a, perhaps, not always appreciated advantage in stating a problem in terms that the children understand. A child may be able to add eight cents and five cents and four cents with perfect ease, while a demand to add eight rods and five rods and four rods would make him feel sure that the unfamiliar "rods" have complicated the problem in some way, that will make simple addition impossible. Of course, there is always the danger of the fascinating appeal of the familiar object, as in the case of a small child, asked a problem beginning,- "A farmer sold his cow, which had cost one hundred dollars, for one hundred and twenty dollars. What did he gain?",- who asked, after a long and interested consideration of the problem, "Why did he sell his cow?" On the whole, however, the familiar is a less dangerous distracting influence than the unfamiliar, in most cases. The importance of establishing and maintaining self-confidence is much more important in dealing with the child than with the adult. The teacher must, therefore, take his function as repair boss very seriously, and endeavor to see that the desired output results, in every case, at the conclusion of the smoothest work period possible.[17]

The Ninth Function, The Inspector.

The inspector is responsible for the quality of the work done, and for the quantity of the product made.[18] He is also responsible for the quantity of spoiled work. He is expected to stand by the worker during the first complete cycle of work, that is, while the first piece is made, in order to see that the worker knows how to do the work, can do it, and does do it properly. He also inspects all work when it is finished,- but the first inspection insures that the greater part of the work done, and probably all of it, shall be of a very high quality. For example, suppose the worker is to drill latch handles at a drill press. When he is ready to make the first handle, the inspector comes to the drill press, and remains there, watching him, until the first handle is completed. He then inspects the finished product. If this is right, and has been made according to the instruction card, there is every likelihood that the worker understands thoroughly what to do, and how to do it, and that he will be able to finish his task in the set time. When the task is finished, the inspector comes again, and inspects the remaining product. The first inspection is felt to be so valuable in the plant that enough inspectors are provided to insure that one shall be at hand during the performance of all first cycles.

Such inspection would also be of great value in the school room. Our present day methods would make first inspection difficult to install. However, a recognition of its value might lead to its introduction during study periods, when the teacher could pass from one to another to insure that each understood the method by which any new piece of work was to be done. Where individual work occupied large percent of the school hour, individual inspection is a simple problem. With class written work, and especially with frequent written tests, such inspection becomes more difficult, but the amount of waste that such inspection eliminates has never been appreciated. Any careful consideration of habit will make it plain that doing things constantly in the wrong way is an extremely dangerous process. High quality will most quickly be obtained where first inspection is insisted upon, and where final inspection becomes a secondary, though necessary, process.[19]

The Tenth Function, The Individual Worker.

As the chart shows plainly, all lines of connection extend to the individual worker. These lines, as read downward, represent paths of authority; as read upward, paths by which direction, or teaching, may come.[20] It is not always easy to have it plainly understood, in the industrial plant, that the individual worker is, after all, the culminating function, and that by the success of the individual worker can the success of the whole management be estimated.

It is much easier to make this plain in the school, where the success of the pupil is universally regarded as the test of teaching. The teacher, in every capacity, is the source of authority and of information. The lines in the chart are also read upward, in the industries, as lines of possible promotion. It is not impossible to read them so also in the school, for, whether consciously or not, if the teacher is acting in all of these functions, the pupil will learn how such functions operate, and will get some instructions as to how he may himself succeed in teaching. In every case, the lines are lines of relationship, which show how closely the whole organization is tied together.

The Maintenance Element.

As the organization is functionalized according to the chart, as the planning is separated from the performing, and the duties of the various members of the organization are grouped under functional heads, maintenance is provided for by keeping the channels of interconnection open, and by making each member of the organization feel that he is a necessary part for the successful operation of the whole. The fundamental point is the insistence on the social nature of the organization. The spirit of cooperation is, after all, the strong maintaining force. The high pay and good working conditions draw the men, but it is the social spirit that holds them.[21] It is the spirit that leads to confidence that the high pay and good working conditions will continue. It is the boast of the scientifically managed plant that any department can run, even though the individuals in it be changed.

A right social spirit must also be the maintaining force in the school. It has long been reckoned that the final test of a well managed class is the way it behaves under a "substitute" teacher. The proper division of responsibility helps here, so does the proper incentive, but that intangible thing, the spirit of cooperation, which we most demand, is the outcome of the recognition of social ideals. To install and maintain changes, the teacher, like the industrial manager, must have a definite plan that will appeal to the social spirit, and must enlist this social spirit during every step of the installation, and finally trust to the social spirit for the maintenance.

Summary of Part I

In Part I. we have stated the general principles of waste elimination. We have endeavored to show what Scientific Management has done to eliminate waste, and to show that, because of the close, though not always apparent, relationship between the plant and the school, it is possible to apply methods which have proven successful in the plant to the school, We have, then, attempted to show the theories that underlie waste elimination in the plant, the actual practice in such waste elimination, and the methods by which Scientific Management is installed and maintained. It is now our purpose to turn to the school room, and to show how these methods, which have proven successful in the industries, may actually be applied in the school.

References
1. Gilbreth, F. E., "Primer of Scientific Management," p. 36.
2. Gilbreth, F. E., Paper before University of Toronto Engineering Society, March 8, 1912.
3. Taylor, F. W., "Shop Management," Harper Edition, Pages 100-104.
4. Taylor, F. W., "Shop Management." Harper Edition, Pages 109-110.
5. Day, Charles, "Industrial Plants," Ch, VII.
    Taylor, F. W., "Shop Management," Harper Edition, p. 102.
6. Bagley, W. C., "Class Room Management," Ch, XIV.
7. Gilbreth, F. E., "Primer of Scientific Management," Pages 16-18.
    Taylor, F. W., "Shop Management," Harper Edition, Pages 102-103.
8. Gilbreth, F. B., "Field System," "Concrete System," "Bricklaying System."
9. Gilbreth, F. B., "Office System."
10. Taylor, F. W., "Shop Management," Harper Edition, Page 103.
11. Dodge, J. M., Dartmouth College Conference on Scientific Management, Pages 142-152.
    Taylor, F. W., "Shop Management," p. 103.
12. King, I., "Social Aspects in Education," Ch. XVI.

13. Taylor, F. W., "Shop Management," Harper Edition, p. 100.
14. Bagley, W. C., "Class Room Management," Ch. IX.
15. Taylor, F. W., "Shop Management," Harper Edition, p. 101.
16. Gilbreth, L. M., "The Psychology of Management," p. 74.
    Taylor, F. W., "Shop Management," Harper Edition, p. 101.
17. Colvin, S. S., "The Learning Process," Pages 268-269.
        "   " " "Human Behavior," Ch. IV.
18. Taylor, F. W., "Shop Management," Harper Edition, p. 101.
19. Gilbreth, L. M., "The Psychology of Management," p. 75.
20. Gilbreth, F. B., Introduction to "Symposium on Scientific Management and Efficiency in College Administration." Meeting of S. P. E. E., June, 1912.
21. Lewis, W., "An Object Lesson in Efficiency," Paper before Congress of Technology, Boston, April 10, 1911.

Part II

Application of Waste Elimination to Teaching

CHAPTER I
The First Step, The Survey, Recording Present Conditions

What a Survey Is.

The first step in attacking any problem is to have all the facts thoroughly before one. The first thing that it is necessary to do, then, in eliminating waste in teaching is to find out exactly what we are doing at present. This is prerequisite to planning the changes to be made. We may determine this present practice more or less successfully by thinking over the matter, and having an outline of the present procedure clearly in mind. We may, perhaps, progress even faster, if we discuss, the matter with some one, and state our present practice orally. However, the only satisfactory way to know what we are doing is to write it out in detail.[1] This has been clearly proven.

The Need of a Written survey.

The first rule for survey making is, then, "Record present practice, or procedure, in writing," or, as we word it in the industries, "Reduce present practice to writing." The need of making a written record has been demonstrated in the industries. Our own experience has shown us, from the start, that the written record is the only record accurate and definite enough to be depended upon.[2] Oral discussion stimulates to invention, but, where the matter under discussion is to be referred to later, the written record is imperative. Written records fix responsibility. Written accounts, or records, prevent the confusion that arises from forgetting.

Advantages of Written Records.

There are other advantages of the written records besides their value as statements of existing facts. One of these is that information possessed by individuals in the organization is put into definite form, and thus becomes available to all who are interested, or who can profit by it. Cooperation becomes easier. Another is that the necessity for much oral repetition is eliminated. A third is that, if records made by several engaged along the same lines of work are compared, common practice and good practice will become apparent. It was an appreciation of these by-products of the written record that led to the making of the "Systems" in the industries, which are still used as cooperation builders, and as furnishing the reasons for using the methods prescribed. A "System" is a collection of directions for the members of an organization, or for a group of such members, the reasons for the directions being included in every case. The first draft of such a "System" is, of course, practically a survey. A "System" in such a sense as this, if applied to school work, would result from a group of teachers in a school building doing different grades of work, or from a group of teachers scattered throughout the community doing the same grade of work, writing out their practice and the reasons for it; comparing their reasons; and formulating the results into a set of common rules, or directions. The first records submitted by the various teachers would here constitute the survey.

Difficulties of Making a Survey.

It is not easy to make accurate records. In the first place, few of us are trained to make accurate observations. We find it difficult to know just what we are doing, much more difficult to describe this in words. We find this true in the industries, where the skilled producer is often absolutely unable to describe his methods in words. Ask the skilled operator of a machine to tell you, while away from his machine, the process that he devotes his days to performing. In the average case, after a few minutes thinking, he will reply, "I must watch myself do it, while I tell you." Even when you go with him to the machine, he will not be able to put the process into words. Probably one reason for this is the fact that the work done frequently, and especially the work done rapidly, soon becomes a habit, and requires few of the higher mental processes for its direction.[3]

The writer has gotten surprisingly similar results while questioning teachers. "Exactly what is your method of presenting a new subject in history?" might be a typical question. To this the reply often is, "Why let me think.----Well, come and watch me." It was noted on hearing a large group of teachers comparing notes on methods of teaching spelling that seventy-five percent were unable to state what they actually did, but quoted instead the general directions given them by supervisors as to what they should do. Possibly this denoted simply a desire to formulate their practice into standard terms, but it suggested to the hearer at least a possible gap between theory and practice.

In the second place, it is difficult to record present practice exactly, because the procedure will seem to vary. It is not easy to decide whether the thing observed is really worth being called "Procedure," or whether it is a variation that has sprung up to meet the need of the occasion, and that may not be used in the future. The solution to this difficulty is to record the thing as it happens, and note the variation from the usual practice. In the industries we find it extremely difficult to make the observer do this. If he fails to note the variation, and notes the general procedure only, he may omit what might be a better element of a method. If he notes the variation, but fails to note that it is a variation, we get no true idea as to what the usual practice is.

In the third place, it is difficult to make an accurate record, because we feel constantly an unwillingness to record things just as they are. We at once think of better methods of doing things, and are tempted to record these, instead of the methods which are actually used. We found this to be true in first making the records of office practice. The records were made by those actually doing the office work, and the first records handed in were almost always of different, but so-called "better," methods that the workers had decided they would like to use. Even a trained recorder is often hampered, if he knows what is expected to happen, or wants very much that something should happen, as he is unconsciously inclined to make his observations favor the desired results. This is the case, even, of the scientist working in his laboratory. He finds it difficult to remain absolutely unprejudiced. How much more so, then, of an observer not a scientist, who has not had a specific training as to the value of facts. The teacher will find these same difficulties in making an accurate record.

Need of Detailed Records.

The necessity for, and the insistence on, describing each element at length will sharpen the observation, provide for including variations, and make accuracy imperative. It becomes easy to make detailed records when one realizes that even the apparently unimportant is really of great value. This has been proven in the industries. A detailed and accurate record was made of the process of operating a drill press. The aim was to derive a standard method for this operation. The records, which, in this case, were made with the most accurate devices of motion study, showed upon investigation not only elements needed for the standard method, but also records of habit, records of hesitation, and other records that have psychological value. Take another example. A series of records were made of an efficient method of folding a piece of cotton cloth. In order that no detail might be omitted, several observers made these records. One of these observers, having particularly acute hearing, made a record of the sounds registered by the hands of the folder upon the folding board. This record was compared with the various observations and mechanical records, as to what was seen during the folding process. The sound record showed one tap which was not recorded on the sight records. The folder was questioned as to an extra tap, implying an extra motion not in the standard series. This she at once admitted using, with the result that the standard method was ultimately made less fatiguing by the elimination of what proved to be an unnecessary motion.

That a detailed record is possible and is available has been demonstrated by Miss Stevens' admirable critical study of class room practice.[4]

Who Can Best Make the Survey.

The survey may be made by the person doing the work, or by some other person. Both methods are used in the industries, though the second is preferred. Each has its advantages. In the industries, if no expert investigator is available, the organization makes its own survey. If it is plain that an investigator shall ultimately be secured, the organization may profitably make its own survey as a part of the preliminary work.[5] The survey made by the person doing the work is of value in enlisting his cooperation and interest in the work, and in starting him to think in improved methods. If the worker is capable of recording his methods at all, a survey made by him will be of real value to him and the organization.

The two methods are also available in the school room. The teacher may feel that no outside observer can understand the real facts as he does, and may desire to make his own survey; or no trained investigator may be available, and the teacher may thus be reduced to making the survey. On the other hand, he must recognize that an outside investigator will be far more apt to get an unbiased record of facts. The experience of the writer has been that even the most broad-minded of teachers doubts the ability of any outsider to make an accurate and adequate record of his practice. Especially is this the case if the investigator has industrial rather than teaching experience. This feeling has some justification, yet, as we study surveys, we see more and more that survey making is a specialty.[6] It requires a natural aptitude, a general training in observation and exactness, and a special training in survey making to do a really fine piece of work.[*] However, whether an expert survey is made or not, the teacher must undoubtedly make his own survey in order to cooperate fully and heartily in planning the changes to be made.

The Scope of the Survey.

As for the elements that this survey should cover, there is much more danger of including too little than too much. We want an exact, detailed picture of what happens, let us say a photograph in distinction from a portrait. We want the realism and detail that the photograph gives. No matter how careful we are, we will undoubtedly find, as we proceed, that we have gradually made changes from the methods used at the start. We have emphasized the need for detailed records, the question now arises, "Should the survey include reasons for existing methods, and recommendations for changes?" It undoubtedly should, but these should be plainly labelled as reasons and as recommendations, and should be kept distinct from records of practice.[7] We must be careful not to under-valuate elements because we find excuses for them, and, on the other hand, not to over emphasize elements because we recommend them. The professional standing of the expert, his training, and his experience insure that he will not succumb to these temptations. That they are temptations, no one who has made a survey doubts. A review of practice in recording in the industries will substantiate this.

---

* See Appendix C.

The "Materials" Survey.

The survey made will include various departments, or parts, which will take up different aspects of the general subject. One of these will be the survey of handling what might be called the "materials," that is, the consideration of the school room as a work room with individual work places; the storage and handling of stores and tools, that is the various working equipment; and the method by which the materials are routed to and from the individuals using them. In the industries such a survey is made by using what is called a "route model" Such a route model for a room that would correspond to the average school room would consist of a wooden board, or a sheet of paper. On this would be marked the location of the various work places. These would be represented by small pieces of paper, or cardboard, pinned on to the foundation board. The paths of materials passing thru this room would be represented by different colored strings. These would be held in place by pins, and would represent graphically the lines over which various kinds of material travelled, in order to get from their starting points to their destinations. Besides the large model, which is usually kept in the plant, in order that all interested may study it, it is often found good practice to make small models of the same type of such a size and shape that they can be easily carried home by anyone interested, and studied there. The teacher will do well to make such a model of her class room. Not only can she study it where and when she likes, but it will serve as a most admirable record of the condition of things at the start at later times, when the trend of changes made will be of great interest.

The "Individual" Survey.

The other types of surveys to be made deal more directly with the human element. Of such a type is the individual survey, that is to say, a record of all the information available concerning the individuals composing the group studied. The average teacher can, of course, make no adequate survey of the individual pupils at the time at present at his disposal. That such a survey is possible is brought out in such books as Wallin's "The Mental Health of the School Child,"[8] where it is advocated that each pupil be put thru eight tests, which will determine his mental, moral, and physical capacity, in as far as these can to-day be accurately measured. But at least it is possible now to list the information concerning each individual that is available. We certainly have records of name, parentage, home address, age, with, perhaps, supplementary records of medical inspection and school progress. We are tempted sometimes to feel that our records are fairly complete. Yet, when compared with the type of records of "materials used" kept in an industrial plant, or with the employment records there used, we realize that the schools still have something to learn as to "labeling" the material with which they work. In the plant much of the information concerning the individual is gathered by the employment bureau, which is, as we have said, under the disciplinarian function. One Western philanthropist has used the employment records of his enormous plant to affect the home conditions of his workers, and with most gratifying success.[9] Before a man is "taken on" at this plant, he must give certain information concerning himself and his home life. A member of the employment staff, who is also a social worker, is then sent to investigate the report, as given by the applicant. He goes to the home, becomes acquainted with the family, verifies every statement made, and adds such information as he obtains by personal observation. As soon as there is an available vacancy, the applicant is sent for. He is told that his home conditions must come up to a certain standard before he can be employed. For example, his home must be clean; there must be a certain number of cubic feet in the house for each individual living there, etc. If his living conditions do not come up to the requirements, he is given an opportunity to better them, and a later chance for a position, if one is available. Thru this simple type of investigation the living conditions of a surprising number of people in the town where this plant is located have been bettered. Not only those who work in the plant, but those who desire and hope to work there, are making their home conditions more sanitary. As a by-product of this relationship between the plant and the home, the managers of the plant came into close touch with social conditions among their workers, and are able to make adjustments with the least amount of disturbance possible. A large organization having plants in various parts of the country, keeps the histories of its men in such form that a man applying at any of their plants can have his history forwarded to that plant, and can secure a position, if one is available, or at least a place on the preferred list, if his former connection with the company has been satisfactory. As this organization employes men in trades whose members are migratory, much time to both the men and the organization is saved by this plan.

Both of these ideas are applicable to the school records.[10] The average teacher feels that he has not time to investigate the home conditions of his pupils closely, and too often comes in touch with them only thru a case of discipline. Yet, educators are discovering more and more that school records and school conduct depend largely upon home environment, feeding, etc. It is encouraging to note that in some cities and cooperating country districts a social worker is becoming a member of the school staff, and is doing the work in home investigation, which must be done before satisfactory individual records can be kept. The writer heard recently of an industrial school that plans to employ an expert to make such investigations not only to trace the antecedents of the pupils, but also to serve as an aid in adjusting courses to their needs. Not only will carefully kept school records be an enormous aid to the teacher, they will also be a help to the child throughout his entire life. Nothing could be a greater help in vocational training, vocational guidance, and placement than a history card describing the child's life. This, to be ideal, should be begun by the parent, be continued by the various teachers under whom he comes, be submitted to the vocational counsellor, and, finally, to the placement bureau of the industrial plant. But, disregarding all these valuable by-products, the teacher can well afford, for his own advantage, to make as accurate and detailed an individual survey as possible.

The "Sociological" Survey.

The third type of survey to be made might be called a "sociological survey." This will set down the condition of social life in the school room. We may not go so far as to classify school rooms as monarchies and democracies,[11] as has been done, the monarchy being the school room in which the entire power of governing lies with the teacher, and the democracy that in which pupils and teacher share in the government; but we must in some way define and describe the relationship between pupil and teacher, and pupil and pupil. We should record also the results of this relation, or, at least, the existing condition with regard to cooperation. Not that this cooperation, or lack of cooperation, is the result of the form of government only, for that may simply be one of the factors, but simply that we may study what exists.

The sociological survey in a plant is often made at what are called foremen's meetings, or "smoke talks." These are gatherings of groups of the organization, or of the entire organization, to discuss the problems of common interest. They furnish an excellent opportunity for noting the amount of interest of the individual in the organization as a whole, the relation between the various individuals, and the general spirit that exists.

A similar test of the social conditions in the school might be the transforming of the class into a self governing group for a short period several times a week, as was described in an earlier chapter, and the discussion of topics of general interest.[12] The social relation that existed during this conference hour, and its influence upon the regular session of the class would be an excellent test as to the type of social spirit existing.

The Fatigue Survey.

The fourth type of survey is the fatigue survey.[13] This is most important in the industries. It is only recently that we have realized that fatigue is of two kinds, necessary and unnecessary. Unnecessary fatigue must be eliminated. Necessary fatigue must be estimated, and proper allowance for overcoming it must be made. In the industries we go thru the plant, and note the fatigue that exists. Without stopping to investigate its causes, we immediately provide adequate rest. We then study the causes, and attempt to cut out all unnecessary fatigue possible. We do this by providing proper equipment, better methods, and better adjustment of the worker to the work. Where necessary fatigue exists, we provide the best resting devices possible. We make a special record of all chairs, foot-rests, arm-rests, etc., of any type, for these are concrete enough to arouse instant interest in the subject.

The school is far in advance of the plant in the study of fatigue.[14] The average teacher has for centuries kept the fatigue of the pupils constantly in mind, eliminating unnecessary fatigue, and providing adequate rest for all necessary fatigue. Similar work has recently come to be done in the industries. Especially have the schools paid attention to the desk and the chair, to changing position to overcome fatigue.[15] It is, however, not generally recognized that the subject of fatigue has, as yet, been most inadequately investigated in every field. The more one studies the literature, the more clearly one understands that no one has a great amount of knowledge as to how to measure fatigue.[16] This is both discouraging and encouraging. It is discouraging, because it means that have little accurate data to work with. We do not know. We know no better way of measuring fatigue than by measuring the quality and quantity of output, which is most unsatisfactory, especially when we have to do with children, and can rely little upon their ideas of their own capabilities. It is encouraging in that the field belongs to anyone as yet. Those who are doing the pioneer work are glad to state this, and to state also that careful records of existing conditions, no matter how fragmentary, are of great value in working towards the standard we all seek. It is not necessary for the teacher to be trained enough to be able to explain why the conditions that he notes exist. If he will make a careful record of what actually happens, he will be contributing to the scientific study of fatigue. There are records needed as to the amount of output observed after short or long periods of intense application. There are records needed as to the existence of initial spurts and end spurts, that is, as to whether a pupil does a larger amount of work than the average amount during the first few minutes of the work period, or during the last few minutes before closing time.[17] A study of Prof. Thorndyke's book on "Work and Fatigue. Individual Differences" will make apparent the problems that it is possible to investigate, and will add interest to the fatigue study that one makes, no matter how simple and elementary it may be, in that it will put one in touch with the fatigue studies of the masters. The teacher should, then, record, as best as he can, what fatigue exists; what he is doing to eliminate fatigue; the fatigue devices in use; etc. A method of fatigue study in the industries, which is in preparation, hopes to give some suggestions, which may also be of use in the schools.

The "Aim" Survey.

All of the surveys so far mentioned come under the general grouping of recording actual practice, that is, telling just what we are doing. The aim survey attempts to determine and set down where we are going and why.[18] In the industries such a survey is also a part of the work of the employment bureau, which is responsible not only for hiring men, but also for supervising their promotion and progression. The applicant for employment in a scientifically managed plant states, either in a written report or in a conference with some member of the bureau, not only what he has done, and what he desires to do immediately, but what are his ultimate industrial aims. He gives details as to his qualifications for the position he desires to fill, these including not only his industrial experience, but also his schooling, his reading, and the things that he is doing outside of work to prepare himself to fulfill his aims. The topics discussed include the following: "Kind of work wanted now," "Kind of work wanted later," "I want to change my position because I am reading and studying the following," "I am especially interested in the following subjects." Thru the information thus recorded the employment bureau is enabled to outline not only the man's aim, but also the necessary steps towards its fulfillment. As for the aim of the plant as a whole, it is not often stated in such concrete terms, but we find it embodied in the highest type of scientific manager, who aims to promote his men even though this means sending them to better positions in other organizations if all the positions in the home plant of the type called for are filled, and to maintain and encourage a feeling of cooperation by rejoicing with the worker over an unduly high rate.[19]

The school is to be congratulated in having made a more intensive study of aims, and the literature of education is rich along these lines.[20] It is for the individual teacher to review these various aims, and decide which are the aims that are governing his work. The first step in the process is to answer in the simplest way possible the question, "What am I trying to do?" It may be that you are simply filling the board requirements, that is to say, that the thing you have in mind is to do the work assigned you exactly as it is assigned, and to make of your pupils the best possible group to go into the next grade. This is, perhaps, a rather short view, a rather restricted aim, but it is by no means one of which one need be ashamed. It is practically being a specialist in putting a group of pupils thru a restricted amount of work in a restricted time, and trying to do this in the most efficient way possible, leaving the responsibility for ultimate aims with some directing authority. The point here is, if this is a fact, to record it honestly, and to try to record also the reason. This may be that you think it is the best thing to do, or that it is all you have time to do, or that it is all that you are expected to do) or that you believe the efficiency of the school is best furthered by your so doing, or that it is all you believe you can do, in that the pupils seem only able to take in work of this sort.

In the second place, your aim may be to fit pupils for college. The requirements of the college board may take the place of the requirements of the local board of direction, or, in other words, the local board may be willing to give the directing power, in this respect, to the college board. Note here just <u>what</u> is the case and <u>why</u> it is the case, that is, whether you are in a college neighborhood, where to go to college is the ideal,- or whether your local directors feel that their judgment is not so good as the judgment of the college board, or whether your pupils are mostly from the "college going class," whose parents desire that they receive such training, etc. Note also your own opinion on the matter, whether you believe that what you are doing is the best thing, or not, that is, your attitude towards it.

Third, you may be training pupils to go to work, to "fit in" best in the industrial world. It might be possible that in this case you are training many of them to go to college first, but the general idea, in this type of training, is, perhaps, that the <u>work</u> should be the first consideration, and the college simply secondary. Probably, in many cases, the idea is that, while the pupil hopes for more training, he may have to go to work at almost any time. The training must be such that he can enter an industry when he is forced to. At least, you will want to record, as best you can, when your pupils expect to go to work, and to what degree your training prepares them to go into this work.

Fourth, you may be aiming to make citizens of your pupils, to prepare for life in the nation. You may be doing this by simply having this idea in mind, and directing your entire training towards general fitness for citizenship, or you may be doing it by modeling the class government on some existing form of state or national government, or you may be doing it in the German sense, by training each pupil with the primary aim of making him useful to the state.[21]

Fifth, you may be endeavoring to make specialists, to prepare pupils for some very definite type of work either physical or mental, or a combination of the two.[22] You will have two points to note under this heading,

    a.   In how far do you aim to encourage the specialty?
    b.   In how far do you aim to supplement, or balance, a specialty by giving an "all round" training?[23]

Sixth, you may simply be training for happiness, to prepare the pupil, in as far as you can, to live a contented and happy life.[24]

It is not to be supposed that you have one of these aims only in view. Your aim may be a composite of many, or all, of these. These are, at least, types for consideration.

A prominent educator has said that every teacher has in mind a hierarchy of aims. These are the remote aim, which is set, or suggested, by the social consciousness, or the Zeitgeist; the approximate aim, which is often determined by the superior authorities; and the immediate aim, which is generally under the direction of the teacher. For example the ultimate aim might be to develop the individual to his highest social efficiency. The approximate might be making a good citizen. The immediate aim might be teaching cooperation in class room activity. Now, if the teacher were giving a history lesson with these three aims in view, he might assign each pupil a definite and different part of the information to be brought in, thus realizing the immediate aim of securing cooperation in the class room exercises. At the same time he might emphasize those traits in the character study and those events in the part covered worthy to be taken as examples by the upbuilder of the state, thus realizing the approximate aim; and he might consider in his assignment letting each pupil bring in that part of the work, which he could readily, because of his individual peculiarities, make most interesting to the class, thus realizing the ultimate, or remote, aim. A realization of these aims demands not only the formulation of an aim for a term, or an aim for a particular course of study, but also the need of a particular, specific, and definite aim for each daily lesson. This lesson aim, or lesson plan, does not involve a stereotyped method of presentation that excludes deviations to meet the situation and the inspiration of the moment that illuminates teaching. It simply provides the planning to which the performing must ultimately refer.[25]

The "Method" Survey.

The sixth type of survey accompanies the fifth, and records the methods which may well be used in fulfilling any aim. The industries answer the question of method in two fashions:

1. Adapt your method as far as possible to your learner.
2. When in doubt, use as many methods as possible.

As an example of the first:[26]- A gang of French Canadians were put at doing some construction work by a foreman who spoke no French.

The Canadians neither spoke nor read English. The method used in teaching them what was to be done was the object lesson, the only method available and adequate. The men were carpenters. An English speaking carpenter was instructed as to what was to be done. He made, on his work table, a sample of the "form" the Canadians were to make. The Canadians were, then, led to this "form", and informed by gestures that this was the type of work to be done. The results were eminently satisfactory. As an example of the second:- A new worker in a plant is to be set at a type of work which he has not done before. It is necessary that he receive the fullest information possible.[27] He will be given a written instruction card that contains a full description in writing. He will also be given drawings, and, perhaps, a stereoscopic photograph of the object to be made. Besides this, he will receive oral instruction from his gang boss, and, probably, a demonstration, after which he will make a sample article under supervision. He may be shown the completed object, if that is available. If he cannot follow the method as shown by the demonstrator, because the motions involved are too rapid, he will be instructed by means of the motion picture film, where the rapid motions have been recorded and can now be seen, and where the method can now be repeated as often, and performed as slowly, as the learner desires. The motion picture film is an enormous aid in this teaching. It is a well known fact that fast motions differ from slow motions, and that even the most skilled demonstrator, attempting to slow down his method in order to teach it, will use different motions when working slowly than he uses when working rapidly. The motion picture film records these fast motions, and, then, thru controlled projection, enables the learner to see them and copy them at whatever pace is most profitable.[28]

The study of methods is far more advanced in the school than in the plant, and the teacher has received from his earliest training instruction and experience in the relation of method to pupil instructed and subject presented. This should enable the teacher, along with the lesson aim, to formulate the method to be used in such a way as to cover the need of the subject, the aim of the hour, and the capabilities of the individual pupils to be taught.

The Speed, or Pace, Survey.

The seventh type of survey might be called the "speed," or "pace," survey. This is made in order to determine how much we are doing, and where we are placing the emphasis. Such a survey in the industries consists of various charts, which show the amount of work on hand to be done, and the relative amount of this work accomplished each day. A speed chart will enable any member of the organization to see at any time whether the plant is on time, ahead of time, or behind time, and what the difference between the planning and the performing is. The chart also includes notes as to the reason for the existing conditions, and is another excellent example of the working of the exception principle.

In the school this seventh type of survey is also an accompaniment of the aim survey. We must note how long it takes us to present a certain subject according to a certain method, and, then, in estimating our progress in fulfilling our aims we must note whether we are ahead of or behind our program, to what extent, and the reasons.

We plan to cover a certain period during the history lesson of the day. We find that we cover about half this period. We note the fact, and also the reason, which may be that the assignment was too long, that some topic proved so interesting that its necessary elaboration cut short the amount covered, that the method selected proved inadequate, or any of a half dozen other reasons. The reason is important, as is also the fact that the amount we have lost on our schedule must be added to the program of the remaining time.

The Survey and the Waste Elimination Program.

The survey gives us, as we have seen, an account of the limitations within which we work, and an idea of the lines along which progress will be most profitable. It is possible now to outline a program of actual waste elimination. Just as we have taken the survey along two lines,

1. The handling of the material element,
2. The handling of the human element,

so we may take up our actual application of waste along the same two lines. The material element may be considered as a whole. The human element, however, will be easiest considered under two headings:

1. Waste elimination that affects the physical side.
2. Waste elimination that affects the mental side.

It is to these that we must next turn.

References
1. "Educational Surveys and Vocational Guidance." Teachers
     College Record, Jan., 1913.
   Report of the Commission Appointed to Study the System of
     Education in the Public Schools of Baltimore. U. S. Bureau of
     Education Bulletin, 1911, No. 4.
   New York School Inquiry. July, 1913. Made by Bureau of
     Municiple Research.
2. Gilbreth, F. B., "Field System," Introduction.
         "   "   "   "Office System."
3. Bagley, "Educational Values," p. 4l.
       "   "The Educative Process," p. 115.
   Colvin, S. S., "Human Behavior," p. 8.
         "   "   "   "The Learning Process," p. 47.
4. Stevens, R., "The Question as a Measure of Efficiency in
     Instruction."
5. Gilbreth, F. B. and L. M., "Fatigue Study," Ch. II.
6. Ayres, L. P., "The Public Schools of Springfield, Ill. Educational
     Section of the Springfield Survey." Russell Sage Foundation.
7. Reports of Superintendent of Newton Public Schools, 1912,
     1913.
8. Holmes, W. F., "School Organization and the Individual Child,"
     pages 134-139.
   Wallin, J. W. W.
9. Ford Plant, Detroit, Michigan.
10. Gulick and Ayres, "Medical Inspection of Schools," Pages 56-57.
    Hoag and Forman, "Health Work in the Schools," Pages 240-
      250.
11. King, I., "Social Aspects of Education," p, 291.
    Article on "Democratic Government of Schools," J. T. Ray.
12. King, I., "Social Aspects of Education," Pages 377-393.
13. Gilbreth, F. B. and L. M., "Fatigue Study," Ch. II.
14. Bryant, L. S., "School Feeding," p. 215.

Burnham, W. R., Bibliographies on Educational Psychology, "The Causes of Fatigue," A. Mandelstam.

Dresslar, F. B., "School Hygiene," Ch. XIX.

Sandiford, P., "The Mental and Physical Life of School Children," Pages 161-166.

Terman, L. M., "The Hygiene of the School Child," Pages 401-406.

Thorndike, E. L., "Educational Psychology," Vol. III.

15. Dresslar, F. B., "School Hygiene," Ch, V.

Terman, L. M., "The Hygiene of the School Child," p. 82.

16. Goldmark, J., "Fatigue and Efficiency."

Imbert, M. A., "Etudes experimentales de travail professionnel ouvrier:," "Sur la fatigue engendree par les mouvements rapides, etc."

Mosso, A., "Fatigue."

Offner and Whipple, "Mental Fatigue."

Thorndike, E. L., "Educational Psychology, Work and Fatigue, Individual Differences." Vol. III.

17. Thorndike, E. L., "Educational Psychology," Vol. III., Ch, III.

18. Thorndike, E. L., "Principles of Teaching," Ch. I.

19. Taylor, F. W., "Shop Management," Harper Edition, Pages 142-143

20. Bagley, "The Educative Process," Ch. III.

O'Shea, M. V., "Education as Adjustment," Part II.

21. Beckwith, H., "German Industrial Education and Its Lessons for the United States," U. S. Bureau of Education, Bulletin, 1913, No. 19.

Farrington, "Commercial Education in Germany."

Kerschensteiner, G., "The Schools and the Nation."

22. Bloomfield, M., "The Vocational Guidance of Youth," Ch. 1.

23. Thorndike, E. L., "Principles of Teaching," p. 1.

Colvin, S. S., "Human Behavior," p. 309.

24. Farnell, W., "Notes of Lessons in the Herbartian Method," Page VII.
25. Gilbreth, F. B., "Tuck School Conference on Scientific Management," p. 361.
26. Gilbreth, L. M., "The Psychology of Management," Ch. VIII.
27. Gilbreth, F. B., Paper for the "Annals" of the "American Academy of Political and Social Science," April, 1915.

CHAPTER II
Waste Elimination in Handling the Material Element

Types of Changes to Be Made.

As we have already considered in reviewing the theory of waste elimination, changes to be made should accomplish, at least, three results.

> 1. They should result in definite savings. No changes should be made simply to try out another method. We must be sure that the change contemplated will be, or is apt to be, a decided improvement.
> 2. The change must make an appreciable saving. Especially in doing the first work in this line, it is necessary that we have actual and considerable results, this, in order to encourage ourselves and those with whom we are working, and also in order to perfect our method by working at a problem that will give a plain and easily appreciated result.
> 3. The waste elimination should result in demonstrating methods of waste elimination to all interested. The teacher and the pupils should learn by doing the work, and by observing it, how waste elimination is done.

There may well be other results as by-products, but these three we must have.

Methods of Making Changes.

It should have been clear in our discussion thus far that all waste elimination may be translated into terms of making human energy effectual. This we term in a short phrase "motion study." Motion study is the measurement of motions in order to accomplish the largest amount of work of high quality with the least expenditure of effort, and with the least amount of fatigue possible.[1] If we consider our waste elimination methods in this light, the actual class room problems become very definite. As we study the materials, where they are placed, and how they move, the work places, and the arrangement of the various tools and stores upon them, and the general working conditions of the worker, we can easily note the effect of each element upon efficient motions, and upon consequent waste elimination. The rule in the school room should be to take over the results of industrial investigation, whenever these can be made useful. We know that such results are available for applying motion study to as exact a degree as is possible.

There are various methods of making motion study. It is possible to do acceptable work with no devices, simply by counting. It is possible to use the ordinary clock found in the school room. The stop watch method is more difficult to use, and the teacher is seldom, if ever, trained in its use sufficiently to make his results of great value. The micro-motion and cyclegraph methods of making motion study will be described at length in an appendix. They are available to any teacher who has sufficient time and enthusiasm to devote to the work. Without considering these more scientific methods of measurement, the teacher can do much thru observation and the simplest of experiments.[2]

General Working Conditions.

As we step into the school room, we note, first of all, the size; then, the color and lighting; then, the ventilation, temperature, and humidity. The average school room is too large for its purpose, which is the giving and the receiving of instruction. The size of the room is, of course, governed by the type of work being done.[3] However, a laboratory, or a room where individual work of any kind is going on, may be far larger than the average class room, and be perfectly satisfactory. Recitation rooms should not be larger than to accommodate comfortably a class group. Such a group, it has been demonstrated, should not exceed twenty-five, and can to advantage be smaller.

The average school room of to-day has sufficient window space to provide for ample sunlight, and has also provision for artificial light, in case daylight proves inadequate. There is, however, not always sufficient attention given to providing artificial light when it is necessary.[4] The writer observed in one specific instance a class that seemed dull and uninterested transformed at once into an attentive body of students when the artificial light was turned on. "Gloomy" weather affects not only seeing ability, but also the spirits of the students. Moreover, glare is not always noted and prevented. An excellent example of disregarded glare may be found in the average public library, where the electric lights are attached to the desks. It is often almost impossible to place one's book in such a position that the glare from the light does not strike the page, and render reading extremely difficult. Unnecessary fatigue from glare is not such a constant fact or in the average school as it is in this type of library, since most of the light is daylight, and the effect of the glare is, therefore, only transitory. The average pupil will not notice this glare, or, if he does, will not take any means to remedy it. It is noteworthy that most of us will stand great inconvenience from lighting, rather than go to the trouble of making the slightest physical effort to overcome it. Particularly is this true of the child, who has no idea of the serious effects of eye fatigue, and of the decrease in general efficiency which may result from lighting that is defective in any way.

Color is seldom a serious problem in the school room, as the economy of leaving walls uncolored, or of using inconspicuous tints, appeals to the financing authorities.[5] In the industries the color has not been seriously considered except where it could be utilized in working equipment, as an aid to classifying materials, or as a means for attracting attention. For example, different pipes used for different purposes are always marked with different standard colors, and these can be quickly located. Certain forms are always of certain colors, and these can be identified wherever they are. In the office force, each member of a group has his own colored ink for rubber stamps. Thus one recognizes the stamp immediately from the color without needing to decipher the letters. The writer has noted no application of this principle in the school room, though it might well be applied. Teachers consume considerable time finding any particularly desired set of papers. If the class used one color for arithmetic, another for composition, etc., some of this time certainly could be saved. Where different kinds and sizes of paper are used, such as brown paper for drawing, slips of paper for mental arithmetic, lined paper for spelling, etc., there is a saving of time, but the underlying principle is seldom applied as far as it might be. Our discussion of color has led us far afield from the question of general working conditions. However, all parts of waste elimination are so closely linked together that a few excursions here and there into related lines may serve to illustrate the general principle, rather than to distract the attention.

At the present day, the average class room is amply supplied with ventilating devices. This seems to be, however, no absolute assurance that it is properly ventilated. The importance of ventilation can scarcely be over-estimated.[6] We have noticed a close correlation between dragging class work and lack of ventilation. This was particularly the case with a physics class, whose members demonstrated themselves during the laboratory period as bright and interested, but during a recitation period seemed extremely dull, although the teaching was interesting, and bore upon the laboratory problems. The poor ventilation might well have been the cause of the dullness as the observers found themselves extremely dull after a short time I although much interested in what was going on. On the other hand, the classes visited that demonstrated most interest in their work, and accomplished the most in the least amount of time, invariably worked with windows wide open, and with cool fresh air blowing thru the rooms.

The effect of temperature and humidity have also been closely observed in the class room.[7] Such effects have been found to be striking in the industries. So true is this that no careful motion studies are ever taken without recording the temperature and the humidity existing.[8]

Individual Working Conditions.

Under individual working conditions we may consider especially the pupils' and the teacher's desk, chair, and clothing. We might also consider posture, at least in so far as it is affected by these.

The desk and the chair should be adjustable, not only with relation to the pupil, but with relation to each other.[9] The desk should, of course, be so placed that the lighting will be the best available. It should also be placed with reference to distracting influences. In the industries work places are always arranged so that as few people as possible may pass behind the worker, as we find that this greatly distracts his attention. It is, perhaps, not so much a matter of placing the pupil's desk so that no one can pass behind him, as of arranging that as few people as possible shall pass behind him while he is working. There should certainly be consideration of distracted attention in placing the work place. The work place must also be arranged to allow of social, as well as individual, activities, but this will be considered later. In the majority of day schools desks and chairs are well adjusted, but in some of the night schools we find pitiful conditions existing. Grown people are trying to sit in children's chairs, and working at desks whose discomfort can only be realized when one tries to use them oneself for several hours at a stretch. When one considers that light and heat and teaching are cheerfully provided for these ambitious students, one wonders why the question of an appropriate individual work place has been so seldom seriously considered.

The teacher's desk and chair seldom receive the same attention as do the student's, probably, because the average teacher spends but a small percentage of his time during school hours at the desk. Fortunately for the teacher, his work makes a flat topped desk imperative. A flat topped desk is a demand of efficiency in the industries. Nothing is more difficult to eliminate than the wasteful roll topped desks. The teacher is indeed fortunate that he need not contend with this difficulty. Besides its flat top, the average teacher's desk has nothing to recommend it. It provided accommodations neither for what he has in it, what he would like to have in it, nor what he ought to have in it. The teacher's chair is no better. It is neither adapted to working, nor to resting. If its purpose is to keep the teacher on his feet as much as possible, it succeeds admirably. One can think of no other purpose which it could serve.

One hesitates to touch upon the subject of clothing, it has aroused such violent and such bitter discussion.[10] The average American school child's clothing defies every law of hygiene and beauty. Miss Ida Tarbell's criterion of clothing seems the best yet established, "Is it appropriate?" The average school child's clothing is not appropriate. Strange to relate, the simplest yet most appropriate clothing is oftenest found in the expensive private schools, which lay great stress upon good health and good taste in clothing. In the average public school we find clothes that are uncomfortable, glaring in color, and extreme in style. There is no excuse for this in the class where it most generally exists, which is the well-to-do class, since inexpensive ready-made clothing that is hygienic and artistic can be had for less than the price of the usual inappropriate costumes worn. The effects of this inappropriate clothing are more far-reaching than might be expected. In the first place, it is often distinctly unhygienic, being too thin or too tight. In the second place, it certainly is a distracting influence, leading to undesirable competition. This applies not only to garments, but also to shoes, style of hair dressing, etc. The boys' clothing has not the same faults as the girls', though the fads for wearing insufficient underwear, gaudy colors, and sweaters instead of shirts, all have their far-reaching bad effects that affect more than physical conditions. We must consider that the curriculum is full, and that time for new subjects is difficult to find, but, surely, an enormous amount of waste in money, in thought, and in effort would be eliminated, if the coming generation could be taught the value of appropriateness in dress. The same arguments will, probably, be advanced here, as are advanced in the industries, when we endeavor to standardize working clothes. We at once hear of "the freedom of the individual." We hear also that "the poor worker has no other chance to wear the things that appeal to her except at work." Some parent will doubtless say, "Surely, the private school girl can afford to wear a uniform during school hours, as she has all sorts of outside amusements and entertainments at which to wear bright clothes." The answer to this is that the average child who wears inappropriate school clothes does not lack outside opportunities to wear other clothes, and that usually the clothes, worn to school would be inappropriate anywhere. As for individual freedom, one is entitled to it only when its use does not interfere with the freedom of others. Absolute freedom as to the choice of school clothing does interfere with others, and with the social spirit of the group.

So far as we know, lectures on appropriate clothing from the teacher have not a great deal of effect. It might be more effective, if the class took up the matter themselves. It has proven so in the industries.

There the custom is to call the workers together,- it is usually the women workers,- and to show that there is no reason why one should not have appropriate work costumes, as well as appropriate "sport" costumes. The workers are, then, asked to design themselves what they would consider appropriate and artistic "atelier," or studio, gowns. They are shown as model gowns worn by artists. Such gowns are not only artistic and simple, but appeal because of the class of people who wear them. It is customary for workers in laboratories, both men and women, to wear gowns, or aprons, the material handled making the advisability of wearing such gowns immediately apparent. Younger children might be appealed to by the uniform idea, which appeals also to the young workers, such as the messenger corps, who are pleased and proud to wear specially designed work clothes. Another feature of the solution of the clothing problem in the industries has been the fact that those occupying more important positions have been ready and glad to adopt any standardized clothing suggested. This has influenced the members of the organization in less important positions to follow their examples. In a well-known factory in the Middle West, which is run on the most progressive plan, a kimono apron, well suited to the type of work done, is offered to the women workers in the plant at a very low rate. It is well known among the workers that the office force, and even the wives of the head men in the organization, wear these aprons at types of work for which they are suitable, and this helps to give them a standing that they might otherwise lack.

It would undoubtedly be a help in the school, especially with younger children, if the teacher would wear, at least during the installation period, some modified form of the work uniform suggested. The teacher can certainly go as far as to wear a school costume that is a model in its appropriateness. We note that many teachers do so. One teacher, in particular, whose class work is remarkably efficient, it was noted, wore low heeled rubber soled shoes. These, with her general attitude of preparedness, mental and physical. seemed to have a strong influence upon the pupils. We note in the case of the nurses' uniform. both undergraduate and graduate, and in the case of the cap, or marked sweater, or other symbol of college standing, that costume has value as it is a mark of attainment. Being this, it is worn with pride. The same thing is true of cadets' uniforms, of Boy Scouts uniforms, etc. The question of clothing may seem unimportant, but its influence. economic, social, and individual, is enormous. It would certainly be a wonderful thing for this country if school children, as a body, could be convinced that efficiency and appropriateness, the two being more often synonymous than is supposed, are the real tests of clothing.

The effect of clothing on the social spirit was noted at a school where, because of the nature of the work, the pupils came for certain hours only during the day or week. The pupils were mostly girls. The younger ones were accustomed to take off their hats, as well as their coats, upon entering the school, but many of the older ones wore their hats, especially for class recitation. It was noted that those who took their hats off seemed to enter into the social spirit far more readily. There not only was a feeling of "at homeness," but there was more attention devoted to the work, this not only because the attention was not distracted by observing new and attractive headgear of others, but also because the more or less uncomfortable hats did not constantly suggest the lesson being over, and the wearers going on to some other work or play. The girls were all asked to remove their hats being told that the social spirit of the class room would be better. They agreed readily, and a decided improvement was immediately noted. As with everything else, a habit was soon formed, the sooner, because it was an easy and comfortable habit to form, and the good results have continued.

The influence of proper clothing upon posture has been often noted. Proper adjustment of desks and chairs also affects posture.

Supplementing these and the talks that the teacher gives upon the subject should be charts from the Posture League.[11] The League is now enabled to furnish every teacher applying with a large and attractive chart, that pictures correct posture. Such a chart is an incentive towards correct standing and sitting that only those who have shown it to young children can realize.

Room Equipment.

We turn now to the general equipment of the room, its placement, and the relation of the various articles to one another.

We may consider, first, the teacher's table, or desk, and chair. We have already referred to these, but not to their relation to the pupils' desks. The teacher's desk is almost universally placed in the front of the room, this doubtless so that he can see all the pupils, and be seen by them, easily. The writer has never known, however, of any attempt to measure exactly the advantages of having the desk so placed. Doubtless much depends on the purpose which the desk is used by the teacher. In one case, the teacher practically never sits at her desk during the working school day. She uses it as a supply table. It is covered with photographs of past pupils, flowers, etc. It is extremely ornamental, and doubtless showing the pictures of successful past pupils acts as a stimulus to the present class, but, being what it is, and not a work place during school hours, it has no excuse for its position in the middle of the front of the room. The teacher walks around it and into it, as she teaches, and would do far better to move it to some place, where it could be seen during school hours and used at other times, yet not impede her progress, for she is one of that type that accomplishes most when physically, as well as mentally, active. In other school rooms, much of the time pupils actually reciting stand in the front of the room. Here again, the teacher's desk is often misplaced for the type of work that he desires to do. We have seen a splendid social spirit aroused in a class by allowing one or another to stand in the place usually occupied by the teacher's desk, and address the class, or debate with the class. The teacher, meantime, occupied one of the pupils' chairs, and became a member of the group. It was also noted that in a class in harmony much difference in social atmosphere was created by a change in the placing of the piano. This was at first placed so that the pupil playing had her back to the rest of the class. This immediately gave her a feeling of being a performer with an audience. The piano was moved so that the pupil faced the class. This change, with a few introductory remarks by the teacher, made the player feel that she was contributing towards the class improvement and pleasure.

As for the arrangement of the pupils' desks with relation to one another and the teacher's desk, the arrangement in the average class room, that is, parallel lines and rows of seats, is extremely inefficient.[12] In the first place, it is difficult to place individual pupils properly with relation to the teacher, who must almost inevitably come into close touch with those in the front of the room only. In the second place, the method of seating is no aid to seeing that the teacher's attention is properly distributed. The good teacher's attention will, doubtless, be so distributed thru some other plan for distribution. The seating will offer no assistance.

It has been noted, with inexperienced teachers especially, that they soon fall into a habit of calling either upon the front rows, or the back row, leaving a large portion of the class neglected during any class period. In the third place, this usual seating arrangement is a decided damper upon developing a cooperative spirit in the class. It is a prime necessity for arousing cooperation that all may look easily at the person who is speaking to the class. The present seating means that a large proportion of the pupils must sit in, or twist their backs into, uncomfortable positions, in order to look at the pupils reciting. Of all the school rooms visited, but one recitation room seemed ideal. The pupils' desks were arranged in concentric semi-circles about the teacher's desk. The teacher had nothing but approval for the seating arrangement, but complained that so few students could be placed in the ordinary floor space. The answer to this objection is, of course, that the school rooms are not properly designed. We note that the average room for science lectures and demonstrations, designed so that every pupil can see the demonstration, allows of pupils seeing one another easier than does the average recitation room. At one private school visited the English class met in a special conference, or seminar, room. The pupils sat in comfortable chairs, drawn into an informal semi-circle, and a most excellent social spirit prevailed. This was here practicable, because no written work was done during this period. With the present school room such grouping seems impracticable. However, there is nothing impossible about it. There is no reason why a large modernly equipped school could not have special rooms where written work only is done, and other rooms for conferences. Properly designed chairs with arms are adequate equipment for any short written exercise. Programs, outlined further ahead and more in detail, would be needed in order that the proper class might reach the proper work place at the desired time, but this would soon become a matter of routine. If, as is being strongly urged, the well developed social spirit is the most desirable incentive, radical means must be taken that this social spirit may grow. A proper seating is certainly one of the factors. In one specific instance, where the chairs were easily moved, the chairs had stood in the usual lines and rows. They were now moved to form a large semi-circle, there being, perhaps, twelve to fifteen in the class. As far as possible no other changes were made, it being merely suggested to the teacher that the new arrangement would allow the children, who were all small, to see better. Improvements were noted at once. Every individual was called upon, and the teacher, as well as the pupils, became more cooperative.

Another element of school room equipment is the blackboard.[13] There is much discussion as to the use of blackboard and the value of blackboard work. This we must consider later. We have to do here with the placing of the blackboard. It is certainly a great waste to put a blackboard anywhere where it cannot be seen easily from any part of the room. Yet, in the average school room the blackboard encircles the room at a certain height, whether it is useful or not, this, probably because it costs little more to put a blackboard all the way around the room than half, or three-quarters, of the way around. As a result, therefore, much blackboard space that is not fit to be used is used to the consequent daily discomfort of the class. Space that might well be utilized for other purposes is thus worse than wasted. Many school rooms could be transformed into artistic, as well as efficient, work places, if blackboards were placed only where they were useful, and the other spaces were properly utilized. As to the finish of the blackboard, this is too often determined by what the janitor, or some one else in charge, considers makes a good-looking, or easily dusted, surface, rather than by what proves an excellent surface upon which to write. Almost every teacher can testify to waste through "beautifully oiled" blackboards. The general use of the blackboard is as a place upon which the teacher may make demonstrations. Therefore, ample blackboard space must be provided convenient to the teacher and in full view of the pupils.

Another element of school room equipment is the waste. This may not seem, at first thought, a very important element, but its placement has a decided effect upon the ease with which tidiness in a room can be secured and maintained. There is a great difference as to the practice of the use of the waste basket in the school room. In the first place, many different types of waste baskets are used, some of open weave, that are self-evidently poor containers, as pencil sharpenings and other fine pieces of waste sift thru to the floor. If there is but one waste basket, it is too often placed under the teacher's desk in place supposedly convenient for the teacher's use. This position, however, means that the teacher is constantly disturbed, if the pupils are allowed to deposit things in the waste basket during school hours. Another arrangement is to have the waste basket by the doors where the boys pass out of the room. With this placement it is customary for the boys to empty their desks of waste before intermission, and to deposit this waste as they march out of the room. In some cases the girls are allowed to pass their waste to the boys just before intermission. This is often an occasion for considerable disturbance. In one case where this was pointed out there were two available waste baskets. The teacher placed one at the boys' exit, and one at the girls', thus allowing each pupil to deposit his waste for himself, as he left the room. The teacher himself, it was noted, with this arrangement made many trips to the waste basket during the day to deposit waste. A third waste basket, or some smaller receptacle for waste, for the teacher's use, that could have been kept empty by a pupil, would have bettered conditions here. Not every school room has three, or even two, waste baskets, and the same scantiness of supplies with regard to proper pencil sharpeners is also noted. The waste in sharpening pencils with a knife often borrowed from the teacher, thus demanding time to make the request and time for the pupil to go to the teacher's desk and get the knife, there is also waste of poorly made points, dirty hands, etc. With good pencil sharpeners as cheap as they are, and the necessity in school rooms for providing work during periods of unavoidable delay, there is no excuse for not functionalizing pencil sharpening, and providing adequate equipment for the work.

Another element of school room equipment is the clock. There is much discussion as to the proper placing of the clock in the industries, as well as in the school rooms. In the shops, for years, it was the rule that no clock should be in the work room, as it was supposed that the workers wasted time looking at the clock. Actual measurement showed, however, that where no clock was present much more time was wasted looking at watches, or asking one's fellow workers for the time. The present practice in the industries is to place a clock in every work room where it can be seen by every worker. The office workers each have an inexpensive watch as part of the desk equipment. This is hung over the desk, where it can be seen with the least amount of effort possible. This has been found good practice. The same would doubtless be true of the school room. The pupils are bound to know What time it is. Less time will be wasted by putting the clock where they can see it easily. The "time wasted" in looking at the clock will be wasted anyway. The clock is not the cause of the waste. It is simply an object that happens to attract wandering attention. With an appreciation of motion study and time study, the clock becomes an efficient tool. It is consulted of necessity, and acts as an incentive. The teacher should take this on faith, and early in the program see that the clock is properly placed.

It is customary for the writer in suggesting possible changes in equipment always to mention early the proper placing of the clock. It is surprising the number of objections to moving it which are encountered. These range from "But it has always been there," thru "The janitor will not like the work," "It will leave a bare space on the wall, "The children will spend all day looking at it," including a surprising number of replies, that all indicate the human dislike of making changes. The clock incident might be considered a test case, that will show early and clearly the teacher's attitude towards actual physical changes involved in waste elimination. As a test of actual differences caused by different placing of the clock, some experiments were made with a class of ten young women during several class hours. The small, portable clock used was placed with its back to the class, where no one but the teacher could see it. During the latter half of an hour period every girl in the class asked her neighbor, at least once, what time it was. This usually occurred after the teacher was seen to glance at the clock. Ten minutes before the hour was up several began to gather their things together, preparing to leave. The next hour that the same class assembled the clock was placed so that the class could see it easily. There were, of course, no questions as to the time. There was considerable glancing at the clock, but no one started to pack up her things until the class was practically. There was no attempt here to suggest the use of the clock as an efficient tool, as it was not desired to complicate the variables. The experiment indicated possible saving from replacement alone.

Another part of the working equipment is the calendar. This is used by every member of the class several times, often many times, in the day, according as there is little or much written work. Yet the calendar is seldom placed where it can be seen easily by all. The proper calendar will have large, plain figures, and it will be the duty of some one to put a horizontal line through each day as it is passed, that is to say, that up to the present day of the month all dates will be cancelled by a heavy horizontal, preferably red, line. This is good office practice in the industries, and even a five year child will soon note whether the cancelling is kept up to date or not. The writer has frequently urged teachers to move calendars, that were in dark corners, or places seen with difficulty, to the front of the school room, and has received the objection, "But I have too much in front of the room now." Yet an inspection of what was there often showed ornaments, that could as well have had a less conspicuous place, and materials such as maps, used for a part of the day, and sometimes not every day. Such material could easily be adjustable, and be put in place, when needed, by some member of the class specially assigned. If nothing except material constantly needed was given the important position in the front of the room, there would be no need of overcrowding.

The ornaments of various kinds offer a serious problem in themselves. Such are pictures, growing plants, and the flowers, that the children are so fond of bringing. Any one can close his eyes, and recall a long line of teacher's desks, covered with growing plants, shedding leaves and blossoms, and with more or less rickety vases of floral offerings for "teacher." These certainly add not only to the beauty of the school room and to cultivate a love of nature, but also to the spirit of cooperation; but a large supply of them certainly form no part of the work place. A plant table is inexpensive and easy to secure, and allows of the plants getting the air and sunshine that they need. The cut flowers may be kept on the plant table, or provided with hanging vases, that can be easily seen, yet out of the way. Such vases are to some extent available, and certainly there would be a supply, if the need were realized. Even in the industries we find the greatest need for respecting the tastes of the individual regarding ornaments. It is not uncommon to find a space on the wall in front of the worker's work bench covered with calendars and magazine covers, illustrated pages from the papers, photographs, or other ornaments. These are never destroyed, or disparaged, in any way, but it is insisted that they shall not any interfere with the work place as a work place. The worker is usually quick to see the advantage of this. The same thing is not always true of the teacher, who fears to wound the pupils by moving their gifts from the very important places which they have occupied. Yet the problem has been handled with such skill by some that a happy solution is certainly open to all.[14]

We turn, finally, in examining room equipment to the equipment for containing tools, stores, and worked materials. By "tools" in the industries we mean the things with which we work. By "stores" we mean the things upon which we work. By "worked materials" we mean things that have been worked upon once, and will be again. A typical class room "tool" is a pencil. A "store" is paper. A "worked material" is a paper written by the children, and not yet corrected by the teacher. Tools and stores are usually kept in a class room in cupboards or cases, worked materials in the same, or similar, cases, or in the drawers of the teacher's desk. There may be also a supply table, a bookcase, and a large dictionary and chair, possibly other things. The efficient tool room or store room in the plant is, called a "one motion tool room," or a "one motion store room." The school tool and stores stations should reach this ideal as nearly as possible, that is to say, one should be able to take anything out and put it back again with but one motion, or, at least, with as few motions as possible. Things that are used oftenest should be placed most conveniently. In the industries no tools, or stores, are taken out by any but those directly in charge, that is, no worker takes out, or puts back a tool or a store for himself. It would be a wise thing, if this could also be done in the school room. If not, the next best thing is to allow any one to any take things out, but no one but the particular person assigned to put things back. This is common practice in the efficient filing room, as it is also in many libraries. The mistakes occur in putting things back into the wrong positions. A basket, or some other container, is provided nearby, into which things with which one is finished, or that he does not. need, are placed. The person in charge, then returns the article to its place when he has time.[15] If this seems impractical, as a first step at least label every shelf, box, and drawer to reduce handling time. The shop uses mnemonic symbols, that is, a combination of letters and figures, to represent words and phrases and help the memory.[16] These are perfectly practicable in the school room, especially with older children, but labels in longhand with the ordinary name of the material or tool will answer.

It is a question whether the teacher's desk is proper place to keep worked materials. Much depends, doubtless, upon the amount of equipment for holding tools, stores, and worked materials available.[17] There are worse places than the teacher's desk. It is certainly discouraging to the class to see carefully prepared papers lying exposed to dust on a supply table, or notebooks in the laboratory on a table near the running water.

Containers and Contained.

It will be a great help in keeping materials of various kinds in order to provide as many containers as possible, boxes for pencils and crayons, compartments for the various kinds of paper, etc.[18] These may be of two kinds. First, a permanent part of the containing equipment, that is always to be used for materials at rest. Such will be the compartments into which the various kinds of paper can be put. A great advantage of these containers is the indication that they give as to the amount of supplies on hand, and the warning that they automatically give the teacher that more supplies are necessary. It must not be forgotten that to do efficient work there must be not only enough supplies to provide for the ordinary working place, but also sufficient for the elasticity station, that is to say, there must be material on hand, in case any more is needed in an emergency. Other containers will be on the packet principle, that is, devised for moving many units easily at one time. Such are pencil boxes, that are used in distributing the pencils, an eraser, mechanical drawing instruments, etc., to be carried to the desk, and used during the drawing period, then returned to the tool cupboard until the next period. Little has so far been done in the school room towards devising containers. The ordinary boxes in use are seldom devised to preserve the materials they contain in the best state possible, nor do they provide that the material can be taken out and returned with the least number of motions possible.

The Relation of the Work Place to Tools and Stores.

It is thoroughly recognized in the industries to-day that a work place is a place where work is done, that it is not an attractive condition when it is bare of work and of equipment. Unless the desk must be used for some other purpose, there is no reason why the working equipment, such as pencils, should be stored away every time it is not in use. One is constantly surprised in going thru class rooms, and especially laboratories, during school hours to find room after room with desks and tables absolutely bare, no one even attempting to set up or take down working apparatus. In a scientifically managed office one desk drawer is always set aside for company supplies that are available to anyone. It is, then, possible for anyone going to any work place to get, at least, enough material to enable him to make a record, to leave a note, or to do the most pressing work of the moment. In the office desk the upper left-hand drawer is devoted to this group supply station. The same idea might be applicable in the school, making it possible for any one to find, at least, paper and pencil wherever he went ready for his use. We do not find in the industries that these privileges are abused, and the supplies carried off. Their purpose is understood, and the entire organization cooperates towards the maintenance of the plan. The same would certainly prove true in the school. Where the school supplies the paper and the pencils, it certainly seems an enormous waste for pupils to carry this elementary working equipment even from one desk to another. It has been objected by one who is almost a faddist on hygiene that no one should use another's pencil because of the danger of infection, since so many have the habit of putting either the pointed or blunt end of a pencil into their mouths. If this feeling prevails, let us insist on individual pencils, but, at least, supply paper.[19] In the same way crayon and eraser should be at standardized positions at certain intervals in the tray below the blackboard, if blackboard work is used. So also a pencil and a pad should be in some way attached to the dictionary, and the chair needed in using the dictionary should always be in front of the dictionary, and in a fixed relation to it. The red pencil for crossing off the calendar should be attached to the calendar. Wherever possible working equipment should be fixed at the work place, its maintenance in proper condition being entrusted to some special person. These are the elementary changes in handling the materials element that can actually be made by the teacher at the start.

If he is ambitious, and willing to begin on himself, the teacher may well, at the same time, transform his own desk into a working model. This is invariably done in the industries, The first step is to draw a plan, showing exactly what is to be kept in the desk, and where. This plan is kept where it can be seen by the lower priced or less skilled worker who is to see that the desk arrangement is maintained. The desk must be flat topped. The upper left-hand drawer must contain company supplies, that is, supplies available to all. The desk in the industries is cross-sectioned, as is the plan. Every piece of working equipment that the user considers necessary is placed by him on the plan in exactly that place where he desires it be. There is always an in basket, labeled "In," and an out basket, labeled "Out." The out basket is red. Both baskets are of wire, as the material is moved in and out by a boy, who, because the baskets are made as they are, can see from a distance whether there is anything in the "Out" basket for him to attend to. There are also the rubber stamps required, a pencil rack, and any other equipment which the user feels essential. A plan of each drawer is made in the same way. The stationery of all kinds is kept in specially devised containers. The company drawer is arranged as follows: The front six inches are devoted to two small boxes, or packets, each $9\frac{3}{4}$x$5\frac{3}{4}$x$1\frac{1}{4}$. These boxes are identical, and are divided by pasteboard into ten small compartments. In these are kept pencils, erasers, rubber bands; i.e., the usual office supplies. Between the two boxes is a card that says, "Replenish contents of tool box." When supplies of any type have run out in the top box, the user moves the lower box into the upper position, and throws the supply card into his "Out" basket. The boy in charge then sees that the supplies are renewed. The user may leave the desk in any condition he pleases. It is the duty of the boy to put the desk into exactly the standard condition that the plan indicates. It should be, to say the least, not tactful to enumerate the contents of the average teacher's desk. We find "How about standardizing your own desk?" a fighting question. However, we recommend such standardization not only as furnishing a model to the pupils, but as furnishing an admirable instruction to the teacher in search of a method of standardization.

The pencil rack in the plant has been a source of arousing great interest in motion study. It is customary in every plant to ask all interested to design pencil racks that will require the least motions possible to deposit or pick up a pencil, and that will, at the same time, maintain the pencils in the best condition possible. The result is not only a rack that is efficient, but also a greatly increased interest in the subject of motion economy.

Routing Materials.

The problem of routing materials might be taken up as a part of the consideration of the materials element. However, in the school room, for the present at least, most of the routing will be done by having the teacher, or the children, move the materials, rather than by using any mechanical means. We shall, therefore, consider the routing under the problem of physical motions in considering the human element.

Tests of Effective Changes.

It is a pleasure, as well as a stimulus, to test each change towards waste elimination, as it is made. We not only use the three tests outlined in the beginning of the chapter, that is to say,

1.   Does it make savings?
2.   Does it really serve as an example of waste elimination?
3.   Has it taught us the methods of motion study?

We further test by asking whether the change has enabled the higher priced man to be relieved, and a lower priced man to do the work. These tests an efficient change must pass. As we review the changes suggested, we will see that practically all of them do allow of such functionalization of the work. It is provided not only that material be better placed and better handled, but also that the teacher is relieved and that the pupil receives training thru the actual work and thru the added responsibility. The proportion of success that we have attained in these various lines will determine how successful the experiment has been. If we have made much material saving, we can afford not to question too closely the amount we have learned. If we have learned methods of waste elimination, we may not be so strict in our demands for large savings. If we have relieved our high priced worker, and trained in a lower priced man, that alone justifies the changes. We must test every change by all these criteria and any others that may suggest themselves before deciding as to the value, or lack of value, of the changes.

References
1. Gilbreth, F. B., "Motion Study."
2. "Micro-Motion Study," Industrial Engineering, Jan., 1913.
3. Dresslar, F. B., "School Hygiene," Pages 30-41
4. Cornell, W. S., "Health and Medical Inspection of School
    Children," Pages 153-155.
    Dresslar, F. B., "School Hygiene," Ch. IV.
5. Dresslar, F. B., "School Hygiene," Pages 80-81.
6. Cornell, W. S., "Health and Medical Inspection of School
    Children," Pages 155-173.
    Dresslar, F. B., "School Hygiene," Ch. XI.
    Terman, L. M., "The Hygiene of the School Child," Ch. X.
7. Dresslar, F. B., "School Hygiene," Ch. XIV.
    Terman, L. M., "The Hygiene of the School Child," p. 155
8. Benedict, F. G., "Studies in Body Temperature," American
    Journal of Physiology, 1904, XI., Pages 145-170.
    Gilbreth, L. M., "The Psychology of Management," p. 111.
9. Cornell, W. S., "Health and Medical Inspection of School
    Children," Pages 180-190.
    Dresslar, F. B., "School Hygiene," Ch, V.
    Terman, L. M., "The Hygiene of the School Child," Pages 80-81.
10. Burks, F. B., "Health and the School," Ch. XIV.
    Munroe, Paul, "Cyclopedia of Education," Article on "Clothing
    of School Children."
    Pakes, W. C. C., "School Hygiene," Ch. XI.
11. Bancroft, J. H., "The Posture of School Children."
    Burks, F. B., "Health and the School," Pages 272-274.
    Cornell, W. S., "Health and Medical Inspection of School
    Children," p. 464 ff.
    Terrnan, L. M., "The Hygiene of the School Child," Ch. VII.
12. Shaw, E. R., "School Hygiene," Pages 26-27.
13. Shaw, E. R., "School Hygiene," Pages 27-29.
    Dresslar, F. B., "School Hygiene," Pages 41-49.

14. Kotelmann, L., "School Hygiene," p. 165.
15. Gilbreth, F. B., "Office System."
16. Benedict, H. C., "The Mnemonic Symbolizing of Stores Under Scientific Management," Industrial Engineering, July-August, 1912.
    Colvin, S. S., "Human Behavior," Pages 290-291.
17. Hope and Brown, "A Manual of School Hygiene," p. 135.
18. Kent, R. T., "The Tool Room in Scientific Management," The Iron Age, Sept. 4, 1913
19. Dresslar, F. B., "School Hygiene," p. 337.

Observations Illustrating the Handling
of the Material Element

XIV.

Observation

A harmony class, of young women meeting at ten-thirty on a gloomy winter's day. The subject of the hour was analyzing a melody, which should have interested the class. However, the class seemed to become more dull and uninterested as the hour progressed. The observer finally noted that the sun had gone under a cloud, and that the room was becoming gradually darker. The artificial lights were at once switched on. The class immediately became attentive, and continued so thruout the remainder of the hour.

Comment

This seems a clear case of the bad results of poor lighting and of the good results of adequate lighting. The light was at no time too poor to prevent the pupils from seeing properly, but the dullness seemed to act as a depressing force.

XV.

Observation

A 6 B grade. The teacher showing the observer different sets of class papers. The arithmetic papers were all on plain white paper, the spelling papers were ruled slips, the drawing was on brown paper. The same thing was noted in visiting a third grade room and inspecting the papers. Each style of work was done on a different size or texture of paper.

Comment.

The ease with which the teachers found any set of papers desired led one to feel that much more could be done than is at present done to save time by the use of different kinds of papers, and also by the use of different colored papers. Where two classes are in the same room a different color for each class would save handling time.

XVI.

Observation.

A class in high school physics observed during the unprepared period. An examination was to take place the next day, and every pupil was supposed to bring up points upon which he was in doubt to help him in his preparation for the examination. In spite of this incentive for steady work the class seemed extremely dull and heavy. The observer and the friend who was with her soon began to experience the same feeling, and noted that all windows were closed, and that the air seemed warm and close.

Comment.

This is an apparent case of the bad effect of the lack of ventilation, and was contrasted at once with the good work observed in the physics class of the same grade where the work was done with open windows, though there was not the incentive of preparing for an approaching examination.

XVII.

Observation.

Second grade pupils writing in copy books. Teacher passes back of the seats, and stops to observe the writing carefully. Observation shows that in practically every case the pupil either stops, or does much poorer work while the teacher is observing.

Comment.

We see here plainly the distracting influence which, the observer believes, is created because the teacher stands back of the pupil where the pupil cannot easily look at her. It might be suggested that the teacher stand where the pupil can observe her as well as she can observe the pupil.

XVIII.
Observation.

A class of adults learning English in an evening school. This class consists of perhaps fifty, as there are two teachers. There are among these many tall men, although the class is Polish. It is noted that the seats are the regular low chairs used by fourth or fifth grade pupils. The adults seem very uncomfortable.

Comment.

In the industries efficient performance has been greatly increased by providing proper chairs. A queer thing about the situation in this evening school is that the observer saw several rooms with larger seats not in use.

XIX.
Observation.

A primary school. Noted in infant class that, while there were many pictures, plants, etc., all were placed so as not to interfere with the carrying on of the actual work done in the room. The best available space was used for blackboards. The table that one sees in other places often covered with plants served as an admirable supply station. The usual surplus of ornaments, children's work, etc., seen in the average school room had been used to decorate the hall, which in most schools remains unornamented. Here the decorations were low enough for the children to enjoy. The school is old and unattractive in its construction features, but has been made a thing of beauty and an efficient work place by the thought devoted to it by the teaching staff.

Comment.

This admirably illustrates the importance of an efficient work place, showing, as is demonstrated also in the industries, that efficiency does not mean eliminating adornment, but rather placing it properly.

XX.
Observation.

A physics class room in a high school for both girls and boys. Noted the unsuitable dressing of the girls, especially the elaborate hair ribbons which are now in style. These not only cut off the view of those sitting behind such a bow from the board and the desk where demonstrations were being made, but seemed to require constant adjustment by their wearers.

Comment

This is a typical example of the distracting influence of unsuitable clothing. The observer contrasted with this procedure the behavior of a group of girls of similar age at a school where a simple uniform is insisted upon. Standardization seems the proper remedy.

XXI.
Observation.

A first year high school class room. The teacher's desk is in the middle of the front of the room less than two feet from the front row of pupils' desks. It is impossible for the teacher, or pupil reciting, to stand comfortably where she can be seen by all. Every inch of the desk is covered with books, photographs, flowers, etc.

Comment.

The teacher's desk has absolutely no excuse for its position. It is evidently used as a supply station rather than a work place. Efficiency would demand that it be moved to the side of the room.

XXII.
Observation.

A teacher's desk in a first grade primary class. Several classes are in the room, and it is the custom for the teacher to call the class reciting to form in line at the front of the room. There is no room in front of the desk for the pupils to line up. They, therefore, form a line from the side of the desk to the side of the room. The teacher who sits at the desk naturally hears the pupil standing next her far better than those at a distance.

Comment.

Here also the desk seems to be little used as a work place during school room hours. It might well be moved to the back or side of the room. The pupils could then stand directly in front of the teacher, or form a semi-circle about her. In her chair without the desk's intervening she would be in a far better position to encourage the proper social spirit. Here again we have the improper placing of materials.

XXIII.
Observation.

A second year high school English class. The teacher's desk is in the front of the room, but somewhat to the right of thee center. The teacher sits at desk when making records or hearing recitations, but stands at the center of the room when giving a teaching lesson. Pupils stand at the center of the room during certain subjects when reciting.

Comment.

The pacing of this desk is admirable. It fits into the teacher's plan of running the class room as far as possible like a debating society or club.

XXIV.
Observation.

A harmony class of young children. The piano, which has formerly been placed so that the one playing it has her back to the class, is turned so that the player partially faces the class, while, at the same time, the class is enabled to watch the player's fingers.

Comment.

With this change in the placing of the piano the interest of both player and class increases. The player, seeing the attentive audience, realizes that she is playing for, rather than to, them. Again we have here the beneficial effect of properly placed material.

XXV.
Observation.

An ungraded room in a grammar school. The pupils are those who have fallen behind their grade, or proved unruly in the regular class room. The seats are arranged in a semi-circle about the platform on which the teacher's desk is located.

Comment.

This arrangement seems particularly fortunate here, as the children are in the room because of ill adjustment of some sort. Therefore, it is particularly necessary to gain and hold their attention easily. The teacher commends the arrangement highly. Critical observation confirms her recommendations. Such seating might well be used in every class room.

XXVI.
Observation.

A science lecture room in a high school. The seats are arranged as in the amphitheater of a hospital. The observer notes the ease with which the pupils follow the demonstrations on the instructor's table and at the board. The ease with which all can follow the recitations of anyone is also remarked.

Comment.

This, while doubtless too expensive an arrangement for an ordinary class room, certainly shows the benefit of the semi-circular arrangement of seats.

XXVII.
Observation.

A senior English class in a private school. The students use large and comfortable chairs with arms for writing material. Seats are drawn into an irregular semi-circle with teacher at the center. The observer noted not only, the physical comfort of the class, but also the ease with which written and oral work was handled, and the presence of the recognized seminar spirit.

Comment.

Here again the seating was an important influence. The same girls were observed in other classes where regulation desks and desk arrangement existed. There was an immediate return to the stereotyped school room attitude.

XXVIII.
Observation.

A sixth grade class. There are blackboards at the front and rear of the room and on one side, also a small blackboard between the windows on the fourth side of the room. The front boards are covered with maps, pictures, and programs. In demonstrating or explaining work the teacher uses the side board, sometimes, if she is walking about the room, even the rear board or the board between the windows. Glare makes the rear board and the board between the windows difficult to see.

Comment.

Many of the things on the front board could equally well be in less conspicuous places. Maps, etc. could be rolled up. The slight saving of the teacher's time in her not having to walk to the front of the room to see the board is not compensated for by the strain on the children's eyes and attention through the use of the other boards.

XXIX.

Observation.

A sixth grade. A similar arrangement of blackboards as in the last room described, although this is a different room and teacher. Half the class sent to the board. Because of the light fully half this work cannot be comfortably read by any pupils seated, or by most of the pupils at the board. Inspite of this fact much blackboard work is done. The attention of class seems to wander during the time that the blackboard work is being explained, read, and corrected.

Comment.

If blackboard work must be used, surely it would be wisdom to send fewer to the board at a time.

XXX.

Observation.

A first grade class. The lighting is admirable. Blackboards are on front and rear walls and one side wall. The blackboards are elaborately ornamented with fancy drawings and mottoes. The pupils, sent to board for half an arithmetic lesson and also for a spelling lesson, are obliged to take great care to avoid the ornamental drawings, and often to write in a cramped position.

Comment.

Fewer ornaments would be more pleasing, and such as are used could easily be put higher up where they would be out of the children's way.

The children are extremely short, and use perhaps a half to two thirds of the board space, leaving at least a foot of clear space around the top.

XXXI.
Observation.

A third grade class. The blackboard extends around four sides of the room. The room has light from two sides, and it is difficult to read work on a large part of the blackboard. The entire class is sent to the board, and a different example dictated to each child. At the end of five minutes the work is stopped, and the children in turn read what they have written on the board. It is impossible for a large number of the children to follow the work. The teacher herself is obliged to move from place to place to read what is written, and the observer, who sits near the teacher's desk, finds it impossible to see a great deal of the work.

Comment.

Here again we have poor working conditions. Fully half of the blackboard space should never be used, or, better still, no blackboard should ever have been placed there. This latter method would have left the space available for other use.

XXXII
Observation.

The same third grade room described in example XXXI. Teacher demonstrating an arithmetic problem. She pulls a portable blackboard to the front of the room, makes sure that every child can see it, and then sets to work.

Comment.

It seems strange that, realizing as she does in this case thoroughly the necessity for having the whole class see the work, this same teacher should fail to appreciate how poor the class use of the blackboard space in the room is. This shows clearly the need for a close study of the work place in the school room. This teacher is very able and progressive, and has the children's welfare in mind. It is simply that the problem of standardizing every work place has never been properly presented.

XXXIII.

Observation.

A sixth grade class. There are two wastebaskets in the room, one under the teacher's desk, one at the door through which the boys pass in leaving the room. The girls are supposed to pass their waste paper, etc. to the boys at recess and closing periods. The boys deposit this material in the wastebasket as they pass through the door. The wastebasket under the desk is for the teacher, and is not supposed to be used by the pupils. The pupils are observed, however, to go up and deposit paper in the teacher's wastebasket during the recitation hour, though infrequently.

Comment.

The plan of having a fixed time and method for depositing the waste is admirable. The trouble here is in the lack of sufficient equipment. There is considerable confusion when the girls pass the paper, etc. to the boys. At the observer's suggestion the teacher's wastebasket is placed at the girls' entrance, and the girls are made to deposit their own waste as they go out. This works very well, and the former confusion is done away with. However, now, the teacher makes occasional trips to one or the other of the wastebaskets to deposit her own scrap paper. This, is, of course, a serious waste. The teacher should immediately be provided with a wastebasket herself, or some receptacle for the waste that a pupil could empty at set periods into the larger wastebasket.

This illustrates several points. The first is the poor placing of available material. The second is the lack of available material in the average school room. Wastebaskets are so cheap that it is extremely inefficient to consider their cost as compared to a few minutest time saved in the class room. This illustrates also the danger of the teacher's making any change until she understands thoroughly the principles and practice of Scientific Management. Without such understanding a small apparent saving may actually result in a much greater loss of time and effort. By carrying her own material the teacher violates the fundamental law of functionalizing the work. She also makes of her own work place a place much poorer than it originally was. It also emphasizes the importance of the serious consideration of the problem of handling paper, both used and unused. Professor Bagley brings out the inefficiency of having unused, used and, especially, torn bits of paper on and in the pupil's desk. This is a problem of education, as well as of management, that is often neglected.

XXXIV.

Observation.

A fifth grade class of girls. Written lesson being done with pencils. During the twenty minutes four walk up to the teacher's desk, borrow the teacher's knife, and sharpen their pencils None are reproved. No record is made.

Comment.

The time actually spent on the papers must vary considerably, if time is spent by some pupils in sharpening pencils. There is no excuse for sharpening pencils during working periods, nor is their excuse, in these days of inexpensive and excellent pencil sharpeners, for using a knife. Neither should each pupil sharpen his own pencils. The remedies are

1. To provide a pencil sharpener.

2. To have the sharpening done during periods of unavoidable delay.

3. To have the work so functionalized that the sharpening is done by one person as a reward, as special training, or for some other very definite reason.

XXXV.

Observation.

A class of ten older students at the Music School. A small portable clock stands on the piano so placed that it can be seen by the teacher, who is supposed to consult it in order to complete her work within a set time. During the lesson hour such pupils as have watches frequently consult them. Those who have none ask their friends for the time. As the close of the period draws near, the class become restless, and begin to prepare to leave.

Comment.

The whole trouble here is the wrong placement of the clock. The industries have proven that a proper work place includes a clock or watch easily seen by the worker. At the suggestion of the observer the next time this class assembled the clock is placed so that it can be seen by the class as well as the teacher. The result is no consulting of watches. The class remain attentive to the end of the hour. The average teacher believes, as does the average oldtime manager, that the clock is a distracting influence. Common sense should suggest that it is more distracting to desire constantly to see something that one cannot see, or can barely see, than to have this thing in plain sight where one can look at it, and then dismiss the thought of it from one's mind.

XXXVI.

Observation.

A sixth grade class room. The calendar is on the side blackboard in a corner of the room, so placed as to be easily seen by the teacher, but seen by only a few of the pupils. The pupils are expected to place the date at the top of all written work. Whenever a written exercise occurs pupils ask the date, jump up from their seats to look at the calendar, or walk to the front of the room to look at the calendar.

Comment.

With the present day practice of dating each paper the calendar is an important part of working equipment. In this case the observer suggested placing the calendar in the front of the room. The teacher objected that there was no room. Yet various pictures, serving as ornaments only, occupied places that would have been admirable for the calendar. The observer also suggested cancelling all dates past with a vertical red line as is done in the industries. The teacher objected to the extra work involved on her part. The observer urged that a pupil be delegated for this task. The teacher doubted whether the results would justify the expenditure of effort. This illustrates the lack of study of the efficient work place. It also illustrates the average teacher's failure to understand the principle of functionalization. If waste elimination means anything, it means taking work from the teacher, and either eliminating this work entirely, or passing it over to the pupil in such a way that it furnishes some training.

XXXVII.

Observation.

A sixth year class. The front eight inches of the teacher's desk occupied by growing plants and by four glasses full of flowers. It is noted that the teacher is obliged to handle other materials on her desk with great caution, also that every time a pupil approaches the desk the teacher finds it necessary to insure that the pupil does not tip over the flowers, nor break the plants.

Comment.

The observer urges the teacher to move the plants to a shelf or table near the window, and to have hanging vases for the flowers, or add the flower glasses to the plant shelf. The teacher objects that the pupils will think this shows lack of appreciation of their gifts. She says also that the flowers have "always" stood there. This illustrates a prevalent lack of appreciation of what a work place, means. The flowers would be equally ornamental and pleasing out of the way. It also illustrates a tendency we all have to feel, that what has been established a long while has necessarily some good reason for existing. The remedy is to apply accurate measurement.

XXXVIII.
Observation.

A fourth year class. The plants are arranged on a well placed and attractive plant table near the window. The teacher's desk is thus left free for working. The teacher tends the plants herself, and spends much time and effort watering them, pruning them, etc. She shows great nervousness every time pupils approach the plant table.

Comment.

Upon inquiry the observer found that many plants are the gifts of the pupils, and that the pupils greatly desire to tend the plants. The teacher, who is a great plant lover, evidently fears that this amateur tending will have bad results. Here is an admirable chance to functionalize the work, relieving the teacher and training the pupils. The admirable placing of the plants simplifies this whole problem so that the change could easily be installed.

XXXIX.

Observation.

A small school. All the supplies, extra paper, pencils, etc. are kept at the school storeroom where they are handled by a special teacher, and where they may be purchased by the pupils at any time. No extra equipment is in the rooms. Pupils leave recitation frequently to go to storeroom and purchase supplies.

Comment.

This method of handling supplies is excellently, especially handled as efficiently as it is here, where a sufficient stock for everyone is always in the building. The trouble here is that the class room practice is not standardized. Pupils' supplies should be inspected during daily periods, and it should be insured that each one has laid in not only sufficient stock for the work planned, but also enough for an elasticity or reserve station. As supplies are bought by pupils, all of whom are plentifully supplied with money for the purpose, there is no problem on that score, though there is some need to for administration as to waste of materials.

XL.

Observation.

A second grade class. Supply cupboard in back of room. Here are kept paper, pencils) drawing pencils, supplementary readers, in fact all sorts of supplies. Because of the nature of the work supplies are taken out and put back constantly. The teacher, during the time the observations were made, got the supplies from the closet and distributed them. The pupils upon completing the work took the supplies back and put them in the cupboard. At the beginning of the session the supply closet was immaculate. At the end of the session the supply closet was a jumble of confusion.

Comment.

While the original appearance of the closet indicated that the teacher herself had a place for everything and everything in its place, it was evident that the places were not indicated in any way, and that the children were accustomed to putting back supplies where they chose. The teacher admitted spending much time between sessions straightening out the supply closet, but seemed to feel that this was unavoidable when working with such young children. There were several ways to handle this situation. The simplest would be for the pupils to get the materials, and for the teacher to put it back, if the pupils deposit the material with which they have finished on some bench or shelf near the closet. This would mean somewhat the same procedure for the children and less work from the teacher, who during the straightening up process was accustomed to move the confused material from the cupboard to the shelf or table to do the sorting. It would be much better to mark each shelf in the cupboard plainly, thus indicating where the various things were to go, and to insist that the pupils put back their supplies in an orderly fashion. Better than this would be to have one or two pupils do this work for the entire class during a delayed period. The teacher might object that this would use a pupil's time that should otherwise be employed, but pupils of this age need just such training as handling these supplies would afford. Here an excellent opportunity for functionalizing the work is neglected, one that the Montessori system would certainly utilize. The work might be passed from one group to another, this affording work to all without delaying the class.

XLI

Observation.

An ungraded room of grammar school pupils. These were grouped into various small classes for the different branches of work. Supplies were in a small cupboard at the front of the room, well placed near the corner. A large supply table stood near the cupboard, also near the teacher's desk. All supplies for the day, books, paper, pencils, etc. were observed to be arranged in orderly fashion on the supply table. During the entire morning everything needed was obtained by the pupils, this most expeditiously. The teacher, upon being asked, said that the supplies were taken from the cupboard before school in the morning by the monitor, and arranged according to a definite plan for the entire morning session.

Comment.

The practice here is excellent. Through this and other waste eliminating devices the teacher and class accomplish an enormous amount of work.

XLII

Observation.

Drawing class. Pupils of high school age. Special teacher giving instruction. Supplies are all kept in a cupboard at the rear of the room. After the arrival of the special teacher one pupil distributes paper, another lead pencils, a third colored lead pencils. It is thus about seven minutes after opening a session before the class is prepared to listen to the teacher and set to work.

Comment

All such passing of supplies should be done before the class hour, especially in the case of a highly paid special teacher, who visits the class but seldom, and every moments of whose time is valuable.

CHAPTER III
The Human Element, Eliminating Waste in Physical Motions

The Relation Between Wasted Time and Physical and Mental Motions

We decided in discussing waste elimination as regards the human element to divide such study into a consideration of the physical element and of the mental element, that is, of physical motions and of mental motions. This is an arbitrary and not very satisfactory division. All physical motions, of course, imply a mental element, and all mental happenings express themselves to a greater or less degree in some form of physical activity.[1] However, there are certain acts, that, if observed, show more prominently the mental side. It is on this basis that we shall consider, first, how to simplify the physical procedure, leaving the more complicated mental element for the later discussion. When we consider wasted time in the school room and in the industries, we find that both wasted motions and wasted thought are involved. When we consider efficiently used time, we find that it involves a better thinking process, and a simplification of the physical motions actually used to perform the work. For example, a teacher wished to test the success of a short explanation that she had given of a certain method in arithmetic, that had seemed puzzling to the class. She, therefore, said, "Take a sheet of white paper. (This was a standard sheet, perhaps, 6"x9".) Tear off a strip that will be six inches wide and one inch long. Write the answer to this question on the paper." The question given formed the test as to the understanding of the method. The class received in this simple manner a lesson in economy in the use of materials, a training in judgment as to what a paper 6"x1" actually looked like, the physical exercise of folding over and tearing off the strip, and the added mental exercise of giving accurately the answer to the problem. This method might be criticized from a motion study standpoint in some respects. However, it serves as an excellent example of the possibility of mental and physical training.

The Proper Distribution of Time.

Closely related to the above discussion is the proper distribution of time between mental and physical work.[2] In the average elementary and even secondary school the only physical work that is done is such an amount as is prescribed as exercise, added to the amount involved in distributing and collecting supplies, and in otherwise preparing for and clearing up after mental work. The matter of time given to exercise should be governed by the amount of necessary work involved in school work proper.[3] We must all agree that too much allowance for exercise is better than too little, but surely it is wasteful to assign periods to unproductive activity, when productive activity would have as excellent physical results. The amount of exercise and the distribution of exercise periods is a part of the fatigue problem, and cannot, therefore, be determined by any offhand judgment.

As for the distribution of time between "Get ready," "Do the work," and "Clean up," in the average school work the "get ready" and "clean up" periods are occupied largely with physical work, while the "do it" period is occupied with mental work, the physical motions, if there are such, being usually a matter of recording. The proportion of time that the actual working time is to the time spent in getting ready and in cleaning up must be carefully investigated.[4] Of course, "cleaning up" time could be reckoned as part of the preparation time for the next work, but this is really not a fair method of estimating, since so considering it will give us no help towards standardizing the task time. In the industries task time includes always time for getting ready, time for doing the work, and time for cleaning up. In the class room, for example, if an arithmetic test were given, in the task time must be included time for distributing needed supplies and tools, that is, papers and pencils or pens; time for working the examples and setting down the answers; and time for collecting the papers and putting the pencil, or pen, in the temporary, or permanent, resting place. Most teachers are greatly surprised to find how much of the time during class room hours is actually used, at present, in getting ready and cleaning up.

There are various methods of cutting down this time. One is by having this part of the work done during the intermission, or before or after school hours, either in the school plant, or at home.[5] In some schools there are rules prohibiting the pupils being in the school building for any considerable time either before or after school hours, this, apparently, because it is thought that their being there would necessitate the teachers' being there also. Surely, it is false economy to prevent the child's spending extra time at work at a profitable work place, if he so desires.[6] We have often wondered why some arrangement is not made whereby pupils who desire to do home work at school during the afternoon or evening hours may find it convenient to do so. The average home is not equipped with the proper work place at which the child can study.[7] It would not be necessary that every teacher be at the building. It would not be necessary either, perhaps, that anyone of the regular corps should be in attendance for such work, but surely some one of age and capacity to supervise might be on hand, so that preparation work of any type desired might be done at the pupil's convenience. If the pupil so desire, much work of the type of recording in notebooks might be done at home. The restrictions on certain types of notes to be submitted for college entrance demand that they be done in the school under the teacher's supervision, but all notes are not of this type.

Another method of shortening preparation time is by considering the desk as a work place, and having more than sufficient supplies constantly on hand, so that there need be far less frequent replenishment of supplies than is at present the custom.

A third is by utilizing periods of unavoidable delay. For example, in many schools it is the custom to stop recitation several minutes before the gong for passing sounds. Many teachers make efficient use of this time by getting ready for the next work period.

A fourth method would be by using the younger and less skillful pupils to do the preparation and "clean up" work. This method might be helpful, in the elementary school. There is no doubt that every child should learn how to handle physical materials. Probably this training should come much earlier in the school course than is now the custom. Under our present practice of having primary and grammar grades in the same building, it would seem perfectly feasible to so arrange the work that primary children might be sent into the grammar classes to attend to the distributing and collecting. This would be entirely in accord with the Montessori theory and practice that is receiving such an enormous amount of consideration in the educational world to-day.[8] The burden of making this innovation would rest largely upon the teachers in the kindergarten and primary grades, who have shown themselves, in many respects, remarkably willing to adjust themselves to any conditions that will better develop the pupils.

The aim of the waste elimination here is to enable as large a percent of the school day as possible to be devoted to the actual work of learning. The method to be used depends upon the particular conditions existing, but all methods should be considered and utilized to as great an extent as possible.

The Problem of Routing.

The problem of routing in the class room covers the routing of the pupils and the routing of material. The routing of pupils considers getting the pupils into the class room and to their seats, getting them from their seats to the board and back, or to some recitation place and back, or to needed materials and back, or from the desk out of the room into the hall and the school grounds.[9]

Routing of pupils is better handled in the average elementary than in the average secondary school, this for several reasons. In the first place, it is felt that the older pupils will be hampered by the restrictions of the formal grouping of the elementary schools. In the second place, the pupils in the secondary school do not move in groups, but as units. In the elementary school the pupils probably form in line in the yard. They march into the building, often to some rhythm from a bell, or a drum, or a more or less ambitious band. They march thru the cloak room and to their seats in orderly lines. There they are seated at once, or upon signal. In the same way the class often march as a group, or in small groups, to the board, or the recitation line, and back to the seats. Very much the same method is employed in leaving the room, "stand," "pass," "in lines," etc. Certain elements of this method may be questioned, such as making all pupils stand by the seats until the command to be seated is given. It may be suggested that they could profitably sit upon reaching the desks, or work places, and begin immediately to prepare for the first lesson. However, there is the advantage in the present method of unified action, of cultivating social spirit, and of the grace of standing while greeting the teacher, and until given permission to be seated. In the private school the pupils usually enter and leave in less strict order, but are expected to shake hands with and courtesy to the teacher, while saying "Good morning," or "Good night." This would, undoubtedly, be considered to consume too much, time in the large classes of the public schools, but time is always relative to the results achieved, a thing we often forget.

The elementary school usually does not face the problem of one group of pupils entering, while another is leaving. This is the usual custom, except at intermission periods, in the secondary school. It has, perhaps, not been realized that there are many elements of the secondary school passing problem that resemble the problem in the primary and grammar schools. One is getting the pupils from the room into the hall. In almost every case the class leaves the room as a group, while they enter the room individually. Another is the problem of getting to and from the board, and to and from supply stations. In the average school room it is possible, and perfectly feasible, to use two doors for passing. Yet seldom does one find all pupils entering from one door, and leaving by the other. still less often does one find all pupils leaving the room, walking either to the back or the front of the room, as has been assigned, and those entering, approaching the desks from the opposite direction. The result is that in the average secondary school much time is wasted by crowding in some places, and distinct lack of crowding in others. Because such conditions are widely prevalent, an excessive amount of time is often allowed for passing. Pupils dawdle from one room, and from one work place, to another, and acquire habits of slow motions, that it may be difficult to break. The best remedy might not lie in a better routing of pupils, but in an incentive to reach the next work place more quickly, and to spend as little time as possible in transit. However, until this desirable condition prevails, something could be done by better routing. A fine example of excellent routing during the class period was noted in an ungraded class, where it was necessary for the teacher to handle many small groups during one class period. The recitation line was put at the side of the room, as far from those studying as possible. At the appointed time, at a single word of command, group one passed to the recitation line. An assigned pupil handed his book to the teacher as he passed to place. The recitation was then conducted. At another word, the first group returned to their seats, the one who had given his book to the teacher recovering it as he passed. At the same time the second group was filing into place on the line, a pupil here also handing his book to the teacher. In a surprisingly short amount of time the second group were reciting and the first group seated. The entire procedure for the day was carefully outlined at the start, and an enormous amount of work covered. Many elements of this routing method, doubtless, were applicable only to the specific problem there considered. Other elements would prove available in any class room routing. Yet, we often see the following procedure: Group one completing work at the board, group two working at the seats, Teacher: "Those at the board pass to the seats." Pause, while group one seat themselves. "Those who were at the board now take books and study. Those who were working at the seats pass to the board." A proper routing would handle both groups at the same time, and, at the end of half the previous passing time, permit the teacher to begin work with the second group at the board.

This brings up one element of the blackboard problem. Those who advocate work at the blackboard seldom realize the amount of time actually used in getting ready for, and cleaning up from, such work. If blackboard work is as valuable as some believe, such time may be well spent, but it must be estimated as part of the price paid for blackboard work.[10]

Where monitors handle various parts of the work, it may be often noted that these are poorly routed, or, perhaps, poorly placed. The blackboard monitor is seated in the back of the room, when most of the erasing is on the front board where the teacher demonstrates. The supply monitor is seated as far as possible from the supply closet, etc. Improvements in functionalizing the work may make changes in the routing of such monitors unnecessary, but while the monitors are used the routing is important. As for the routing of materials, as little of this as possible should be done during school hours. Eliminating waste in routing, however, depends upon developing such social spirit as would make it possible to keep proper supplies in desks, providing containers in desks to hold perishable materials, etc. Under present conditions it is felt that a large amount of the routing must be done during school hours. Some teachers make it a custom that every bit of written work shall be collected the moment it is finished, this, perhaps, partly because they feel that, if not collected, the work will become soiled, and also that it may distract the pupil's attention. Yet, we have frequently seen classes accustomed to turning papers written side down upon their desks at the end of a test period, or a written period, and starting at once on another type of work, with no apparent distracting influence from the completed papers. These were collected during a later "delay" period. No one who has not observed distributing and collecting in many school rooms could imagine by how many methods it is possible to do these things. Each pupil may pick up a sheet of paper in passing to his place; or the front pupil in each row may pick up enough paper for his row, this paper being ready piled for him or not, as the case may be; or a monitor, seated anywhere in the row, may come to the teacher, or supply table, or supply closet, or any other place, for enough for his row; or one pupil may pass around and supply the entire room; or the teacher may pass around, and lay a sheet of paper on each desk; or a dozen other varieties of distribution may be employed. The collection may be done in as many different ways, the back pupil usually collecting for the row rather than the pupil in front. The papers may be passed from the back, or across rows, both in distributing and collecting. The remarkable thing is how many of these methods may be used in the same class at different times. Now, one method, even though it be not the best, is better than many methods, even though these all be good ones. The standard method eliminates the need for making constant decisions. The teacher's attitude during the distribution or collection is interesting to watch. It often seems difficult for him to shift the responsibility for any portion of the work upon the pupils.[11] Seldom does the teacher say, "Class collect papers," and then turn to other work. If there is no standard method, there must be a delay, both of teacher and pupils. The pupils wait either to decide for themselves, or to have the teacher decide, the specific method to be used. Even if there is a standard method, the teacher will often watch the distribution or collection, as though it were the most important process, until the papers are in the appointed resting place. The trouble here is the lack of a well thought out detailed plan.

There are two suggestions that might be of use in school room routing. One is to route pupils and materials at the same time, if this is feasible, that is, to allow pupils, who are passing, to bring with them completed papers, and deposit these at a convenient place, as they pass. The other is to make sure before standardizing a method that the method is the best one used.[12] For example, the teacher might. spend much time standardizing the method of having the back pupil of each row collect papers, and might train himself to utilize the time during collection for other work, only to find that the method of having the collection made during intermissions was far more profitable with his particular class. The improvement of the first method would not mean time wasted, in so far as teacher and class received training in motion study and waste elimination, but the time could surely have been better utilized in substituting the better method and progressing from that.

Better Use of the Blackboard.

If blackboard work is to be used, and the final discussion of this comes under the discussion of mental motions, the blackboard should be improved as a work place. Each child should find, upon arriving at the blackboard, crayon and eraser near at hand. The pupils should at once take the crayon in the right hand and the eraser in the left hand, and should hold them thus during the entire period of blackboard work. There is a great waste in laying down the crayon to pick up the eraser, and the eraser to resume the crayon. The crayon should be held at such a slant that it will not squeak. It is possible to standardize the proper position. Pupils should be taught to write heavily, so that the work will be legible. If the work consists of repetition of problems that are alike except for certain numbers, nothing should be erased except those elements that are to be changed. This is a matter demanding careful consideration. We have seen two teachers endeavoring to apply motion study consume a far longer time deciding what to erase, and actually erasing and making substitutions, than would have been taken by erasing the entire work and starting anew. This, again, is an example of the profitableness of separating planning from performing. On the other hand, we have seen ten problems, precisely the same except for the figures, erased in their entirety and rewritten, when a few strokes of the eraser and writing in a few figures would have allowed the pupil to proceed at once to the actual solution. The class must understand why the problem is erased altogether, or in part, if the motion study attempted is to be of any value.

To what extent work not actually in use should be erased from the board should be determined by a study of attention.[13] If the attention of the class is distracted by the filled board, time spent in erasure would be profitable. If not, such erasure can well be left to some later "delay" period. Uncorrected work often acts as a distracting influence upon pupils who have returned to their studies. The teacher has postponed correction until a later period, or, perhaps, has decided not to mark the work. The pupils do not know this, and are, perhaps, hoping for a chance to correct mistakes before the teacher's inspection. Often an entire class will find it impossible to concentrate upon the next task under these conditions. This is a serious disadvantage of blackboard work. Work on paper could be collected, or turned over, or otherwise disposed of, so that it will not distract attention.

If the class is to observe either teacher's or pupil's work on the board, as has already been said, only such board must be used as can be plainly seen by all. This seems self-evident, yet one frequently sees the teacher with a front board space available, use a corner or side board, because it is handiest to him at the moment, rather than the better board, that may be but a couple of steps away.

Excellent unison work on blackboards has been frequently observed. In one case, where musical dictation was going on, the class stood with erasers in left hand, crayon in right. The process was as follows:

1. Listen.
2. Think.
3. Tap the rhythm.
4. Write heads of notes.
5. Write stems of notes.
6. Mark bars.
7. Mark values.
8. Mark meter.

The teacher gave the command for each type of work, the pupils responding in unison. The results were admirable, in so far as the class' enjoying the work was concerned. An excellent opportunity for noting the characteristics of performance and of mistakes was afforded. Some worked too slowly, others too rapidly. Some seemed hampered by a cramped position. Some seemed compelled to stop constantly and correct mistakes, although the sequence of operation and method of procedure were carefully outlined. Differences in reaction time were noted, as also differences in willingness to respond. The same type of work might have been done at the seats, but it would not have been so easy to note the performance of many individuals at the same time. The class was small, so that all could take part at one time. From this arises the question as to possibility of setting a time that will not push some and delay others,- but the object of this work, which covered but a few moments, was to secure unison in performance, and this certainly was accomplished.

Eliminating Unnecessary Motions at Seated Work.

In considering motions made at the desk we must consider,

1. Whether the motion made need be made at all.
2. Whether, if made, it is being made by the most efficient method possible.[14]

We must ask, first of all, "Should the work be done at the desk, or in some other position?" If the work is not done at the desk, do we leave the desk because we are cramped from sitting there too long, or because the work can be better done away from the desk? Work should never be done away from the desk because one is tired from desk work, if the work can be done most efficiently at the desk. It is better to allow time for necessary change of position, and then return to the desk, than to attempt to do the work at a less profitable work place. If desks were arranged so that writing might be done either standing or sitting, as bookkeeping is done, one class room problem would be solved. We would be enabled to continue at written work far longer than we now believe possible, if that were desirable.

As for writing, there is a question as to whether this is best done standing, or not. There is no question that much reciting should be done standing, in order that the pupil may become accustomed to speaking when he is on his feet. This is well demonstrated by the pupil who has been tutored and allowed to sit while reciting, and his consternation, when made to stand and recite before a class. Doubtless, much of the lack of adjustment arises from the unfamiliar presence of many others during the recitation, but this is not the only element. We have seen pupils in private schools, accustomed to sitting while reciting absolutely at a loss for words when requested to stand. We have also seen pupils accustomed to standing unable to express themselves well while seated, and immediately fluent when allowed to stand in the accustomed position. Here, again, arises the question whether the pupil should stand at his seat, seats being arranged as in the ordinary school room, or should walk to the front of the class to recite. If the object is to give the self-confidence and the social feeling that are so important, undoubtedly he should stand where he will face those to whom he is speaking. We note the practiced public speaker at any meeting rising and walking to the front of the room, often to the platform, almost unconsciously, as soon as he has indicated and received permission to speak. It is not, perhaps, the function of the school to develop finished orators, but certainly nothing gives one a feeling of preparedness and effectiveness more thoroughly than to feel that one can address any audience, if he knows the subject in hand. It would, then, be profitable to so functionalize the class room work that, for a certain percent of the day at least, the pupil could become a speaker, and stand in that relationship to the class, not of a repeater of others thoughts or words, but of a contributor, at least to the extent of expressing personality in the method of expression.[15] On the other hand, why rise to give a word or a phrase answer? Suppose a class of small children giving word answers to simple problems in numbers. They bob up and down. "Five fives?" "Twenty-five," "Five sevens?" Thirty-five." "Five nines? Forty-five." Etc.

"But," you will ask, "how standardize class room practice?" Simply by doing the same thing in the same way every time. It is not necessary to do everything in the same way every time.[16] There may be considered, perhaps, to be involved the question of showing respect to the teacher, but there is really no reason why one should stand for certain types of reciting any more than for writing. The attitude of respect is that attitude that is prescribed for the particular situation. Another question to arise is the question of raising hands to indicate desire to recite, completion of work, noting a mistake, desire to ask a question, or some other condition. As an indication of having completed work, raising hands is certainly a wasteful motion. One teacher has substituted laying the right hand flat on the desk. Another has her class indicate finishing one problem and readiness to start another by moving the hand containing the pencil to the next line below on the paper. Raising the hand to ask a question during written work is particularly wasteful, when, as is often the case, the child lays down the pen, or pencil, before raising the hand. This is frequently seen. As for raising hands to ask questions during recitation, this is, perhaps, allow able, if the raised hands really indicate a desire for information, as it is a check upon attention. It is always interesting to note the practice when hands are raised to indicate a desire to recite. In many cases, especially with younger children, it will be found that those who raise hands are not really prepared to recite, and raise their hands either as a matter of habit, to imitate others, or for some other reason. Again and again we find pupils who, when they get to their feet, have no idea even of the subject under discussion. There seems to be some almost automatic response. The teacher says, "Those who know raise hands," or, "Who can tell?" and almost every hand in the room is raised immediately. Of those who really are not prepared, some have a more or less confused notion of the subject, but some seem perfectly dazed, as though their entire response to the teaching had expressed itself by raising the hand. A signal must stand for something to be of value. Possibly one trouble with the hand raising signal is that it has been used for so many purposes. Surely, if children indicate desire to ask a question by hand raising, desire to recite by hand raising, etc., there is room for confusion.

There has been much discussion of waste thru a needlessly large number of questions asked by the teacher.[17] One element of this waste will be the constant raising of hands, which is also an element of the repose in the class room. As for raising hands while others are reciting to indicate mistakes in the recitation, this seems a doubtful practice. The reciting pupil is frequently embarrassed, interrupted, or confused by the hand raising. This practice is supposed to stimulate the pupils. This it possibly does, but it is doubtful whether the reward is sufficient to compensate for the critical attitude that the class takes, and the discomfort of the pupil reciting. Oftentimes the hands are raised when no mistake is made, the reciting pupil loses confidence, and the recitation is ruined. The class should certainly have an opportunity for constructive criticism at the close of the recitation, but allowing and even encouraging an interruption by such hand raising, though it be made as noiseless as possible, establishes a discourteous and unsocial habit. Nothing can be said to excuse the practice of waving hands to indicate desire to recite. One frequently sees a class, or a large proportion of them, waving hands violently, sometimes even snapping fingers, and half springing from their seats, to indicate a desire to recite. Such nervous tension and extreme enthusiasm are not indications of close attention. This has been tested by asking a class that was undergoing a paroxysm of hand waving to write down the answer they desired to give. The results proved emphatically that close attention had not been given, or at least that the teacher's explanation and the question asked had not been understood, although all surface indications signified a most successful teaching session. If the raising of hands is to be retained, it should be used to indicate but one thing, that is, a desire to ask questions.

Another waste in desk work is the copying of material by the pupil, such as copying problems in written work, writing down home work, etc. The amount of time consumed in such copying is seldom appreciated. What possible advantage can such copying serve? If the pupil is to get practice in writing, he had far better get it while writing original compositions. If the object is accuracy, that can be acquired thru constructive work. The unfortunate part about this copying is that so much of it is done at times when every moment should be utilized for real mental training. If the copying were done in "delay" periods, or towards the end of the session, when the work drags a little, it would not be so serious. But no. Part of a test period at the beginning of the day when every one is keyed to constructive work is used for the mechanical work of re cording that could as well be done by a typewriter, or a printing press. The matter of expense is, of course, a factor generally considered. In how many schools commercial pupils are typing material that is of no value to themselves or to anyone else, simply for practice in acquiring speed and accuracy. These pupils might well prepare test papers that could be passed to the teachers needing them. The same thing is true in many schools or communities where boys are learning printing. If the time now spent in copying were carefully estimated, and that time were devoted by the children to learning to run a typewriter, we firmly believe that they would be able to supply themselves with test papers, and to learn to operate the machine at a respectable pace. This has, so far as we know, not been tried in the schools. In the industries the office boys have utilized time saved by eliminating waste in other operations in learning to run the typewriter, and with excellent results. The problem involved in supplying typewriters to these pupils will, doubtless, seem to many to make this plan ridiculous. The trouble with present conditions is that the various branches of our school activity have not, as yet, learned to cooperate. One type of school lacks something that another type of school is producing, the second having no outlet for its products. School rooms lack equipment, such as waste-baskets;

and plant tables, while the pupils in the manual training schools are making articles for which there is no particular need or use. Girls in the cooking class are preparing food with no particular object except learning to cook, while in the next school they are facing the problem of feeding ill-nourished children. In the same way, training in finger-wisdom that could be given by printing standard work sheets for arithmetic and other school subjects is lacking, while classes everywhere are wasting time doing written copying. In some cases, where lack of funds has made cooperation necessary, it has been tried, and has proved most successful. In one specific instance where funds ran low, the girls in the cooking class cooked the school lunches, thus saving the expense of an outside caterer. However, when funds were available, a caterer was again put in charge, and the cooperation ceased. There is such splendid opportunity here not only to eliminate waste and make actual savings, but also to instill a working, social spirit that one wonders it has not been recognized and utilized long before this. Mr. Courtis has demonstrated beyond the possibility of a doubt that printed test sheets furnish an ideal method of testing arithmetical ability. It is surprising that his pioneer work in this line has not a greater following. In the industries the entire matter of copying would be settled by the actual cost. If thirty copies were needed, what would be the cost of typing them? What would it cost to print them? Would thirty be all that would ever be likely to be needed? Or would thirty more be needed, or, perhaps, a hundred, within a few months, or a year? The actual cost would decide the method. It must be remembered that in almost every type of work, no matter how small the class is, there are other classes in the school, in the town, in the state, in the country, who are doing or will do work that is identical, or might easily be made so. Here, again, proper cooperation would make printed sheets of all kinds so inexpensive that no one could afford to substitute any hand work.

An added advantage of the printed question would be that it would be formulated with such care that there would be little opportunity for confusion on the part of the pupil as to what was meant by the question. When the question is written on the board by the teacher on the spur of the moment there is often confusion as to the exact meaning. This is at once apparent when we note the number of questions asked by the pupils during the copying time, and while actually setting to work. The printed question would be formulated with care and tested on a typical class before being put into final form.[18] There is, at present a restriction in many college entrance requirements that will not allow of the use of printed sheets. However, college entrance requirements, as well as other things, are subject to tests for efficiency, and should not be used as models without having first been submitted to such tests. In the college class rooms, however, printed outlines and printed tests are frequently found, and receive emphatic endorsement from many professors and students. The writer has also seen printed texts used with great success in teaching harmony. An enormous amount of time was gained by not requiring the pupils to copy the music that was to be analyzed. The staff and the notes were given, the pupils marked the names of the chords, and marked also the phrases directly in the books. It is felt that in this day the average student of music does not become a composer. Hence, there is little necessity for skill in doing the actual notation of musical notes. The same thing applies to the school. If we are aiming to make scribes of the pupil, it might be wise to include a large amount of copying, but now little scribe work is actually done to-day.

Standardizing Procedure.

We have spoken before of the loss that occurs from performing the same act by different methods. We should include some specific examples of this here. One striking lack of standardization in our schools is in the case of handwriting. In one third grade class recently visited the teacher said that the pupils had been taught three styles of handwriting during the three years that they had been at school. The resulting penmanship was all that was needed as a comment on the efficiency of this process. Now in this day of tests and with the splendid work that has been done in testing handwriting,[19] there seems no excuse for not determining what type of result in handwriting is desired. This being known, to determine the best method of securing this type is simply a matter of time and careful measurement. Lacking a standard, the teacher should at least be able to insist that a single method be used. However, to-day the decision as to this seldom lies in the teacher's hands. He has, however, the privilege of insisting that the pupil use the same handwriting for all written work as is used during the penmanship practice period. This, in many cases, is not done. Pupils assume a certain position of the body, arm, fingers, etc., during the penmanship period, but write any way they choose during other periods. The result is a conflict of habits that can have no satisfactory outcome[20]. The question of speed enters here. The pupil's rapid writing often differs greatly from his slow writing, try as he may to make the two similar. Teachers do not always consider this fact in making assignments. This is especially true of home work, where the teacher has no means of checking as to whether the work assigned did require more time than he allowed, or not. Any one who has watched a child struggle with home work must have heard, "I can do as much as he told me to, but not the way he wants it done," or, "I can do it the way he wants it done, but not as much as he told me to. You just cannot do all that right in the time he set." Some parents have found out by actual experiment that, even with an adult mind attacking the problem, the child's statement was true. Standardization of requirements is imperative.

Another waste from lack of standardization is in having no form for assigning home work.[21] We frequently hear in assigning a history lesson, "Take page 2, section 3; take also section 4, page 3; take also page 5, section 4, etc." This method of assignment does not allow of the pupil's using ditto marks. It thus takes longer to write down the assignment. Moreover, in some cases, upon getting home, the pupil doubts whether he has recorded the assignment correctly. The first assignment was page 2, section 3. The second was, according to the record, section 4, page 3. Was it not, perhaps, page 4, section 3? So many textbooks to-day have parts, chapters, sections, paragraphs, sentences, etc., that there is much danger of confusion in assignment unless a standard is made and strictly adhered to. The lack of a standard form for written work and home work also means wasted time for the pupil, and a more serious waste of time to the teacher in examining and correcting the work.

Another waste in lack of standardization occurs when pupils are forced to use a long method of notation, unless speed makes some shorter method imperative. Abbreviations and ditto marks may be frowned upon during class demonstrations in written work, yet the teacher, if pressed for time, will use them without apology, and will permit the pupil to use them, if the work must be finished within a few moments. Now, if there is a short method of notation that is perfectly comprehensible, why not use it constantly, so soon as the pupil understands the meaning of the abbreviation or symbol? Other teachers will allow no crossing out in certain types of work, insisting on careful erasure. In periods of stress the pupils are encouraged to discard the eraser, and draw a line thru any errors. The pupils seldom understand the reason for permitting a thing at one time, and forbidding it at another, and credit the teacher with lack of decision, or with being arbitrary. Standardization will prevent this. Few pupils are too young to appreciate the value of motion study as applied to all physical work. They can understand that the crossing out process requires less motions than the erasing. They can appreciate the motion saving in the ditto marks, and thru this appreciation they gain an appreciation of time and of efficiency. However, this motion study and the standardization of practice come with orderliness of class room procedure, which is an almost universal goal, and which forms such an easy transition to cooperation under the proper guidance.[22]

Functionalizing Physical Work.

There is a splendid chance for functionalization in applying waste elimination to the physical work in the school room. The first endeavor is to relieve the teacher of all work possible. Many teachers do such work as collecting and distributing papers, feeling sure that they thus save time, and that they are more efficient in handling materials than the pupils. They fail to realize that they are using strength on non-productive work that is really needed for teaching, which is the teacher's true work. In most cases, however, the teacher's doing the work is the result of lack of planning, and of the inward conviction that so many of us have that we can really do things a little better and faster than anyone else. Every teacher is supposed to develop the Montessori attitude of doing nothing for the child that he can do for himself. A strict application of the practice that underlies this attitude will result in the desired functionalization. The teacher who erases the blackboard, marks the calendar, distributes the supplies, waters the plants, etc., not only uses strength needlessly, but also deprives the pupils of opportunities for cooperating and developing responsible capability and actual physical experience. Moreover, he often robs the class of time that the class needs for actual instruction. Take a specialized teacher, like the drawing teacher. The class receives, perhaps, but one hour a week, or less than that, of much needed specialized training. If this teacher gives one minute of this time to work that some less specialized person could do, he is depriving the class of a valuable opportunity for instruction. The teacher does not realize that in performing many of these physical acts he distracts the attention of the class from the instruction that he is giving. We all know that "the moving object distracts the eye."[23] What, then, can we think of a teacher who, while giving an explanation that demands attention, moves a chair, erases the board, distributes test papers, or performs any unnecessary physical activity. Careful planning will do much to eliminate such waste immediately, but amusing results occur when the procedure is not carefully outlined. In one instance, a teacher had been convinced that she wasted much time in erasing the board herself. She therefore decided at once that during the next period two pupils should erase the board for her. They were simply told that they were to relieve her of erasing the board. The result was comical. Several times the pupils dashed up, only to be sent back to their seats, as the teacher was not ready to have the work erased. At other times when the teacher was ready the pupils did not realize this, as no signal had been agreed upon, and a long pause ensued, while the pupils were summoned, erased the work, and returned to their seats. There was ample board room to provide that no erasing need be done till the end of the period. However, the teacher had accustomed herself to use but a small space, and seemed helpless to write beyond this. Rushing in changes without considering every bearing of the situation often leads to results such as the one described, and to the after effect of the teacher's considering all efficiency methods as confusing and overpraised innovations.

On the other hand, a teacher with a carefully thought out plan can functionalize work most successfully. One of the most successful teachers ever observed has found written work profitable, and has obviated using much of her own time for correction by correcting the first few papers, and then allowing those with correct solutions to correct the papers of others. She must, of course, inspect the final results, but saves much time during class room hours, and is able to proceed much more rapidly by functionalizing this inspection work. How much other routine work could be done by the pupils? Copying of records, making of charts, inspecting supplies, devising routing systems, all of these types of work, if done by the pupils, would relieve the teacher, and train the pupil himself. The work must, of course, be done under supervision. In the industries we find that no work of any type can be passed without inspection, that no worker, however skilled and specialized, and however high in the organization, can be exempted from inspection. We cannot expect to succeed in the school room, if we functionalize the work and then put all the responsibility upon the pupils.[24] Division of responsibility unavoidably accompanies division of work.

The Relation of Speed to Efficiency.

Too often the amount of speed attained is considered a satisfactory test of efficiency. It is far from being this. If quality, immediate and permanent, is maintained, then speed and amount of output are good tests, but never speed without consideration of quantity and quality.[25] What use to teach a lesson in half the time, if the pupils do not understand it? What use for pupils to complete a test in a short time, if the work is not correct? What use to accomplish a large amount of work, if the output is not up to standard? In the industries we lay much emphasis on the habit of speed, but we insist always that the right motions shall be used. We thus put the most exact test as to quality. The same thing must be done in the school room. Perform the physical work with the greatest amount of speed possible, but insist always that the prescribed method be used without deviation. For example, you may insist that your pupils write rapidly. If so, you must insist that the pen be held in the proper position, and moved with the proper motions. If you do, the writing must be of the standard legibility and appearance desired. Speed alone is of slight value as an inspection test. The speed with which work is conducted in the class room is no indication of efficiency. The writer has observed certain nervous types of teachers rushing classes thru one kind of work after another. The pupils flew to the board. The teacher spoke at top speed. The work was put onto the board with speed.

Almost before it was completed, the class rushed back to their seats, and this process was continued throughout the entire hour, and, in fact, day after day. The investigator had the curiosity to review carefully a set of tests of this work. There seemed to be almost no permanent impression made upon the pupils' minds, yet there certainly were some valuable results of the teaching. The class had learned to respond promptly to directions. On the other hand, if quality is properly provided for, the habit of speed is most valuable, and that it is a habit no one who has observed school room and industrial practice can doubt.

The question of speed attainable is a question of individual differences. However, there is a percentage of improvability, and up thru that percentage we can undoubtedly go.[26]

In considering the efficiency of our changes in procedure we must, then, consider speed as an element, but always as an element. Here, again, as in testing the "materials" element, we consider savings made, and also experience in waste elimination gained thru making the changes. With these always in mind we may attempt to calculate the value of what we have done, and the lines along which future improvements can best be made.

References
1. Calkins, M. W., "A First Book in Psychology," p. 354.
    Imbert, A., "Evaluation de la Capacite de Travail d'un Ouvrier
    Avant et Apres un Accident," "Les Methodes du Laboratoire
    appliquees a l'Etude directe et pratique des Questions
    ouvrieres."
    James, W., "Psychology, Advanced Course," Vol. II., P. 372.
    Stratton, G. M., "Experimental Psychology and Culture,"
    pp. 268-268.
2. Bagley, W. C., "Class Room Management," Ch. IV.
    "   "   "   "Educative Process," Pages 340-344.
    Kotelmann, L., "School Hygiene," Ch. VIII.
3. Barry, W, F., "School Sanitation," Ch. XIV.
4. Bagley, W. C., "Class Room Management," Ch. III.
5. King, Irving, "The High School Age," Ch, XI.
6. Johnston, C. H., "The Modern High School," Ch. XI.
    Terman, L. M., "The Hygiene of the School Child," p. 277.
7. McMurray, F. M., "How to study," p, 305.
8. Fisher, D. C., "A Montessori Mother," Ch. II., III., IV.
    Montessori, M., "The Montessori Method," Ch. XII.-XIV.
9. Bagley, W. C., "Class Room Management," Pages 37-47.
10. Bagley, W. C., "Class Room Management," p. 39.
11. McMurry, C. A., "Conflicting Principles in Teaching," Pages
    108-110.
12. Gilbreth, L. M., "The Psychology of Management," Pages
    179-180.
    Taylor, F. W., Paper 1119, A. S. M.E., para. 51, para. 98-100.
13. Pillsbury, W. B., "Attention," p. 243.
14. Gilbreth, F. B., "Motion Study."
15. Johnston, C. H., "The Modern High School," p, 239.
    Parker, S. C., "Methods of Teaching in High Schools, Ch. XI.
16. Gilbreth, L. M., "The Psychology of Management," p. 138.
17. Parker, S. C., "Methods of Teaching in High Schools," Ch. XX.

Stevens, R., "The Question: as a Measure of Efficiency in Instruction: A Critical Study of Class Room Practice."

18. Gilbreth, L. M., "The Psychology of Management," p. 158.

19. Ayres, L. P., "A Scale for Measuring the Quality of Handwriting in School Children" - Russell Sage Foundation, New York City, No. 113.

Starch, D., "The Measurement of Handwriting," Journal of Educational Psychology, Oct., 1913.

Thorndike, E. L., "Handwriting," Teachers College Record, Vol. II., No. 2, March, 1910.

20. Colvin, S. S., "The Learning Process," Ch. III.

21. Johnston, C. H., "The Modern High School," Ch. X.

22. Parker, S. C., "Methods of Teaching in High Schools," p. 43.

23. Colvin, S. S., "The Learning Process," Pages 269-270.

24. King, I., "Social Aspects of Education," p. 297.

25. Gantt, H. L., "Work, Wages, and Profits," p. 19.

26. Thorndike, E. L., "Educational Psychology," Vol. III. Part II., "Individual Differences and Their Causes."

Observations Illustrating Eliminating Waste
In Physical Motions

XLIII.

Observation

A sixth grade. Teacher giving a test in arithmetic sent out by the superintendent. A certain time is allowed for this test. It is noted that the teacher counts the time from the beginning of distributing the supplies to the end of collecting the papers.

Comment

All time up to the time when the first question is dictated thru the time the last question is answered is working time, and such time only. Other time is getting ready and cleaning up time. If this time is included in the test time, all sorts of variations, having to do with distribution of materials, etc., will affect the results. The method should be standardized, and all time except working time excluded.

The Courtis tests are to be recommended in that the entire procedure relating to them has been so standardized.

XLIV.

Observation.

A sixth year class. During the entire morning procedure the passing and collecting of material in this class were conducted with no further words of command from the teacher than "Pass pencils and paper" or "Collect pencils and paper", etc.

Comment.

In this case it was noticeable that the entire procedure of transporting the material had been standardized. This not only insured no waste during the process, but, at the same time, formed an excellent habit in the pupils. This also shows the necessity of standardizing the procedure.

XLV.
Observation.

A third grade class in a girls' school. It is noted that all of the pupils have an ample, in fact an almost overabundant, supply of tablets, pencils, crayons, etc. These do not seem to distract the attention, as might be expected, but simply prevent any delays for lack of proper equipment.

Comment.

This room is typical of the entire girls' school where the pupils are encouraged to keep as large a supply of materials as they please in their desks. It is insisted that the supplies be kept in order, and the observer heard no objections from the teachers on the score of confusion in handling desk materials. The observer notes of two of these small girls that they take great pride in keeping their supplies in good condition, and take any dull pencils home to be sharpened, and otherwise insure that everything should be in perfect order. As in the industries, here also we find that an elasticity station does not tend to increase confusion or wastefulness.

XLVI.
Observation.

A sixth grade class. It is the custom in this school to ring a warning bell a few moments before the recess and dismissal bell. The teacher here observed regularly utilizes this period to instruct the class as to what is to be taken up directly after the recess period. Where there is time the pupils place the next book or supplies to be used upon the desk before passing from the room. Where this is not possible the pupils, who seat themselves immediately upon entering the room, begin at once to take out the supplies needed, and, as far as the observer has remembered to note, are always ready to work by the time the teacher, whose duty it is to watch the various lines pass, has entered the room and taken her place at the desk.

Comment.

This well illustrates the possibility of utilizing delayed periods. It may be compared favorably with many classes visited, which came to attention upon the warning bell and sat motionless until the second bell sounded. Such a rest might be advisable during a session. It surely was not needed just before a period of free play. Probably, in most cases, time is not left unoccupied for the sake of rest, but simply because there ill no thought of its being utilized.

XLVII.
Observation.

A large grammar school for both girls and boys. Before each session and at the close of the recess period the pupils form in excellent lines in the yard, and march under the leadership of captains to the various class rooms. At the close of the session and at the beginning of the recess period the pupils rise, form in lines, and the captains, a girl and boy for each room, are responsible for the appearance of the lines. These lines march into the yard and disband there.

Comment.

Not only is it to be noted that all passing in and out of the building is accomplished with the least amount of time possible, but also that the children stand well and go through the entire procedure, as the result of careful training, with a clocklike precision. We have here excellent habit formation as well as efficient performance.

XLVIII

Observation.

A typical city high school. Here the pupils come into the building when they choose and leave when the work is completed. The passing noted is between recitations. There is no order on leaving the class rooms. The halls are crowded. The pupils loiter or rush as they please, chat, laugh, and amuse themselves generally.

Comment.

There is no doubt that certain periods must be devoted to recreation and rest. It is doubtful, however, whether the hall furnishes the desirable place, or the passing time the desirable time for such recreation. It is certain that, in many cases, more time is taken for passing than should be, and that often the confusion is so distracting that the pupils find it difficult to settle down to work upon reaching the new classroom. Possibly, if the pupils were forced to assume the class room demeanor immediately upon entering the room, it might remedy conditions. Certainly there must be some sharp distinction drawn between work periods and rest periods.

XLIX.

Observation.

A freshman class room in a high school. Much board work is done during the class hour. The teacher sends one, sometimes even two rows, to the board. In each case the command is simply, "Rows 1 and 2 pass to the board," and at the end of the board period, "Seats." The pupils rise quickly, and pass in excellent order to what are evidently their accustomed places at the board. They pass to their seats in the same orderly fashion.

Comment.

Here we have routine reduced to habit. The observer notes not only the excellent effect upon the pupils, but also the enormous amount of saving in time. This in the industries would be called excellent routing.

L.
Observation.

A room of fifth and sixth year girls in a private school. At the end of the session, which extends until one o'clock, the pupils sit at attention in their seats, as soon as they have put their working materials and desks in an orderly condition. As each girl is ready, the teacher calls her name. The girl then advances, takes the teacher's hand, curtsies, and in reply to the teacher's "Good-by A", says "Good-by Miss V."

Comment.

This may sound like a complicated procedure, but it really occupies a very short amount of time, which seems well compensated for by the excellent social spirit aroused. The pupils act as though they felt themselves practically the teacher's guests. They are taught through this method courtesy and grace. As the pupil first ready is first dismissed, there is every incentive to come to attention promptly. This, for the situation involved, ss excellent routing.

LI.
Observation.

A large city high school. As in the high school described before, the pupils are allowed to dawdle as much as they please in the halls between passing periods. It is also noted that the pupils are allowed to proceed at an extremely slow pace during laboratory periods. Two teachers consulted at this school say that they find habits of slow motions among the pupils that it is extremely hard to eliminate.

Comment.

Here again we see the necessity for insisting upon standard practice. Work must be separated from rest, and habits of swift motions during work periods insisted upon.

LII.
Observation.

An ungraded class in a grammar school. This class consists of several sections. It is the practice of the teacher to have the class that is reciting form a line on the side of the room near the front. At the appointed time at a word of command a group pass swiftly and directly from their seats to the recitation line. The first member of this group hands his book to the teacher in passing. At the end of the recitation and at a few words from the teacher this line pass to their seats, the pupil who had given his book to the teacher recovering it on his way. While this line was passing, another line pass from the seats to the recitation line. This procedure goes on through several periods without one hitch.

Comment.

This example illustrates admirably the advantages of a carefully thoughtout routing program. The teacher of this class handles difficult work at two to three times the speed that the ordinary class room teacher handles the work. The teacher, when questioned, said, "But I had to think this up in order to get through what I had to do." This is another example of the benefit of the incentive

LIII.
Observation.

A sixth year class in arithmetic. Half the class are sent to the board. At the end of fifteen minutes this portion of the class is sent to the seats, and the other half of the class sent to the board. The seated half do not rise until the others have resumed their seats and their work.

Comment.

There is no reason why in this case, as in the case of the example before, the second section should not pass to the board while the first section is passing to the seats. This would require some little planning in the routing and some preliminary training in its performance, but would soon result in saving of, at least, a short period of time every time this kind of blackboard work is done.

LIV.
Observation.

A harmony class of girls from ten to twelve years old. It has been suggested to the teacher that she wastes much time in erasing the blackboard for herself. She, therefore, decides to use monitors, and requests two girls to erase the board for her. These girls are seated in the back row. Therefore every time they erase the board they are obliged to walk quite a distance, and to pass by, or through, the front rows in order to reach the board. Having received no direction as to when to erase the board and receiving no signals, they frequently rush forward when not warranted, and do not appear when needed. The teacher finally tells them to stop erasing the board, and later tells the observer that the monitors waste more time than they save.

Comment.

This illustrates several points.

1. The poor placing of the monitors, who for efficient service should be placed as near the board as possible.
2. The necessity for separating planning from performing. If the whole plan had been properly rehearsed and signals agreed upon, the results would have been entirely different.
3. The necessity for understanding the full implication of changes before making them, and the danger of having what are really improvements discarded because the one making them does not realize that the confusion is from faulty performance not from a flaw in the plan.

LV.
Observation.

A first year high school class. During one period at least three short written exercises in arithmetic are done by the class, these being interspersed with oral work. In each case when the written work is completed it is turned face down upon the pupil's desk. At the end of the hour the work is collected by monitors at the back of the room.

Comment.

This practice not only saves time in collecting material, but also prevents distraction of the pupil's attention, such as might occur if the written work were left face up. This exemplifies not only excellent routing, but also the maintenance of proper working conditions.

LVI.
Observation.

Various grammar grades. No one who has not visited many class rooms doing comparatively the same work can realize the many possible methods for distributing and collecting papers and supplies. We have noted teachers distributing papers, one pupil distributing for the entire class, pupils in the back seats distributing for the row, pupils in the front seats distributing for the row, one monitor from each row seated anywhere in the row distributing, each pupil taking a paper from the teacher's desk, or from the supply table when passing to place, etc., and a similar variation in the collecting.

Comment.

The important feature here is not so much what the system is that is used, but that the same system be used every time for the same type of work. The great waste seems to be in not reducing the routing here to a habit. Because of this lack not only is the pupil's time lost, but much of the teacher's time in planning and directing the routine each time. We have here lack of standardization and lack of functionalization.

LVII.
Observation.
A sixth grade class. An arithmetic test. The test is so planned that it is completed at the recess period, and the pupils deposit the papers on the teacher's desk when passing out of the room.

Comment.
There are several excellent points to this plan. One is that no extra motions are involved in putting the papers in place, since the pupils pass from the room anyway. Secondly, the teacher can inspect with the least amount of effort possible, standing at her desk and inspecting pupil and paper as they appear before her. Thirdly, each pupil is directly responsible for the condition in which his paper arrives at the teacher's desk. We have here, then, motion economy, a simple inspection, and personal responsibility.

LVIII.
Observation.
A harmony class of small children. The children are sent to the board. Each has an assigned work place bounded by white lines. Each work place is provided with a crayon and an eraser.

Comment.
The speed with which the work is carried on contrasts very favorably with the speed of similar work with less standardized working equipment, as seen in the average class room. A child from an older class comes in a few moments before this class meets, and prepares the work places and sees that they are fully supplied with working materials. The advantages of this are obvious.

LIX.
Observation.
A sixth grade class. The teacher is demonstrating on the board. She happens to use several examples elements of which are similar. She is very evidently trying to practice motion economy, for she erases only such parts of her work as need to be changed.

Comment.
Because of the teacher's inexperience with this method of motion economy she spends much more time making the changes than it would take to erase the entire work, and do it over again. The awkwardness of her procedure seems to attract the children's attention more than the work that she is explaining. There is evidently a habit interference here. For such changes should be made in class until they have been so thoroughly rehearsed in private as to become practical automatic.

LX.
Observation.
A harmony class. The class has been working at the board, and now returns to the seats. The teacher assigns written work, and corrects the work at the board, while the class working. The class find it impossible to attend to the assigned work, but, instead, follow the work of the teacher.

Comment.
This illustrates the impossibility of work under bad working conditions, and the dangers of a distracted attention. If board work is used, it should be corrected while the pupils are looking, in order that they may understand the corrections, and keep their attention concentrated upon the subject in hand. We have here poor arrangement of work and waste of time and attention. The teacher's idea, probably, is to correct the work, and have it erased in order that

more work can be placed upon the board. At least, this is what her practice is. What is meant to save time really results in wasting time.

CHAPTER IV
The Human Element, Eliminating Waste in Mental Motions

The Question of Mental Motions

We have seen that a study of physical motions is by no means a simple thing. There are so many elements involved in even the simplest motions that satisfactory waste elimination involves a large amount of intensive study.[1] The problem of mental motions is a much more difficult one to attack, largely because the subject is so intangible. We must, however, realize that a large percentage of the efficiency of the school room depends upon the methods by which the minds there gathered together act. The purpose of the school room is teaching and learning, and of this process the mental element is the more important part. We must consider, then, the material with which these minds are to occupy themselves, the method is by which they are to work, and the inducement to keep them at the work determined upon. That gives us, then, the same old problem: "What is to be done?" "By whom it is to be done?" "How it is to be done?" and "Why it is to be done?" the "Why" including not only reasons for what is done, but the presentation of these reasons to those expected to do it.

Home Work Versus School Work.

The amount of work to be covered during the school year, the school term, and even during the month, week, or day, is usually laid out in advance.[2] It is, however, often left to the discretion of the teacher as to how much of the detail work, let us say, shall be done in the school room, and how much shall be done at home. We have already discussed. to some extent, the disadvantages of home work, the fact that the average pupil is tired at the time he does the home work, that he has no suitable place at which to do it, and that he lacks the necessary supervision for the type of work often assigned. We might also note that, while the pupils at the school are all provided with the same opportunities, this is by no means true of pupils working at home. One may have time to do the work, a good work place, encouragement, and adequate assistance in case he needs it. Another may have neither time, place, encouragement, nor help, and the remainder of the class may possess to a varying degree the advantages of the happier, and the disadvantages of the unhappier, condition. The pupil who, because of his inheritance and surroundings, has least need for advantageous conditions for home work is the one most apt to have these conditions, while the pupil most hampered thru inheritance and training is, naturally, accustomed to the least home advantages. It is coming to be accepted more and more that the only satisfactory solution of the problem is the abolishment of home work. This can be brought about thru a longer school day, or, we hope, thru more efficient methods of handling the present school day. Before this happier time when home work exists no more comes, however, there are various things that can be done.

That part of the school work that demands least reasoning and that is most attractive and interesting may be assigned for the home work. For example, most pupils enjoy drawing and coloring maps. This makes most satisfactory home work. Copying of corrected exercises may well be done at home. Poems may be learned there, if the pupils find learning poems interesting, as younger pupils, at least, usually do. Among older pupils home work usually includes all work not done in the class period, that is, work to be prepared between one recitation in a given subject and the next. It is expected that some of this work be done in the study period at school, and that only what remains as too much to be done in the study period be taken home. The amount of work demanding supervision that can be assigned under these circumstances depends largely upon the amount of supervision available during the school study periods. However, here too the teacher can often be of help in advising which part of the work be done in the school study period, and which is suitable to be done at home.[3]

As for the amount of home work to be assigned, this should be as small as possible. Until the time necessary to do work, that is, task time, is better known than it is to-day, it will be very difficult for the teacher to have any idea how long the assigned work will take the individual, or even the average student. Many times, as has been before said, the teacher would be surprised to know how much longer the assigned work took the pupil than he had expected. On the other hand, the teacher is occasionally surprised to find the pupil taking much less time to do the home work than was expected. For example, a seventh grade history class was transformed into a club, and allowed to assign their own home work. They immediately and continuously assigned themselves three times the work that the teacher had been accustomed to assign, and accomplished the work with ease and excellent results. If the teacher must, because of pressure of work, assign longer home work than he desires, or than the pupils appreciate, he may do much to make the assignment acceptable by explaining the necessity of the assignment, or his desire that the class advance with rapidity. As always, the question of motivation, or incentive, enters here. The writer has heard a long assignment prefaced by, "I know the home work I am going to give you is long, but this class is capable of going ahead very fast, and I am trying to see how much you can do without getting overtired, in order that we may cover the most ground possible." The assignment that followed was received with interest, and accepted as perfectly satisfactory.[4]

Wherever possible there should be correlation in the home work assignments. This is a simple matter when one teacher has charge of all subjects. It is a matter often little attended to in secondary schools, where many teachers make assignments. This is usually because of lack of cooperation in the planning. The teachers usually know, after the assignments are made, thru the pupils' complaints, that long tasks have been assigned in each department, but the success of each individual plan makes it difficult, at this stage, to change the assignment. If the plans had been correlated earlier, no such burden need have been imposed. The frequent custom of having tests on all subjects come at about the same time has something to do with lack of correlation in assignment. Some nights the pupils must spend up to, and often over the limit of assigned time at the work. Other nights each subject will fall below the time limits in its requirements. Not only is there lack of correlation as to amount of time required, but as to the amount of written work and book preparation needed, and as to the subject studied. Surely, it is wasteful to demand an English composition when the French teacher has asked for a "smooth translation" of a poem; or to make a long mathematical assignment when the physics assignment includes a large amount of mathematics.

The method of making the assignment must also be considered in discussion standardization. In the previous chapter we have spoken of the necessity of using the same form in dictating an assignment.[5] Another possibility of waste lies in needless repetitions. As in other class room relations, many teachers seem to repeat while assigning home work almost mechanically, while apparently thinking of something else. A teacher will repeat question one a second or third time very slowly, while apparently thinking out the terms in which question two is to be stated.[6*] Here again, of course, we have inadequate planning.

As for the form in which home work shall be done, this also should be carefully determined, and well known by every pupil. There should be no confusion as to what form is expected, and the form itself

---

* See Appendix D.

should be of such a sort as to arrange the material in an orderly sequenced that can be easily remembered.

To be of value the homework must be inspect ed in some form or other.[7] In many cases where the teachers complain that the homework is not properly done it will be found that the pupils do not believe that the teacher inspects the homework with care. It is an extremely dangerous thing to let the pupils get the idea that the home work does not receive attention. Nothing will more quickly break up the spirit of cooperation. If there must be delay in inspecting home work, the inspection should be done even more carefully than is usual, and the papers returned punctiliously to the pupils.

The parent who keeps in touch with the child's work can often judge of the spirit of cooperation existing by the child's attitude as to the corrected homework. "How was your last night's homework?" may be asked when the child comes home from school. "I don't know yet," will be the answer. "Miss B. said she would not have time to look at it to-day; but she <u>will</u> look at it, because she said she would, and I will tell you about it day after tomorrow, anyway."

This teacher has inspired her pupils with the belief that she will ask them nothing that she does not expect done, and that she will show appreciation of accomplished work by giving it careful attention. This takes time. It means effort, but in this case, at least, it certainly has paid.

Not only must the home work be inspected, but mistakes must be corrected. The necessity for this will be brought out more in detail in considering written work a little later.

206 Eliminating Waste in Teaching 206

Distribution of Work in School Hours.

Having decided what work can be covered at home and what must be covered at school, we turn next to the distribution of this necessary work throughout the school day.[8] The first question that presents itself is that of emphasis. What are the most important things that we are to teach? In every case they are those things that we expect to be remembered the longest. One successful teacher has said that he always tests his daily program by asking himself, after he has made it out, "Just how much of this will I expect my pupils to remember in a year, in six months, in three months, etc?" and this is an admirable test. The thing that must be remembered the longest will in all likelihood become a part of the working equipment of the individual. Take, for example, spelling. We must emphasize the spelling of those words that will be needed in writing throughout life, that must be a part of the daily writing equipment. Take, again, arithmetic. We must emphasize those things that will be used every day by the every-day man, that is, the method of attack that enables one to reason out a problem, and the elementary processes that underlie successful accounting. We must emphasize next that part of the day's work that forms a connecting link between what has been done and what will be done.[9] For example, in history the period covered in the day's lesson should be treated as an outcome of the past and a prediction of the future. Each day's lesson should be an indispensable link in a chain. We may well have in mind, in every subject, Taine's idea of the literary work as a development of the heredity, the race, and the moment. It is so easy, if one is not careful, to present facts that are disconnected. The emphasis should always be laid upon the connections involved in the lesson. It may be that we will present the subjects in the course of study in the same order each day, and that we will devote the same amount of time to each subject each day. This will depend on the needs of the immediate situation. Even if this be the case, however, the emphasis will undoubtedly shift at different times. Here, as in all planning, we must have in mind the principle of tolerances, that is to say, the amount of variation that we should allow ourselves. "Tolerance" is a word frequently used in the industries.[10] In making a drawing, for example, of a machine to be made, under each dimension is put the amount tolerance, or variation from the measure given, that will be allowed.[11] Certain dimensions must be made within a hundredth, or even a thousandth of an inch, where great exactness is required; other dimensions within a quarter, or perhaps a half, of an inch, where great exactness is not necessary. The result is that the worker puts his closest attention upon those places that require it, and can work with freedom where such absolute concentration is not demanded. This principle has equal application to the school room. The teacher should in planning his program have in mind what tolerances he may use. The relation between this and emphasis is clear.

Another point that arises in the distribution of work is that of seat work versus board work. Now the advantages and possibilities of board work have, we believe, been much overrated. There is little excuse for using board work as a relief from seat work, as the necessary relaxation can be accomplished with much less waste of time by some simple form of standing, or seated, gymnastics. The blackboard is excellent as a means for making demonstrations, either by the teacher to the class, or by some member of the class to the remainder of the class.[12] It should never be used to show anything except correct work. For example, if the teacher knows that a certain pupil has information that would be of value to the class, this pupil may well use the board as an auxiliary to presenting his information. Or, in case the class is to correct their own or one another's papers, one pupil may well put a correct solution on the board. The evil effects of attending to incorrect work of any sort have never been sufficiently appreciated.[13] Much attention is being paid, in these days, to mistakes. It would be interesting to note whether seeing a list of words misspelled by a class written upon the board would not influence many who had previously spelled the words correctly towards spelling a word incorrectly. We realize fully the important rule of habit formation, "Never allow an exception to occur."[14] Yet at times we present the wrong habit to the child in the form of a mistake recorded upon the blackboard, which, if he attends, he must, to a certain degree, tend to imitate.[15] It has been maintained that allowing children to work at the blackboard permits the teacher to see and correct many mistakes with a small expenditure of time. It must be remembered that there are other elements besides the teacher's time involved. Even though it be possible to put every member of the class at the board in such a position that his work can be easily seen, it will require a most complicated program for the teacher to finish correction at the time the pupils finish the work. It is a common sight to see many in the class at the boards after they have finished, waiting for the work to be corrected, and to see others whose work has been corrected waiting at the seats for the teacher to finish correcting the other work at the board. He who defends board work must at least make careful record of the time involved in doing and correcting the board work as compared with the time taken to do and correct similar work at the seats, not forgetting to estimate the danger of individuals' copying one another's errors.

Another question to be decided is the proportion of time to be spent on oral work, compared with that to be spent on written work. We have here involved the element of change that is undoubtedly necessary, the importance of oral versus written expression, the amount of time necessary to get individual response from a large group in oral and in written work, the nature of the work that is covered, and many other variables.[16]

There arises also the question as to the amount of time to be spent upon drill.[17] The educational world has been astounded to hear maintained that forty percent of the pupils in the schools do not improve under drill. By "drill," we mean simply practice or repetition. Surely a certain amount of such drill is necessary, if the proper impression is to be made upon the mind. The danger is that attention will lapse. Repetition without attention is worth little.[18] In the first place, drill must be constructive. It is an enormous waste to drill the entire class on spelling words that the majority of the class spell correctly. One teacher, at least, prevents this by taking care never to give, in a second spelling lesson, words which have been spelled correctly by the entire class, confining class drill only to words misspelled by many, and supplementing this by individual drill on individual misspellings. Another important thing is to drill only on essentials. Drill is certainly a mark of emphasis, and the rules for emphasis apply distinctly to it. When it is as difficult as it is to provide that even the essentials be correctly remembered, we must save drill, a most difficult process to handle, for these important things. In order to hold the interest, as many should be allowed to participate individually and actively in the drill as possible. This implies calling upon as many pupils as possible, and allowing each one but a short time to recite.[19] The result of this will be not only that many receive drill, but that each one receives some training also in self expression. The laws governing the efficiency of repetition have been carefully deduced. These must be constantly applied. Drill that is started with enthusiasm, then dropped, then renewed at unstudied intervals, will be of little value. As for so-called "tests," a great deal too much time is usually devoted to these. A few minutes should be enough to demonstrate whether the class has a grasp of a subject or not. Tests that are reviews should be given under the supervision of the investigations that have been made on the subject. A few minutes at the end of every hour should be reserved for a rapid and immediate review. The intervals that should elapse between later reviews have been carefully determined.[20] The general rules for efficiency in distributing time over the lesson hour would imply, then, time at the beginning of the hour for a review of the preceeding work, in order to find a background for the new work; then time for the development of the new ideas; and, finally, time at the end of the hour for a summary of the new thought and an outline of the assignment, or the work to follow. Here, as in handling the physical side, we have what. is practically the "Get ready," the "Do it," and the "Clean up" time, all carefully provided for and all strictly adhered to.

The Teaching Period.

Besides carefully planning the teaching period and making provisions for variation from the plan, there are certain other suggestions that may be of help. One is the necessity for defining any new terms that are used.[21] In the industries, we are very careful that any instruction given shall be in such terms that it will be understood stood perfectly and easily. This is provided for by standardizing as many different descriptive phrases as possible, and, in addition to this, by providing many types of illustrations, such as drawings and photographs, to make any doubtful term or direction clear.[22] In the school room there exists the same necessity for putting any new matter in such terms that the children will understand what is said easily and quickly. A most successful training teacher has said that one of the chief difficulties with the pupil teachers is their tendency to use a vocabulary beyond the children's comprehension. However, in the school there is the added problem of continually enriching the children's vocabulary. This demands use, and frequent use, of words that are new. Fortunately, children have a faculty for hearing and learning new words. The young child is most ready to indicate that the word is new to him by asking at once, "What does that mean?" The older child is not so ready to ask, but will usually indicate lack of knowledge by a certain blank expression that is easily recognized. In the industries we find all excellent test of the worker's not understanding the direction, or illustration at which he looks, is that he will invariably tilt his head from one side to the other, as if to get a new slant upon what he is reading. When the foreman-teacher sees a workman looking at his direction card with head tilting, he feels sure at once that an explanation is needed. We have noted the same thing in night schools, where the older pupils have not understood what they were reading. The inexperienced teacher has seldom an idea of the limited vocabulary of the child, or of the number of words that he can recite or sing without having the remotest understanding of their meaning. A parent who has answered questions as to practically all words except prepositions and adjectives in the first verse of "My Country 'Tis of Thee," appreciates, perhaps, better the limited knowledge of the child, and certainly appreciates, the difficulty of giving definitions that will be understood. In order that a child shall thoroughly understand a new term, it is necessary not only that it be defined in terms that he already knows, but also that he be encouraged to use it himself, as promptly and as frequently as possible. Encouraging children to make acquiring new words a habit, and teaching them how to do this, will have most satisfactory results.

A second thought to be kept in mind is the necessity, always, of making common elements clear. This, of course, is simply another way of emphasizing the necessity of using association constantly. This, again, is successfully used in teaching in the industries. The standardized phrases always make it possible for the worker to recognize quickly the elements with which he is already familiar that appear on a new instruction card. Knowing these, he usually finds it simple to fit the new elements into the common environment. In the same way, the child should be taught to observe and appreciate quickly old elements that enter into anything new that he is learning. We have found this especially helpful with young children learning a foreign language. A sentence or a phrase of a poem in French, for example, might appear to the child absolutely strange and incomprehensible because several new words appeared. A little encouragement and practice will enable him to recognize all the words he already knows, and to fit the new words into the sense as soon as he grasps their meaning. We have found difficulty here, in that some children are hampered by the formal method by which they have been taught English grammar. For example, the child has been taught that the sentence must be analyzed. Suppose the sentence were, "The sun shone brightly o'er the valley." We must think, first of all, "The sun" is the entire subject, before we can proceed to thinking, "shines brightly o'er the valley" is the entire predicate. "Shines" is the simple predicate, etc. Now suppose this child be given the sentence in French meaning, "The moon shines brightly o'er the mountain." Suppose the child knows the word "shines," the word "brightly," and the word "o'er." You may say, "Give the sense of the words that you know." You may find, however, that he cannot proceed to think the words beyond "the moon," because "moon" is the subject, and he does not know the meaning of the word. In our passion for analysis we have apparently forgotten to teach the child to think in wholes, and to value synthesis as highly as analysis. This same difficulty is often found in teaching a working knowledge of a modern language to a child who has been over trained on grammatical endings, etc. Ignorance as to the meaning of one grammatical ending will block the child's ability to make sense of what he is reading.

Along with the necessity of emphasizing common elements in a subject comes the necessity of emphasizing common elements in different subjects, that is, of correlation of work.[23] This we have already mentioned in discussing the home work. The necessity for this is being realized more and more in secondary schools, though there is still much to be desired, even in the self-evident correlation needed between laboratory and lecture, or class, work in the same subjects. A similar need for correlation exists in the primary schools. We appreciate fully the advantage to the adult in "reading along a given line," or "living in an atmosphere." We do not always realize that the child can get the same enjoyment out of this, and that the enjoyment can be afforded to him easily. Everyone regrets, for example, that the literature lesson must be closed when the children are enjoying such stories as the Arthur legends. There is no reason why the arithmetic problems should not be stated in terms of Arthur's times, the geography have reference to descriptions of Arthur's country, the composition work take up some trait emphasized in the legend, etc. The advantage of this would be not only maintaining an atmosphere, but also adding interest and life to some subjects that are often abstract and dull. This necessity of making all subjects seem interesting and alive to the children is one that is constantly with the teacher. We have spoken, in discussing teaching in the industries of the use of object lessons, demonstration, pictures, etc. The subject will, of course, seem most alive to the child when it is illustrated by an object that he can handle, when there is some definite physical way by which he can participate.[24] Objects that are observed, or pictures, or drawings, or maps of objects, are also helpful. Next to these come vivid imagery, word pictures, etc. Children differ very greatly in their power to appreciate such word pictures, in their power of visualization. It is most necessary to realize this in teaching such an abstract subject as, for example, geometry. Here some members of the class seem absolutely unable to progress, because, in spite of all the reasonable proof, they cannot see that the statements made of the geometrical figures are true. Other children find demonstration extremely irksome, because they visualize so clearly that it is self-evident that the simpler geometrical propositions are true. Such a child is often seriously delayed in his progress in geometry by being forced to explain at length this, to him, self-evident thing, before he understands the mathematical method of attack. If the child be allowed to go on, and to begin his demonstration at the point where he first has difficulty in seeing the geometrical relation of the figures, he will usually be perfectly willing to go thru the reasoned proofs.

There is one danger to be avoided in making the subject vivid, and that is proving things by figures and parables. For example, in singing teacher was heard to say, "Now <u>do</u> is the home note," and to illustrate various intervals by describing trips to and from home, to neighbors, etc. A child later asked the question, "Can we start from <u>fa</u>," that is, the fourth note, to which the teacher replied, "No, we generally start from home." Now, in this case, the figure represented a fact, as probably in most cases the figures, or parables, used do, but one of the most deceiving tricks of the spellbinder is the use of such figures in argument. No one who has listened to an orator swaying an ignorant audience thru false logic masked by such figures can help feeling that even the youngest children should be trained as to the danger in their use. At least, we can avoid arguing in such terms.

A safe method of making the subject vivid is to appeal to as many senses as possible. This is done when teaching music by having the child hear the sound, look at the key of the piano, and <u>feel</u> the interval, all at the same time. It is also done constantly when using the Montessori method. We must not infer that we can improve original capacity by such sense training, but we certainly can perfect such capacity as exists, and make the subject more real to the child. If the teacher himself has a vivid interest in the subject, no matter how abstract and dull it might otherwise be it will usually be vivid and interesting to the class. We can always realize this by reviewing our own experience, and seeing how much more the courses and hours that we remember best were made vivid by the personality of the teacher than by the subject matter presented.

An element of the teaching hour that must be kept constantly in mind is the necessity for repetition. This has a close relationship to the question of drill. There must be sufficient repetition so that the children remember what is studied.[25] Any repetition beyond this point is waste. We have spoken before of the habit some teachers form of repeating while thinking over the ground ahead. As for danger from insufficient repetition, this arises often when the teacher presents the same material the same day to different classes. The writer has observed many times that, where the lesson plan is not carefully made and in writing, the teacher is prone to omit necessary statements with the later classes, feeling that to make them would involve repetition. He has, in point of fact, made the statements to the earlier class, the later classes having heard nothing of them.

The question of repetition enters also into another element of the teaching hour, that is, questioning and answering.[26] Miss Stevens' admirable study of questioning makes clear the waste in needless repetition of questions. The teacher must consider the relation of the number and nature of the question asked to the amount of nervous tension existing in the class room. He must also consider the waste involved by asking too many questions, by using too many words, and by repeating questions. There is also to be considered the method by which the questions are distributed among the class. If the class are called on consecutively, the attention of those who have been called on is very apt to lapse for long periods, or until there is likelihood of the cycle swinging back to them. There is also frequent waste where the person expected to answer is named before the question is stated. In this case, unless a fine social spirit exists, the attention of the entire class except the one individual named tends to lapse, often before the question is asked. As for questions asked by the class, these, if they indicate real desire for information, are always in order. We occasionally see a class accustomed to questioning simply to use time, or to attempt to sidetrack the teacher's attention from the subject in hand. There enters also the form in which answers shall be given. If the object is to train in self-expression, a demand for complete statements in answers is a just one. If, however, the object is the rapid development of a thought, sometimes complete statements as answers cause great loss of time, and act as stumbling blocks in the thought's development. The subject matter in hand is an important element here. As Miss Stevens has said, the average teacher will be astounded to see how little the class themselves are allowed to contribute during a questioning session. The extreme of this is where a teacher may be observed to ask a question, allow the pupils to raise their hands, thus volunteering to answer, and then disregard the hands, and answer the question at length himself. At the other extreme stands the teacher whose questions serve only to make the pupils review old material, and who himself adds no new material to the subject under discussion. Questions from the class often involve interruptions, that are another point to be provided for. The efficient teacher can digress at any time when digression seems necessary, or can handle any interruption satisfactorily, and return at the close to exactly that point in the discussion where he left off. Here, again, the carefully made plan is an enormous help. On the other hand, one not infrequently sees an interruption or digression send the whole thought development out of its path, with teacher and class apparently wandering thru the remainder of the hour. We must provide, as in handling material things, for elasticity stations, that is mental material available for handling unexpected happenings without using up material necessary for carrying out the regular work plan, when return to this becomes feasible.

Any review of questioning will involve that ever present element of the teaching period, the question of speed. Speed must not be confused with efficiency, although it often accompanies efficiency. Too rapid talking by the teacher or the pupils gives an atmosphere of uncertainty and insecurity to the work. On the other hand, rapid talking, if the class has been accustomed to it, does at times hold the attention and carryon the class work at a rapid pace. In order that it may do this, however, there must be a fine social spirit, and an alertness upon the part of the teacher to see the first sign of fatigue, and to provide for overcoming it. The study of emphasis helps one to know where speed is possible I and where it is undesirable. One method of attaining speed that is surely commendable is that of teaching so-called "short cuts," or quick methods, from the start, when such are available and can be understood. Anyone who has watched a class in commercial arithmetic perform miracles in getting answers to problems cannot fail to wonder why other arithmetic classes are allowed to use such round-about methods. Successful teachers of such classes have been asked why these methods could not be used with younger children, or with children not taking a commercial course. In every case such teachers have replied, "Of course this method could be used," and in every case, when questioned, the pupils of such teachers have shown an understanding of the reasons for what they did that equalled, if it did not excel, the understanding of the longer methods had by the pupils of the other classes. If there is an excellent short method, teach it from the start. It is a matter of great interest to specialists on individual development to understand all the long round-about methods thru which the race has gotten results, and their development into more efficient methods. Surely at this time, with a full curriculum and a short school day, there is no excuse for teaching children any but the most efficient most rapid method of getting results. Some of us still object to teaching children simplified spelling. No one, however, considers teaching them the spelling of Queen Anne's or Queen Elizabeth's time. Yet, we still see children doing arithmetic problems by methods that have been abandoned by successful business colleges and business men for years.

Finally, we must consider always the element of fatigue. We must provide, of course, for rest or change where fatigue is apparent, but we must be careful not to confuse other things with fatigue. Real fatigue is exhaustion, not mere disinclination for work.[27] The remedies for the two conditions are entirely different. Much time is wasted in the school room by diagnosing as fatigue many ills that are really caused by lack of sufficient incentive.

Written Work.

The provisions to be made for written work bear much similarity towards those that we have already discussed in speaking of home work. Little is known as yet as to proper length of assignment. We know, however, that the average assignment is not long enough to keep the brightest pupils in the class, or even the average pupils, busy during the assigned time. Experiments in measurement are now going on that will give us some accurate data on the subject. We have spoken of the advantage of written work as a test for knowledge. The entire class can be tested in this way in a very short time most satisfactorily. We have spoken also of the need for exactness in statement. As to requirements, here again the principle of tolerance must be observed. The pupil must know how exact he is expected to be in each part of the work. There are strong grounds for believing that there is a close connection between neatness and accuracy. The pupil who finishes behind the average, that is too say, who does not finish the required amount of work in the given time, is a subject for after school work, where the teacher must function as a repair boss. The pupil who finishes ahead of time furnishes a serious problem. No pupil should ever be left without something to do. It is usually a simple matter to supply supplementary work that will develop the pupils grasp, and especially breadth, of knowledge on the subject, yet will prevent him from getting so far ahead of the class that he needs the teacher's personal direction, which may not be at the moment available. The writer has seen a class working with a splendid social spirit ask for such supplementary work, if the teacher had neglected to provide it. Where cooperation exists among classes, it is possible that the pupil who finishes ahead may be allowed to go to the laboratory and set up apparatus, or study rooms may be provided for the entire school where pupils may go to prepare for other recitations. To allow a pupil to sit without work is a most serious and most prevalent waste in the present day school room practice. Such a pupil not only loses time, but acquires habits of idleness that are difficult to break. The work provided must, however, be attractive. This is absolutely essential. If it is not, the pupil will be encouraged to "soldier." "Soldiering" is undoubtedly in the school room, as in the industries, greatly to be dreaded.[28] By "soldiering" we mean working at a slower speed than is necessary, or pretending to work in order not to be assigned extra work. For this condition worker and pupil are never to blame. The fault lies solely with those who do not provide a proper incentive for the work to be done.

All written work should be inspected, marked, and returned; inspected, because practice without inspection has been proven to be of little value; marked, because the pupil has a right to some definite return for his effort; returned, because errors must be corrected, if right habits are to be formed, and the habit of correctness is more important than a superficial knowledge covering a larger ground. Mistakes must be analyzed by the teacher if adequate programs for future work are to be made.

We have brought out many times in this chapter and the chapters preceeding the fact that the great underlying method by which waste could be eliminated with greatest ease and with greatest satisfaction is by providing the proper incentive. This applies to physical work and to mental work equally. We shall, therefore, turn to this as the final solution as regards both the mental and the physical element.

References
1. Gilbreth, F. B., "Motion Study," p. 6, 7.
2. Bagley, W. C., "Class Room Management," Ch. IV.
3. Parker, S. C., "Methods of Teaching in High Schools," Pages 392-397; 415.
4. Bagley, W. C., "Class Room Management," Pages 205-206.
5. Gilbreth, L. M., "The Psychology of Management," p. 157.
6. Stevens, R., "The Question as a Measure of Efficiency in Instruction: A Critical study of Class Room Practice."
7. Bagley, W. C., "Class Room Management," p. 233.
8. Bolton, F. E., "Principles of Education," Pages 275-277.
9. Hamilton, S., "The Recitation," Pages 144-147.
10. Gilbreth, L. M., "The Psychology of Management," p. 172.
11. Parkhurst, F. A., "Applied Methods of Scientific Management," p. 33.
12. Perry, C. C., "Problems of the Elementary School," Ch. VII.
13. Colvin, S. S., "Human Behavior," Pages 174-175.
14. Colvin, S. S., "Human Behavior," p. 171.
    Hartness, J., "Human Factor in Works Management," Ch. I.
    James, W., "Psychology, Advanced Course," Vol. I., p. 123.
15. Cook and O'Shea, "The Child and His Spelling," Pages 114-115.
16. Parker, S. C., "Methods of Teaching in High School," p. 495.
17. Bagley, W. C., "Educational Values," p. 138.
       "   "   "   "The Educative Process," Pages 328-331.
18. Colvin, S. S., "Human Behavior," Pages 169-170.
19. Bagley, W. C., "Class Room Management," Pages 212-213.
20. Bagley, W. C., "The Educative Process," Ch. XI.
    Colvin, S. S., "Human Behavior," Ch. XV.
    Thorndike, E. L., "Educational Psychology," Vol. II., Pages 193-234.
21. Bagley, W. C., "Class Room Management," Pages 192-193.
22. Gilbreth, L. M., "The Psychology of Management," Pages 153-158.

23. Klapper, P., "Principles of Educational Practice," Pages 350-352.

24. Boyer, C. C., "Modern Methods for Teachers," Part III., Ch. I.
    Ennis, W. D., "An Experiment in Motion Study," Industrial
      Engineering, June, 1911, p. 462.
    Jones, W. F., "Principles of Education," Pages 189-192.

25. Hamilton, S., "The Recitation," Pages 156-158.

26. Parker, S. C., "The Methods of Teaching in High Schools" Ch.
    XX.

27. Thorndike, E. L., "Educational Psychology," Vol. III., Pages 11-
    12.

28. Taylor, F. W., "A Piece Rate System," Paper 647, A. S. M. E.,
      para. 22.
    Taylor, F. W., "Shop Management," Harper Edition, p. 30.

Grouping of Illustrations about a Specific
Line of Class Room Activity

The plan of this thesis demands that the illustrations be grouped, as shown, under topics relating to efficient practice, common or possible in the schools and in the industries. The aim of the writer was so to present the principles and practice of waste elimination as to outline a <u>method</u> by which such waste elimination could be successfully carried out. For example,- in taking up the topic "handling materials," the writer grouped under this all examples relating to such handling, no matter whether these examples concerned laboratory practice, recitation-room practice, board work, seat work, or any other type of activity. Thru a consideration of the principle in all its various applications was thus shown not only the practicability of the methods advocated, but also the scope of their field of application.

The illustrations might have been grouped under the specific situations that they represented. As a sample of the manner in which the data gathered might be re-grouped in terms of a specific line of class room procedure, various illustrations and comments on laboratory practice in a typical high school physics or chemistry class is here included.

Observation

In the typical high school chemistry or physics laboratory course observed, there were found to be two double laboratory periods, or one double laboratory period, or two single laboratory periods.

The pupils came into the room with, or more often without, a text-book, and with writing materials. The workbenches or tables were found bare. The equipment was stored in more or less available supply closets. The laboratory note-books were piled together on a side table or shelf. In one instance noted, the note-books were near the sink where water was running, and several jars of chemicals stood on the table.

The pupils came in talking; if they had not finished an experiment, got out the equipment, carried it to the work-benches, and then started to set up the apparatus. If they were starting a new experiment, they usually waited until the class had assembled, when instructions as to the experiment were given. Not until these instructions were given and understood, was the work of getting out or setting up apparatus started.

The pupils worked in pairs, which is the result, more or less, of chance groupings. If one of the pair was absent, and the other in the middle of an experiment, delays naturally occurred.

Talking and moving about the room was usually freely allowed.

Some time at the end of the period was spent in "writing up" the day's work in the laboratory note-book, or time during the period was so spent, if an experiment was finished before the close of the period. The existing college requirements make this necessary, as the note-books cannot be taken from the laboratory. College requirements also prescribe, in many cases, the exact form in which the notes must be written up.

The practice of the teacher in such a laboratory as this varies. In some cases the teacher helps with the setting-up of the apparatus, or himself gets the supplies from the supply closet. In some cases the teacher reads the instructions from the text-book, and adds any explanations asked. In some cases the class, in turn, read the experiment aloud, the teacher here also adding comments. In other cases time is allowed for the pupils to read the experiment to themselves. The procedure depends somewhat upon whether the entire class is kept at the same experiment, or whether each group is allowed to proceed as fast as they can. The former procedure has been the usual practice observed.

While the experiments are actually being made, the teacher passes from one group to another, and gives instructions or help when this is needed. At the close of the period he may supervise the taking-down and putting-away of the apparatus, or he may do some of the work himself.

This is a generalized statement. of the procedure usually observed. Different variables are, of course, combined in each instance.

As for correlation between laboratory work and class work in the same subject, here also much variation is to be found. In some cases the same teacher handles both class room and laboratory, and attempts to correlate the work closely. In other cases different teachers handle the two branches, but work together, and correlate the work. In still other cases two teachers handle the work, but make little or no attempt to correlate,- both aiming to cover the same ground in a term's work, but not to handle the same subject at the same time. All immediate stages between these three exist.

Comment

The double laboratory periods are evidently the most efficient; this, for the reason that the "get ready" and "clean up" time is cut down. It takes much less time to get ready for and clean up after a double period, than it does to go thru the same work for two single periods. This falls under the law of standardizing procedure,- grouping the "get ready" and "clean up" time, and reducing it as much as possible.

It is a mistake to have the work places empty when the pupils come to work. If, as is the case in some laboratories, no other class uses the work places between the laboratory periods, there is no excuse for taking down the working apparatus and putting it away. It should, rather, be covered, if it is in any way perishable. To dismantle it is as wasteful as it would be to dismantle a workman's machine or work-bench in the industries. If the work place is needed by others, as little as possible of the equipment should be disturbed. The amount of supplies available, the nature of the work, etc., must, of course, govern the practice; but an empty work place is, to an admirer of efficiency, neither attractive nor admirable. This falls under the rule, "Eliminate unnecessary delays."

As for "working materials" not in use, these should be in store and supply places, well classified and arranged, as are the tools and stores in the industries so that they may be obtained with the least amount of time and effort possible. "One-motion store and tool rooms" should be the motto here, as in the industries. These again fall under the law requiring standardization.

As for the handling of the materials, this should, wherever possible, not be done during working periods, unless the process of handling is an essential part of what must be learned in the laboratory. All other handling except this should be done between periods, and has been done successfully by student foremen, who are advanced in their work, and who enjoy the responsibility of helping in this way. It goes without saying that there should be an adequate supply of everything needed on hand, and that the foremen should receive sufficient instruction to do their work efficiently. It is a great waste for the teacher to be forced to do such handling of material as can be done well by less highly trained helpers, or by students. This falls under the law that all work should be functionalized to suit the individuals performing it. In the industries such handling of material is directed by proper routing, which insures definite practice.

As for methods of coming to an understanding of what is to be done,- there is great waste involved in having an entire class read, or have read to them, working directions. The rapid readers are held back by this process. Moreover, it seldom holds the attention of all, and the inattentive must do the work over again. In the industries, this entire matter would be handled thru the instruction cards, which fall under the laws for standardizing and teaching. A written instruction card is prepared for each operation involved, and a set amount of time is allowed for each individual to read his particular instruction card. This practice might well be introduced into laboratory practice. Oral instruction is used simply as a supplement to the instruction card.

The practice of two pupils working together on an experiment is wasteful. The brighter pupil does most of the work, and it is practically impossible to discover which part of the work is done by each pupil. The law of individuality demands, in the industries, that the output of each worker be apparent, and be recorded separately. This practice is equally necessary in the laboratory.

The talking and walking about are wasteful, in that they disturb working conditions.

As for writing up the note-books,- the requirements of the college entrance board cannot be commended as efficient. However, even complying with these, a definite amount of time may be insisted upon for this writing-up. This, in the industries, would be rated as "cleaning up" time. If no college requirements furnish restrictions, the writing-up should certainly be done on standard, printed forms, and at some other time than the laboratory period.

As for correlating the laboratory work with lecture or recitation work,- there is an enormous waste where close correlation does not exist. The half-time schools have demonstrated the possibility of so preparing a pupil for his work, that he can go into an industrial shop, and set to work with practically no lost time. Efficiency would demand that the work be so functionalized that everything possible be done during class room periods, and that laboratory periods be devoted exclusively to experimental work.

CHAPTER V
The Problem of Motivation

The Incentive in the Industries and in the Schools.

The more we contrast the successful shop or school room with the unsuccessful, the more we realize the importance of the problem of motivation.[1] It is the incentive, in the final analysis, that is the moving force that leads workers and pupils alike to do what is best for them individually and as group, and to continue doing it cheerfully and well.[2]

There are many likenesses among the incentives to be found in the efficient school and the scientifically managed plant. In the industries some workers do the work quickly and well because they like the manager, or the particular boss or foreman who is over them. In the same way, in the schools many pupils do as requested because of affection for the teacher.[3] Such liking is an admirable element of the social spirit, but, as we have already noted, true efficiency must not depend entirely upon the presence of any one individual. Such a liking is not, then, an adequate incentive. There are other workers in the industries who work and accomplish much because they like the work itself. It has been noted on many kinds of construction work that, even where the foreman is not popular, the workers accomplish work high in quality and quantity because of pride in the trade and interest in the workmanship. This is particularly true of the older members of such trades as bricklaying, stone-cutting, stone setting, etc., who have the old-time craftsman's pride in their product. In the same way a certain type of pupil who enjoys study will do well in all of his work because he enjoys it, while another will do well in that particular branch, or those branches, that he enjoys.[4] This incentive, however, covers only those subjects towards which the worker, or pupil, has an underlying leaning. There exists in both plant and school what is known as a "habit of work," or a "fashion of work."[5] This may be set either by some strong or persuasive foreman, or teacher, or by a leader among the workers or pupils themselves. It is a strong incentive, and one much to be encouraged, and bears, of course, a close relationship to the social spirit existing. There also exists in both plant and school the factor of competition.[6] In the older type of plant competition was between individuals. In the newer type it is between the worker and his own previous record. This same feature of competition exists in the school, where pupils compete against one another, or against their own record, or as a class group against another class group or their own class record. Another strong incentive, both in plant and school, is the desire for promotion, or for preparation for some future work that one desires to do.[7] Finally, in both there exists the incentive of the amount of pay, or direct reward to be received. In the plant this comes in the form of money, wages paid usually at the end of the week. In the school there is no such money reward, and some other incentive must be provided to take its place. As money is the great incentive in the plant, its non-existence in the school raises a serious problem for the substitution of something equally desirable. Such incentive may be time placed at the disposal of the pupil for some attractive work, or to use as he will, special privileges, some type of foremanship, or any other direct reward.

As for punishments, in the successful plant and school alike punishments are rated as adjustments, the idea being to bring the offending party as soon as possible into working condition, where he is able to work, and to cooperate in the work of the group.[8]

As for differences between the motivation problem in the school and the plant, one important point to be considered is that the ages of those concerned differ widely. The average worker in the plant is an adult, or at least has an adult's ideas as to values. He has also and adult's rights as to decisions as to whether what he gets for what he does is sufficient or not. The pupil in the school, on the other hand, being a child, is appealed to by different things than appeal to the adult, has not a proper standard of values, nor the wisdom that provides for proper decisions. We have before noted that the child in the industries demands an entirely different incentive from the adult. For example, the children who turned over their pay envelope to their parents were only interested when shorter hours with free playtime were offered as a reward, rather than increased pay. The child in the school is, in a way, the final court of appeal as to the success of the motivation used, in that, if he is not interested, he will not respond, but it is not wise to submit the question as to what will be an acceptable incentive to him for decision. A second difference is as to the scope of experimentation possible. The worker in the plant, unless he is reduced to that particular position as the one available job in sight, can, and usually will, leave at once, if the motive for remaining is not strong enough. The average child in the school, on the other hand, is forced to remain even though he be not interested. Therefore, the teacher has more chance to experiment with various incentives, and note the success of each. As an accompaniment of these conditions, it must be noted that, in case of punishment under any but the scientific type of management the worker has no court of appeal, while, except in the most antiquated of school practice, the pupil has always a court of appeal. The third difference lies in the fact that pay in money, while available in the plant, is not available in the school, The pay envelope and its contents furnish a great incentive that the school finds great difficulty in equaling. It has been customary, instead of acknowledging this, to maintain that the concrete reward is out of place in the school room. This is rather inconsistent with the fact that in trade schools, manual training courses, domestic science courses, etc., where the pupil is allowed to take home what he makes and to sell it, if he desires, the reward is extremely concrete, and no one seems to object. Neither is there objection if the concrete reward, which may be money, is removed one step, and presented by the parents instead of the teacher. It may be added that the same thing is true of concrete punishment.

Importance of the Motive.

The importance of the motive can scarcely be overestimated. Upon it upon depends the interest and attention that make it possible not only to do and continue doing, but to learn and continue learning. It influences both physical and mental application. Thorndike has well brought. out the important part that interest, hence the incentive, bears to production and fatigue.[9] He practically advises that in all cases we should experiment with interest first, before deciding that real fatigue exists. We have seen that in the industries successful motivation has been brought about by arousing and holding interest thru the use of incentives that will not injure either the worker or his co-workers. We must aim to supply the same type of incentive in the school. It has been said that the learning attitude implies,-

1. Hopefulness, that is a belief in one's own capability.
2. An assurance of the value of the work done.
3. A knowledge of the possibility of accomplishing the work assigned.
4. A determination to accomplish this work.

We must aim to make this attitude habitual in the school room.

The Use of Competition.

No one who has observed athletic contests, both in the industries, and in the sports, can underestimate the results of competition, or can wish to do away with its good elements.[10] Competition is excellent where it brings out the best traits in the competitors, where it leads to a strenuous and persistent training to accomplish a desired result, and where the competition itself is carried out under the rules of the square deal.[11]

There are, however, dangers in competition to be avoided. One is the danger of being more interested in the fact that one beats others than in the fact that one accomplishes something definite one's self. A second is the danger that the losers will become discouraged. A third is the danger of ill feeling, or, at least, of lack of cooperation among the contestants resulting from the competition.[12] These dangers exist equally in the industries and in the school. In the industries we have avoided them by having the worker compete with his own record. This same practice might be, and, in fact, often is used with success in the schools.[13] This implies that a careful record must be kept of each individual performance, that the individual must be in close touch with his record.[14] It also implies such practice as this. A child during a written lesson will be told, "Decide which word you have written is best made, and start improving from that." Or, again, a child who has written one word twenty times may be told, "Decide which of your twenty words is best written, and make a star over it for a prize." This practice of self-competition will be found feasible in many places during the day's work, arid, especially with small children, arouses interest from the start. Besides the reward of one's own arid the teacher's approbation, the reward of an audience is usually much appreciated. This audience may consist of the class itself, as does the "honor list" on the blackboard. It may consist of visitors. It is interesting to note that, while visitors often distract younger pupils, with the result that interest in the work in hand is diminished, with older pupils the audience acts as a stimulus, and interest in the work increases, as the pupils endeavor to make a favorable impression. Or the audience may be indefinite, as in the case where those doing the best written work are allowed to copy their work in the teacher's book, this to be shown to his friends, or others interested, at some later time. Or again, as in the case of an annual exhibit at a local art club, an audience, of which the pupils themselves may become members, will inspect the results of the best work in drawing and painting done in, all of the schools of the city throughout the year. The advantages of all these rewards, as outlined as possible, are that they are open to all, and that they can easily be adjusted so that the fact that one wins a reward will in no wise prevent another from winning one. Rewards should not be limited to the best, or the three best. They should be open to all who attain a certain standard, no matter what that number may be.[15]

The wisdom of competition between classes is a much discussed point. Surely there is no such danger to class social spirit resulting from such competition as there is from competition between individuals of the class. In schools where class groups are small the written work of the class above that happens to be left on the blackboard has often proved an incentive to the class below. Class records, when posted, have also served as class incentives. In the industries, group competition has proved most profitable.[16] Anyone who inspected carefully the last exhibit of the Committee on Better Industrial Relations in New York, and noted the attitude taken by the different industrial organizations present, must have felt that records and charts of successful practice were most potent and helpful stimuli. Some Committee on Better Educational Relations might well consider an exhibit of similar records arid charts relating to the schools. No one seems to object to competition between schools, and the encouragement of a loyal and enthusiastic school spirit. The underlying truth seems to be that loyalty to one's self, to one's class, and to one's school becomes dangerous only when it refuses to submerge itself in loyalty to humanity as a whole.

If, besides setting up his own best record as something to be overcome, the pupil can be inspired to an enjoyment of overcoming difficulties, so much the better.[17] The training for this should begin long before the school period, in the home. A child less than a year old can be taught to have enjoyment in overcoming difficulties. Where such training has been given in the home the teacher will find little difficulty in continuing it. Where it has not, the training should begin as young as possible. It bears a close relationship to self-confidence, which is a most important element in efficiency.

The Vocational Element as an Incentive.

One of the strongest incentives in the scientifically managed plant is the fact that the worker is made to realize from his first day that everything that does has some relation to his development as a worker.[18] His promotion depends upon the manner in which he does the work given him. There is wide discussion to-day as to the vocational element in the school room. Unfortunately, the word "vocation" has lately come to be restricted, more or less, to some type of work done with the hands. We should return to the earlier meaning, which makes "vocation" the world's work that one selects to do. The writer has been greatly helped by hearing a prominent educator make clear the point that, using this later sense of the word "vocation," the schools and colleges were more vocational a hundred years ago than they are to-day. For example, the college was intended practically only for those who entered the professions of law, medicine, and the ministry. The courses were purely vocational, training those who entered for these life works and for no others. The secondary schools were, many of them, even in this country, of the English type, attempting to do nothing but prepare for the colleges. It is in this older sense of the word "vocational" that we must emphasize the necessity that every child from his young days should have in mind the fact that he is preparing for a vocation, for a life work. He need not, unless economic pressure makes it necessary, decide early what this vocation is to be. He must realize, however, from the start that a vocation he must have.

There is a strange attitude on this question of vocation in our democratic America. The fault lies primarily in the homes. There seems to be a general feeling that a life work is a burden, that the child can be spared and helped by being kept as long as possible with the feeling that he may never have to undertake such a life work. The child is relieved of all responsibility, and is not even told that such responsibility must inevitably come to him. The young child of this type succeeds fairly well in the elementary schools, because of his natural love of activity. The case is quite different in the secondary schools. The cow-eyed gaze of the adolescent, which is so startlingly different from the nervous, attentive attitude that child psychology leads us to expect, is the result of this training. The pupil comes to school because his parents make him, or to pass the time, or, possibly, for companionship, but apparently has no idea that he is supposed to be receiving training to fit him actually to take part in the world's work. Now we do not see this attitude in the average half-time school, trade school, commercial school, continuation school, or in any school where the pupil has any idea of being ultimately useful.

The American attitude towards working with the hands is even more deplorable. When it is possible in a large town, where unemployment is a serious problem, for opportunities for half-time work to go neglected, not by one, but by scores and almost hundreds of boys, there is something wrong with the attitude of the community towards work. We may talk as we will about European caste, and laugh at distinctions between classes. We must acknowledge that we are the real class makers, when we will not allow our children to learn to work with their hands. We fail to realize that one reason why such a wide gap has existed between the schools and the industries lies in the fact that the value of hand work has never been appreciated. Not only does the boy going into a plant to learn a trade find himself handicapped because he is not finger-wise, but also the older boy who plans to become a manager finds himself handicapped by the same ignorance. One great service of scientific management to the world lies in its appreciation of the value of finger wisdom.[19] No one can consider himself a successful scientific manager who is not an expert on motion study, and motion study implies finger wisdom as a fundamental. It is astonishing when we consider the principles that underlie the kindergarten, and the enormous success of the Montessori method, that we take so many children beyond the kindergarten years and deprive them absolutely of the hand training that is so interesting and stimulating. Instead of realizing that the man who will have little opportunity to use his hands, if his vocation calls mostly for brain work, should be afforded extra opportunity for manual training in his youth, we cut him off from such training, often at his fifth or sixth year. The parents are, of course, much at fault for allowing such conditions to arise, but there is also something wrong with the teaching body, when one can hear two such remarks as this in a discussion of teachers within five minutes: "The one who looks forward to working all his life cannot be educated." "There is no reason why a man should not be educated because he can do something." Over against this we place the newer attitude, that no one is educated unless he can actually do something, and that the man who needs the education most is he who looks forward to working all his life.

As for the actual changes to be installed in the school, every pupil should be afforded every day some opportunity to become finger-wise, even if this be only in the handling of the implements necessary to perform an ordinary school room exercise. Secondly, all school room subjects should be so treated as to show constantly their relationship to the vocation, that is, the life work. The writer has investigated carefully for years the reasons given by adults as to why they disliked various school room subjects. Ninety percent of these reasons had as their foundation the fact that the pupil was never made to appreciate the relationship between the school exercise and the later use of the material in life, although the adult questioned was not always conscious of this. Modern languages were hated, because the pupil never realized that they were used by living people, that there was interesting literature accessible, that they were an element in business advancement, etc.; spelling hated, because its relation to rapid reading was never brought out, its use by many as a test of education was not understood, its relation to fluent written expression was unappreciated; history hated, because it was considered remote, because the dates and abstract facts were emphasized at the expense of the human element; arithmetic never appreciated as a necessary tool for commercial success, never appreciated as a developer of reasoning powers. Right here it may be stated that children may be taught, far younger than is usually supposed, to appreciate the necessity for, and the interest of, reasoning. No child that can talk is too young to argue concerning any possession that it desires to have. It is an easy matter to point out a successful argument and the reason for its success. Arguing soon becomes not a harassing experience, but an interesting game. Such vocational interest as this, that is showing, that the subject under discussion is related to every life work, must be a part of all school room practice. If the pupil has decided upon his definite life work, more definite application can be made. Such pupils, however, require less help from the teacher, as we note when we see how simple the problem of motivation is in the night school, the half-time school, and the continuation school. Even if the child has not definitely decided upon, and is rated as too young to decide upon, a life work, the relation of the work to any taste, or tendency, will be helpful. Every child with a taste for composition may be given the interest in the other allied subjects that the exceptional child already has. The long view ahead is also a desirable incentive. If the child appreciates that speed and accuracy in handling the fundamental operations are not only necessary in arithmetic, but in algebra and all higher mathematics, the four fundamentals will become more attractive. If, when he learns to consult the dictionary, he realizes that he is acquiring a method that applies to handling all reference work, this will be an incentive. It is the long look ahead that carries every worker, in the industries and out, thru the drudgery that is part of every day's work. Why not give the child this long look as soon as possible? It can serve as the same stimulus to him.

The Play Element as an Incentive.

We have mentioned the fact that enough interest in what one is doing turns work into play.[20] The truth of this statement depends, of course, upon one's definition of play. If by "play" one means undirected activity that is care-free and purposeless, then work is never play; but activity may be productive, and yet be so enjoyable that it has none of the irksomeness and drudgery with which the word "work" is sometimes associated. We have still too often the idea that nothing is profitable that is thoroughly enjoyed. The industries have disproved this easily. The endeavor to-day is to make all activity done in the plants so interesting, so profitable, that it becomes the worker's happiness to do the work. We have no right to allow the child to leave things undone because he imagines them distasteful to him. However, we have the duty of making every possible subject as interesting and as enjoyable as we can, we recognize at once every man's right, if he does what the world expects of him, to get all the enjoyment out of what he does that he can. This same right is the child's, and it is the duty of the school to help him to secure this happiness. The writer has in mind one of the most efficient class rooms ever visited, where the pupils are preparing for strenuous work in the business world. The teacher believes, and the pupils have been taught, that work done efficiently is always enjoyable. There exists in this room the atmosphere of play of the highest type. It is this atmosphere that is to be strived for.

The Social Spirit as an Incentive.

The great mass of educators to-day believe that the highest incentive towards class room efficiency lies in the development of a proper social spirit, and certainly present day practice tends to substantiate this.[21] Scientific Management believes that cooperation, which is another word for social spirit, is the great incentive in the industries. This would serve as a confirmation of the educators' views as to the school room. Such social spirit makes attendance a matter of course. "They come because they want to," as Perry said a of a group of children, described in his "Wider Use of the School Plant."[22] One teacher notes that a short class meeting at the beginning of the session produces promptness in assembling because of the social spirit involved. Another reports decrease of tardiness, because the principal is accustomed to telephone parents of tardy pupils immediately, and evince a desire to cooperate in making tardiness impossible. It insures promptness in dismissal of one class that the next class may not be delayed, and interest in the work that cuts down the necessity for long passing time.

The first step in developing a social spirit is that the teacher himself feels it.[23] If the teacher truly has it, the class will feel this long before it is explained to them in words. A class coming in to a new teacher perceives his attitude at once The teacher who learns the names of the various members immediately, and can call upon the class individually within a short time, at once demonstrates his social spirit. On the other hand, one may see teachers who do not learn the name of their pupils for days after they have come to them, and the feeling always prevalent in such a class is that the method by which the teacher manifests his social spirit is in the manner in which he distributes opportunities to participants in the class work. Where only the quick ones in the class are called upon, or only the slow ones, or any other group, the class soon divides itself into parts, that do not readily combine into a working whole. The teacher must remember always not only promises and their fulfillment, but also requests that have been made. The class may seem to forget the promise, and say nothing about it, but ultimately some individuals of the class are sure to remember, and, even though the matter never be brought to the teacher's attention, there will grow up a feeling that the teacher is either neglectful, or forgetful, or perhaps prone to promise more than he intends to perform. The writer happened to observe one class at one time that had worked with a fine social spirit, and that was taken over by a new teacher. He had many virtues, but an extremely short memory. The results were that pupils were frequently asked to bring in various outside things that would contribute to the pleasure of the class, but were only infrequently called upon to show or use these things. Promises made one day were forgotten the next. A program in which all had been asked to participate was changed the last moment, as a new idea suggested itself to the teacher. The result was that, though the class admired certain traits of the teacher, the class spirit went absolutely to pieces. Much to the teacher's surprise, after a short time few even brought in anything requested, and attention was indisputably lacking during any assignment of work. In contrast to this stands the teacher who, because of a carefully made out program and a natural interest in the class, never forget what he has promised, and remembers all details of past programs, so planning that each day's work is combined skillfully in a dozen ways with things that have happened before. The attitude of the teacher in receiving questions or answers is another strong indication of the social spirit. One type of teacher will give a question, and receive the answer with the remark, "That was an easy one." Naturally the individual who has answered can feel no triumph in what he has said, and the class is not stimulated toward effort. The same teacher many receive several answers, and, when none is volunteered, remark, "Is this all in the class?" in a depressing tone, which encourages neither those who have, nor those who have not, volunteered. As another example, a pupil makes an extremely good recitation, and the teacher remarks, "You are the only one I feel sure of in this class." The results of this remark are too obvious to describe. Another teacher of this same type may make an exbibit of a slow pupil, this not out of any desire to be cruel, but simply to teach the slow pupil a lesson, and to prod up the class. The results, however, are almost sure to be that the slow pupil is angry, or insulted, and that all semblance of a real social spirit is destroyed. Even worse in its effect is the result of the teacher's inferring that there has been copying. In case there is any suspicion of copying, or other cheating, and the class has knowledge of the matter, the matter must certainly be adjusted before the entire class ultimately. But, surely, because two written exercises resemble one another, there is no excuse for the teacher's remarking to the two writers, "Has there been copying here?" Not only are a large majority of cases of resemblance not due to copying, but the damage done to the social spirit of the class will far exceed any highly impossible benefit to the two rebuked. All criticism of individuals before the class that is designed as a punishment is fatal to class spirit. On the other hand, we have the constructive practice of assuming from the start that each member of the class desires to contribute to the social spirit of the class, and receives anything that is said in this attitude. The teacher who feels this will correct a mistake by some such remark as "Not quite," or, perhaps, as one teacher says with a very young class, that appreciate the play element, "Mary is warm." The important point here is that the teacher's attitude must be always that the class wishes to cooperate, and needs only to be shown the process by which this can be best done. This means, of course, that the teacher truly feels himself at the disposal of the class, and very near to them. In the elementary school, where a teacher and her class spend much time with one another, this attitude is prevalent. It is also found, of course, in the secondary schools, though here it is, perhaps, more difficult to adopt from the start. However, when one sees in all schools special teachers who, some of them, come in contact with the class only once a week, or once a month, and who succeed in establishing, the moment they enter a room, the most splendid spirit of cooperation, one realizes the possibilities in this line. The first few moments of such a teacher in a room will often demonstrate his attitude. The unsocial teacher will begin buy asking, "What was the home work" or some similar question that shows he has not yet adjusted himself to the particular class, or he may, as in one case observed, start in by scolding the class for well-remembered misdemeanors during the last visit. This teacher will be more than apt to forget the names of the pupils, to call upon one and hear another, and to manifest throughout the hour that his time is more valuable than that of the class, and that the class should take anything given in a spirit of thankfulness. On the other hand, the successful teacher will immediately take up the thread where it was last dropped, and will seem for the hour an integral part of the class room group. The class should feel that the teacher's time is valuable, and that it is, therefore, necessary to support him in every way possible. It must, however, feel that the teacher's time is at the disposal of the class, and that the teacher is spared trivial things in order to devote his attention to more important ones. In this way the teacher becomes really a member of the class group. If he feels himself to be one, every remark of such a teacher indicates this attitude. A pupil is inattentive. The teacher immediately says, "Take your book and be with us." Various ones are called upon to lead in the singing, or some other activity. The teacher says, "I am going to ask these pupils to help us out." One pupil is asked to demonstrate a problem that has been corrected by the teacher on the board. The teacher says, "John and I have worked out this problem," the inference being that the work has been done for the class. Such a teacher, instinctively, if a pupil is demonstrating to the class, or addressing the class, takes the pupil's seat, and becomes one of the listening group.

As for the methods by which the class themselves are handled in order that they may develop the proper attitude, it has been found successful with a new class to use considerable unison work, in order to accustom the various members to feel themselves part of a contributing group. It is also well, in giving directions, to include the "why" as often as possible, this being re cognized in elementary school practice, even in such elementary directions as "Class sit at ease," when the class is supposed to stop work and assume an attentive attitude. If the class is noisy, the teacher may say, "If any of you talk, it will mean that some, or all of you, cannot hear me. If you do not hear me, of course, you cannot progress at all." The writer noted the benefits of such an explanation, as used by the teacher of a dancing class of high school age. The pupils were of the age and type to enjoy independence, and were dancing one of the new dances according to their own inclination. The teacher stopped the dancing, and said, Quietly, "This dance is now standardized. You may want to dance it in other places, and, surely, you will wish to be able to dance it with anyone, and to know the standard method." The entire attitude of the class changed immediately. They understood the reason for the teacher's insistence on conformity to the rules, and followed directions at once, and with excellent grace. Some teachers have even gone so far as to take the class into their confidence where a difficult situation was to be faced. Of such a type was the teacher before mentioned, who found it necessary to take older arithmetic pupils back thru a thorough drill in the fundamental processes. But in order to do this the teacher must have a very clear idea of what he wishes to do, and why he wishes to do it, for, as one teacher naively said, "We cannot take pupils into our confidence, if we don't know what we are going to do." The pupils should be made, as soon as possible, to feel that they recite to and for the class. With younger pupils it is easier to make affection for one's class develop from affection for the teacher. It is quite allowable for the teacher to ask, "Who has brought me something?" when collecting the homework for the first few days or weeks, but, as soon as possible, the question should be rather, "Who has brought us something?" This attitude will be fostered by allowing some member of the class to preside over the recitation now and then, or by transforming the class for certain periods into an organization with self-elected officers in charge. The class may become more than a listening body, if allowed to help. In case the pupil reciting needs assistance, the teacher remarks, perhaps, "Let us all tell A so that he will remember," or something of the sort, varying in phraseology, of course, with the age of the pupils. The brave teacher, who is willing to take the final step in allowing the class to cooperate, may inaugurate the suggestion box system, as carried out in the industries. In the plant printed slips are used, which say, "I suggest the following" with a blank space for the suggestion.[24] These are distributed to all members of the organization, or are put in some place where they are available to all. One or more suggestion boxes are then put up in convenient locations in the plant. One may be in the hall, where those going in and out can use it easily, but one will surely be in some inconspicuous place, where anyone who is shy can deposit a slip without being observed. Every member of the organization is asked and encouraged to make any suggestion as to how anything in the plant practice may be bettered, either his own work, or the work of others. The suggestions are read by some unprejudiced person high in the organization, and one or more prizes are awarded at the end of the month for the best suggestion or suggestions. Every suggestion is acknowledged in some way, either by a card that says, "Your suggestion is accepted, and a prize is awarded as follows," or by a card that says, "Your suggestion is received." We thank you for it, but it is not at present available. If available later, it will be used, and a suitable prize awarded." Every suggestion adopted at any time is paid for. The suggestion box idea may be used in the school with simpler apparatus. One box will answer for every purpose. Slips need not be printed, and a reacting of the best suggestion, with the suggester's name, will act, perhaps, as sufficient prize. Some undoubted. improvements will be made with the suggestion box plan. Best of all, the spirit of cooperation will increase. In one school where this has been tried the director was rather disappointed that so few suggestions were handed in. It is to be noted, however, that the pupils stopped complaining to one another of things in thee school practice that they did not fancy. There was no excuse for grumbling to one's self or others, when the opportunity to suggest changes was constantly present and in visible form. We do not always realize that the important thing is not that we can demonstrate that the devices in use are producing something tangible, but that the results show that the use of the devices has been beneficial.[25] We should be able to apply measurement to the results, but we must be very sure that we realize what the results are before we attempt to measure them.

Waste Elimination Methods as an Incentive.

More important than any other incentive for a study such as this is the effect of waste eliminating methods upon the work. We should be able to group and appreciate these effects here. We have seen that elimination of physical waste resulted in better placement, equipment, and routing, in better methods of doing work, in less fatigue, and in habits of using more efficient motions. Now this elimination of physical waste not only cuts down working time and effort, but also arouses interest in work, and, therefore acts as a really positive incentive. In the same way eliminating waste in the mental processes not only affords more time for mental work, but simultaneously arouses interest, that, again, acts as an incentive. The teacher who has shown herself most willing to cooperate with the writer in actually trying waste elimination methods in her class room testifies that she and the class both are much more interested in the work since the methods have been tried. This interest, she believes, has been a very real and valuable incentive. Her experiences parallel the experience of all those who have tried this method in the industries. Not only does the individual pupil become more interested in his work and accomplish more thru the interest, but the class, as a whole, as a social group, becomes stimulated to act as a group.

We have noted the successful use of waste elimination methods demands constant cooperation. This is basic in Scientific Management, and cooperation is, of course, only another word for social spirit. We come, then, at the close of our discussion, to the very point at which we started, to the necessity for cooperation wherever waste elimination is to take place. Waste elimination, as outlined by Scientific Management, is based upon cooperation.[26] It has succeeded in the industries, because cooperation has been forthcoming. It will make greatest headway in the school and plant when these cooperate to use one another's successful methods, and it will make the most progress in the shortest time in the school room when it is understood to be a result of an efficient social spirit.

References

1. Bolton, F. E., "Principles of Education," Ch. XXVI.
    Jones, W. F., "Principles of Education," Ch. III. "Motivation"
2. Gilbreth, L. M., "The Psychology of Management," Ch. IX.
3. Gilbreth, L. M., "The Psychology of Management," p. 304.
    Jones, W. F., "Principles of Education, Pages 109-112.
4. Bolton, F. E., "Principles of Education," p. 682.
5. Jones, W. F., "Principles of Education," Pages 103-104.
6. Jones, W. F., "Principles of Education," Pages 100-102.
7. Gilbreth, L. M., "The Psychology of Management," p. 286-287; 304-305.
8. Jones, W. F., "Principles of Education," Pages 178-186.
9. Thorndike, E. L., "Educational Psychology," Vol. III., p. 120FF.
10. Gilbreth F. B., "Cost Reduction System."
11. O'Shea, M. V., "Everyday Problems in Teaching," Ch. III.
12. Jones, W. F., "Principles of Education," Pages 112-114.
13. Bolton, F. E., "Principles of Education," Pages. 695-700.
14. Gillette and Dana, "Cost Keeping and Management Engineering," p. 7.
    Scott, W. D., "Influencing Men in Business," Ch. II.
15. Diemer, H., "Factory Organization and Administration," p. 5.
16. Johnson, C. H., "The Modern High School," Pages 259-362.
    Lewis, W., "Proceedings of the Congress of Technology," 1911, p. 1910.
    Scott, W. D., "Increasing Efficiency in Business," Ch. IX.
17. Klapper, P., "Principles of Educational Practice," Pages 234-235.
18. Bolton, F. E., "Principles of Education," Pages 700-704.
    Klapper, P., "Principles of Educational Practice," Pages 232-233.
    O'Shea, M. V., "Everyday Problems in Teaching," Ch. X.
19. Gilbreth, F. B., "Motion Study as an Industrial Opportunity," Annals of the Academy of Political and Social Science.
20. Jones, W. F., "Principles of Education," Ch. IV.
21. Lewis, W. D., "Democracy's High School," p. 16.

22. Perry, C. A., "Wider Use of the School Plant," p. 120.

23. Jones, W. F., "Principles of Education," Ch. V.

24. Gilbreth, L. M., "The Psychology of Management," Pages 185-186.

25. Bagley, W. C., "The Educative Process," p. 331.

26. Gilbreth, L. M., "The Psychology of Management," p. 332.

Appendix A

Tests of the Educational Product

Much has been done in the field of measuring the educational product. The results may be divided into various groups of investigations. Some consist of the teacher's investigation of his own as well as the pupil's success by tests, written or oral, given to the class at set intervals in order to determine the familiarity of the class with the subject, and the implied efficiency of the teaching and learning involved. In many communities such tests are given not only by the teacher, but also by the supervising authority. When the latter takes charge of the tests or examinations, a certain standardizing of the requirements for each type and grade of work throughout the entire community takes place. The supervising authority may take up one subject, say arithmetic, and attempt to standardize that completely, so that, for example, each third grade throughout the city may be expected to pass a certain test, and each sixth grade a different test, etc.; or a test that will apply to all grades may be made out, and the time allowed be varied according to the age and grade of the pupils to whom the test is given; or many subjects may be standardized in a less complete way. The model for such standardization is often what is called the "regent's examination," by which pupils of an entire state are examined, at various stages of their progress, according to standard tests. The objections to all such examinations or tests are not so much the method in which they are applied as the method by which they are derived. Comparatively few of such tests are made under such circumstances that one can feel sure that they do furnish an adequate measure of the quantity and quality of knowledge in a certain line that they are supposed to furnish.

Feeling this lack, educators all over the country have attempted to formulate more exact standards that may act as materials for, or supplements to, such tests. For example, Professor Thorndike of Columbia has formulated various scales for measuring different educational lines. As typical of these might be named his scale for handwriting. This was derived by taking a thousand samples of handwriting and sorting them into eleven groups. The steps between these groups are supposed to be equal. The sorting was done by thirty or forty competent judges, and the results of their sorting were carefully compared. The ultimate result gives us, then, eleven samples of handwriting, each of which is submitted as ten percent better than the one that precedes, and ten percent worse than the one that follows it. The criterion is general excellence. To use the standard, one compares the sample of handwriting to be judged with the eleven standard samples, finds which it most nearly approaches, reckons the percent difference, and awards a certain ultimate percent. We have here an objective scale that even an inexperienced amateur may use with some degree of success. There are, of course, several objections to it. In the first place, we may object to the indefiniteness of "excellence" as a criterion of desirability in handwriting. "Excellence" may cover so many terms, "beauty," "symmetry," "legibility," etc., and is also so largely a question of personal preference. The objections rest, of course, upon the number of variables involved in the standards. One thousand samples,- is that enough? Was the handwriting from which these were selected typical of all handwriting, and at the same time typical of the particular group for which the user of the test is planning to use it? Is it possible to make eleven groups with even steps between? Are thirty or forty judges enough, and can we all agree as to their competence? Thorndike himself realizes these objections to which his work is open. He does well to emphasize that the important thing is not his results, but his object. This is to make plain what a standard is, and to attempt to derive such a standare, as a working demonstration of the necessity of such standards. We may object to the Thorndike scale, but we cannot help feeling the value of such scales, and of the principle of standardization of which it is a striking example.

The scale proposed by Ayres for measuring the quality of handwriting of school children offers less variables in that legibility is made the sole criterion. In this test samples of handwriting from schools all over the country were received, the conditions of making the samples and the contents of the samples being made as nearly similar as was possible. Almost sixteen hundred such samples were secured. These were divided into packages, each sample being gone over by ten readers, who each recorded the time that it took him to read the samples. Provision was made against errors thru the readers' gaining speed thru practice. The results were then collected and classified, and from them was deduced a scale that may be used to measure handwriting very much as the Thorndike scale is used.

Hillegas has formulated a somewhat similar scale for composition, and, as have been indicated in the references, scales also exist for measuring work in English, history, mathematics, drawing, etc.

As for the need of such scales, this is well brought out in various articles by Professor Starch, many of which are contained in the "School Review," as noted in the references for Chapter III. The investigations made by Professor Starch and those under him show the wide variation among various teachers in grading the same work, and the consequent unlikeness that unsupervised tests made by the average teacher will be fair and reliable, this, from no desire of the teacher to be unfair, but from his lack of such training as would make it possible for him to be so. Starch finds this to be true not only with different teachers in the same subject, but with teachers as to different parts of the same subject, an example being the emphasis placed upon content, form, etc. His conclusion is that such standard tests and scales, as have been and are being derived, offer the only solution of the problem, and that all attempts at deriving such scales should be strongly commended.

Too much study can scarcely be given to the remarkable work being done by Mr. S. A. Courtis of Detroit, Michigan. The Courtis tests are to be commended not only for their emphasis on the necessity for standardization but for their insistence on the importance of individual differences. No one who has talked with Mr. Courtis can fail to realize that he is a scientist of high rank, who appreciates the importance of measurement, and is willing to abide by the decision of facts, whether this coincides with his preconceived opinion or not. The form, as well as the subject matter, of the Courtis tests is to be most highly commended, and an intensive study of everything published by Courtis will serve as the most complete and instructive introduction to the subject of standardizing the educational product.

Along with attempts to standardize the product come the attempts to determine normality and abnormality in children, and the rate of intellectual progress to be expected at various ages. Binet and Simon have, of course, done pioneer work in this direction by means of testing both normal and abnormal children. They have formulated a series of tests, each of which is supposed to cover the field of knowledge that should be possessed by the child for a definite age, and to include tests that will show to what extent this knowledge is actually present. The objections to these tests are well summarized in Whipple's Manual of Mental and Physical Tests," pages 515-516. Some tests are too simple for the age to which they are assigned, some too difficult, some too mechanical, etc.

Professor Yerkes of Harvard has devised tests covering the same field that he calls the "Point Scale System." He and his followers define their work as attempting to derive standards rather than to apply standards. They have formulated certain tests of intelligence, and allow a certain number of points for passing each of these, and for passing definite parts of them. A child's mental age stands related to the number of points that he is able to achieve in the test. This school has appreciated fully the importance of environment. They maintain that the home and social surroundings of the individual often make it impossible for him to pass tests that might be thought normal for the physical age. They, therefore, record such conditions, and reckon, with the results of the tests, a certain percentage that takes account of the difference in home and social environmental conditions. It must be realized that they are quite right in feeling that such conditions undoubtedly do affect the individual's mental capabilities. However, we must remember that every added variable complicates the problem, and that it is an extremely difficult thing to deal with such a complicated percentage system.

The answer to this entire question probably is that too many variables are involved in all tests up to the present time formulated to handle the situation. Wonderful pioneer work has been done. The future workers must, however, endeavor to take up smaller and less complicated phases of the subject, and to deal for many years to come with simpler problems. If we might attempt to review all that has been done in measuring the educational product from any standpoint, this same criticism would hold true. The problems involved have all been so complicated that it is easy to question the validity of the results. The greatest progress takes place when we reduce the problem to the smallest and simplest elements possible. Devices for making accurate measurements have been invented. If these devices be applied to simple elements and accurate results be obtained, we can then build up standards that will be more nearly unassailable. This is not in the least to decry any of the wonderful work that has been done. In the final analysis, the great value of all this work is in the interest it awakens in the need of measurement and standardization. With the devices, tools, and methods now ready and the interest aroused, the way lies clear for immediate, continuous, and important progress.

Appendix B

Motion Study and Time Study as Methods of Measurement

Motion study and time study are closely related, and, taken together, furnish one of the most valuable means of measurement under Scientific Management. Motion study is the dividing of the elements of work into the most fundamental subdivisions possible, studying these fundamental units separately and in relation to one another, and from these studied, chosen units building up methods of least waste. Time study consists of timing the elements of the best method known, and synthesizing a standard time from the timed units.

The different methods of making motion study and time study have derived their names largely from the type of devices used. There is the counting method, that demands no device; the clock or watch method; the stop watch method; the micro-motion method; the chrono-cyclegraph method; etc.

Excellent preliminary work can be done simply by counting, "One and, two and, etc." Each group, of the number and the accompanying "and," occupy a second of time. After a few moments work with the clock, and a surprisingly short amount of practice, one is able to go on counting regularly without the assistance of the clock, and thus to make one's observations. An ordinary watch maybe used in the same way.

The stop watch method is difficult for an amateur to handle. This for several reasons. A certain amount of time always elapses between making the observation and pressing the stop watch. It is not easy to make the allowance for this reaction time, and for the personal equation involved. In order to take even fairly accurate stop watch time studies, the observer must learn to hold the stop watch in a certain relation between the operation observed and his eye, and to shift his attention from the object to the time piece, according to a rigorously prescribed method. Because of the technical difficulties in making such observations, good stop watch observers are rare.

The micro-motion method of making measurements consists of placing the object or process to be studied against a cross-sectioned background. In the field of observation are also placed a specially constructed clock that can be regulated to any desired speed up to intervals of a millionth of an hour, and also an ordinary clock that acts as a check upon the accuracy of the special clock. The time pieces are started, and the process to be observed set in operation. A moving picture film is then exposed at any desired rate of speed, and the different units or stages in the, process are recorded upon the film, simultaneously with records of the time. The result will be a motion picture film that will show not only method of doing the work, but also the time taken to perform any and every element of it.

The chrono-cyclegraph method of making measurement consists of attaching to the hands, or any other moving part of the operation to be studied, small electric light bulbs that are connected with batteries. The circuit is provided with a controlled interruption that makes it possible for each moving object to record its path in a different fashion, for example, all dots, all dashes, dot and dash, etc. The flashes from the electric light bulb are recorded by any stereoscopic camera, on either plate or film. When the pictures are properly transposed and observed, it is possible to follow the path of any motion cycle thru three dimensions.

The motion study that accompanies any of these methods of recording should be of the same sort. The most efficient method possible should be chosen to be observed. A record of ordinary practice may be made, simply as a matter of interest and a point to start from. The process will then be bettered as much as possible, divided into the smallest convenient and profitable units, and recorded. If other methods of doing the same work seem to possess efficient elements, these also are recorded, in order that all data of any value may be used in deriving the final standard.

The great advantage of motion study and time study as methods of measurement is that they maybe applied to any type of work. The micro-motion and cyclegraph method are the most scientific, yet are capable of being handled with success by even an amateur, if he be earnest minded. Because of the improvement in the processes these two methods are daily becoming more economical. The first cost of a motion picture outfit may seem large, but the accuracy and utility of the results and the wide field of application of the methods make this first cost a less considerable factor than might be supposed.

Because of its very nature, school work will offer an ideal field for the use of these methods. There is no such competition in the schools as there is in the industries. It should, therefore, be possible to establish a central laboratory, or several central laboratories, where excellent methods can be submitted to accurate measurement and standardized. The inventors of the micromotion and cyclegraph methods are glad to put their devices, free of cost, at the disposal of educators, who will surely more and more cooperate towards securing worthwhile standards thru these means.

Appendix C

The Survey as a Measure of the Educational Product

The survey of the public schools of Springfield, Illinois, recently made under the direction of Doctor Leonard P. Ayres, of the Russell Sage Foundation, is a model of what a survey should be, and of how it can serve as a measure of the educational product. Furnished with an admirable table of contents, it is possible to understand and follow its plan from the start.

The first chapter outlines the terms under which the survey was made, the staff making it, and the time and cost involved; the second takes up the study of Springfield and its relation to its schools; the third described the Board of Education; the fourth, the school plant itself; the fifth, the children; the sixth, the teaching force; the seventh chapter discusses the quality of class room instruction; the eighth, the course of study; the ninth, financial administration; the tenth, medical inspection; the eleventh, the high school; the twelfth, the junior high schools; the thirteenth, vocational education; and the fourteenth, educational extension. The chapters vary in length, but run approximately from five to fifteen pages.

At the close of the report we find a collection of the forms used in making the survey and an excellent index. There are also tables, diagrams, and illustrations, that make it easy to visualize and summarize existing conditions. All in all, as has been said, the report is a model of its kind.

It has the advantage of being made under the direction of an expert, with all the data collected by trained workers. It is possible, therefore, to include not only a statement of what exists, but recommendations as to improvements that should be made, and the methods by which they may most efficiently be made. Because of the close cooperation and the friendly feeling between the experts making the study and the local authorities and teachers, we receive not only an accurate statement of conditions, but a sympathetic interpretation of the reasons for these, and an outline of improvements, that is feasible and acceptable, as well as possible and commendable.

The general reader might, perhaps, wish that a resume were included at the close, that would generalize the findings in such a way that they might be utilized by other communities. However, an excellent contents and index make it possible to turn at once, with ease, to the point that demands one's special interest, and the care with which the reason for making a recommendation has, in the majority of cases, been bracketed with the recommendation, makes it possible to generalize the information and to translate it into the terms of one's own particular needs. We must, of course, accept from the outset the authority of the judgment of those making the study. For example, where the report says, "Discipline is good," we must accept their judgment on this point without statement as to the standard on which the judgment is based. In every case, we can at least receive a valuable suggestion as to a field that must be tested or standardized, and an instruction in method that is of even greater importance than the actual knowledge gained from the facts stated.

Appendix D

"The Question as a Measure of Efficiency in Instruction."

Miss Stevens' study is a valuable contribution to the literature of the scientific method as applied to education. Inspired by a natural interest in the subject, and a feeling from preliminary observation that questioning as conducted in the ordinary class room is not an efficient practice, she starts out to investigate present practice thoroughly, and to attempt to formulate a definition of efficient questioning. Her first step is a review of the literature on the subject, which she finds to be fragmentary. Her second is a decision to make, herself, a thorough investigation of present practice. This is conducted along various lines. One is a summing up of her previous observations. A second is a stenographic report of twenty class room teaching hours, this in order to study the data intensively and at leisure. A third consists of one hundred random observations in various subjects, made for the purpose of counting the number and noting the nature of the questions used, and a fourth consists of ten observations of selected classes, each class being observed for an entire day.

The observations of Miss Stevens cover four years, and include classes in public and private schools from the seventh grade thru the high school. All studies are made, so far as the records show, in and about New York City. However, the cosmopolitan nature of the population there, the length of time during which observations were made, the scope of the classes observed, and the varying nature of the types of observation make the records valuable for extent as well as content. In the report, as published by Miss Stevens, are included extracts from the stenographic reports only. These make it impossible for the critical reader to prove for himself every step in Miss Stevens' deductions. However, the scientific method as exemplified in her work is so excellent that one is willing to accept her deductions as careful, and, as nearly as possible, unbiased by the convictions that she held at the beginning of the investigation.

It is interesting to note that all of the data gathered by her and others under her direction, no matter what the nature of the method by which it is made, points to the same conclusions. She is not forced to reconcile what are apparently facts that oppose one another. The conclusions are that an enormous number of questions are asked in the ordinary class room hour, often two or three to the minute throughout the entire hour; that this large number of questions keeps the class at a high nervous tension; that, in spite of this fact, a large percentage of the work is done by the teacher, not by the pupils; that, as a result of this rapid questioning, there is little development of judgment in the pupils, who at best do nothing but memorize in a routine fashion; that the pupils get little or no opportunity for self expression, for individual development, or for becoming self-reliant thinkers. The conclusion of these observations is that efficiency is not in proportion to the number of questions, but is more likely to be in inverse ratio to the number of questions, that is to say, large quantity of efficiency is related to small number of questions.

A further study of the data, however, shows that a small number of questions is not necessarily synonymous with efficiency, that is to say, that quality as well as quantity of the questions asked must be considered. The data is then reviewed in an attempt to formulate a standard for the quality of questions. The results seem to show that there are at least three tests for quality to which a question may be submitted. These are, as worded by Miss Stevens:

    1. "The degree of reflection it stimulates," that is, its
       thought producing power.
    2. "Its adaptability to the experience and work of the pupils."

3. "Its motor power in drawing forth a well rounded
thought and adequate expression for the same."

Miss Stevens would, then, advise that the teacher set up as his standard for quality of questions these three tests, which the questions that he formulates must submit to and pass in order to be efficient, and, as her standard for quantity of questions, six or eight in the ordinary hour.

It is a thankless task to criticise a study as excellent as this. However, it might be wished that Miss Stevens had considered more in detail the broader aspects of her subject. For example, the question is but one test of a successful lesson hour. Its relation to other existing and possible tests might well be pointed out in some detail. It is also true that the question may serve as an excellent tool in other fields than those covered by the three tests. It is undoubtedly true, as Miss Stevens says, that the question is a mighty force in teaching the pupil to think, to use his past experience, and to express himself. It is also a device for rapid review, as a test simply of memory, and where no thought of expression other than to fit the idea into the shortest terms possible is involved. However, all of these limitations of her study are of slight importance. The important thing is that we have here a sane and careful attempt to take up one phase of an interesting subject, considering it from the scientific standpoint. We must admire constantly Miss Stevens' refusal to be carried off into attractive side issues. We must appreciate also that, while she has strong convictions before undertaking the study, she is careful in every case to proceed no faster than the data from the investigations warrant. For example, her results prove that a large number of questions used indicates inefficient teaching. It would be easy to jump to the conclusion that a small, number of questions probably indicates efficient teaching. She is careful not to do this, and to review her entire data before stating that, so far as she has seen, a small number of questions does at least accompany good teaching, if it is not necessarily an element of it. She is also careful, at the end of the investigation to say that what she has done is only one contribution to a field that must be thoroughly investigated, and to desire that her work be rated as a method of attack rather than a valuable body of results. The reader who reviews the work carefully must certainly pronounce both methods and results of great value.

Appendix E

Scientific Management Applied to the School Room

During the months of October, November, and December, the attempt was made on the 6A grade, the children ranging from eleven to fifteen years, to carry on the class in arithmetic according to the practices of scientific management in the industries. Taylor's eight principles underlying good management make these practices clear.

1. The development of a science for each element of a man's work, which replaces the old rule of thumb method.
2. An almost equal division of work and the responsibility between management and workman.
3. A clearly defined and circumscribed task.
4. Such conditions that the daily task can always be accomplished.
5. High pay in case the task is successfully done.
6. Low pay in case of failure.
7. The scientific selection, training, teaching, and developing of the workman.
8. Hearty cooperation between management and men.

How could these principles be applied to the school room was the problem.

The first steps in the reorganization was the cooperation of the teacher and children. The teacher was interested because of her belief in the utility and efficiency of such a system; the children, because of the novelty of the plan and the approval of the teacher.

The next step was to standardize the variables as far as possible. Monitors were given special tasks in the fifteen minutes before school, such as sharpening pencils, passing out papers so that when school began every one might be ready to work with his material there, on his desk. A drawer was assigned for completed work which was collected at noon or night rather than at the completion of each lesson. This device made it possible to start a new lesson immediately upon the completion of the old. There were monitors to keep the storeroom in order and the supplies filled, one to collect and put away unused papers of absentees, one to dust and arrange the teacher's desk, to keep the board erased, the ledges clean and filled. Thus the mechanism of the school room became automatic. Each pupil felt himself necessary to the room, and best of all, work could start promptly at nine o'clock and continue without interruption all day.

According to the method of collecting and passing out papers during the period allotted for a subject, there was wasted on an average two minutes for passing out papers, two minutes for collecting, taking at least four minutes from every arithmetic, language, spelling, history, or geography period, and on two drawing days thirty minutes more.

In mental arithmetic the custom had been to pass out the paper, wait for them to put down their names and number to twenty, and then sit at ease signifying their readiness to begin. These preliminaries took five minutes. The examples were then read, the class doing them as quickly as possible mentally, and at the teacher's command took their pens and wrote the answer. With "pens down" every pen was placed in the ledge and the class was ready for the next example. Experience told the teacher how long to wait between commands, her tendency being to wait for the slowest student in order to encourage him. Fifteen minutes were often required for this work (This counts the time occupied from the giving out of the paper to the receiving of them.).

With the attempt to do the greatest amount of work in the shortest possible time, the children were asked to have their papers placed right in front of them, ink on their pens, and each pen in a position to put down the answer the instant it was obtained. The work became a game in which they were trying to beat a previous record, while the teacher, with watch in hand gave the examples, as fast as the medium pupil could do them, leaving behind if necessary the very slow ones. The results were, where it had taken from twelve to fifteen and even twenty minutes to do twenty examples, five minutes at the least was necessary and ten minutes, at the longest, much depending upon the mechanical aspect of the examples. Thus when twenty minutes were allowed for class work and twenty minutes for written work, we had fifteen minutes for other drill to compare with five or seven minutes allowed in the old method. This one item was valuable indeed where there was so much to accomplish in a short time. The children felt the pressure of the short time, and in consequence had the feeling of having done something worth while when at the end of four weeks they did one of the city tests in three minutes, thereby taking less time than any sixth grade in the city, and at the same time making about the same average as the others.

The remaining time for class work was used in various ways, developing new principles, explaining and drilling upon the old work. The children rarely went to the board, doing any such work at their seats on scrap paper.

The third part of the experiment had to do with their written work. They were accustomed to do five examples in twenty minutes, bright and dull ones being held to the same standard. Those who finished were asked to busy themselves with something else while waiting for the slower ones. The difficulty of the examples was kept as uniform as possible, and five were chosen rather than four or six, since that number was what the average generally accomplished.

The new method was quite different. Now the children were given more examples than the brightest could do, and were told that they were to do as many as possible, greater credit being given to the quick, accurate boy. They were no longer marked according to percents, but by letter,- A, B, C, or F, according as the work was considered excellent, good, passing, or failure. In order that they might work out their own percents, figures being a stimulus to children, the number of examples done and the number wrong were put down like this,- Eleven done, one wrong (11-1). They were made to feel the value of speed and accuracy, both by praise and by marks. At first accuracy and neatness were sacrificed to speed, but that difficulty soon adjusted itself when they realized the need of all three factors in order to secure a good mark. Practically all were interested from the first and remained so, their interest being revived now and then by words of encouragement. The tables show the results of the work.

Much can be done in the schoolroom to make the mechanical side automatic, which becomes the means of giving hours to the school which otherwise would be thoughtlessly wasted. As in business, so in school may the tasks be clearly defined and circumscribed. Praise, or blame, marks, competition, each are incentives to do better work, and take the place of pay which is the main incentive used in the industries. Then, the hearty cooperation between the teacher and pupils makes all things possible.

Perhaps the greatest difficulty of school routine is the constant interruption from some uncontrollable outside force, such as lectures, socials, entertainments, errand boys, and many more which might be mentioned. Much time and energy might be saved were it possible to have questions for each pupil, rather than to have the teacher put fifteen or twenty examples on the board frequently. There would be less eye strain, at least.

Because this method of doing arithmetic makes it possible for the bright pupil to do many more examples than he otherwise would, and thereby gives him greater drill, and because the charts show that the efficiency of all is not lessened but increased, since many more examples are done with little change an accuracy, I would recommend this scientific management as applied to the school room.

A. Mildred Wentworth.

6A Grade

Arranged according to percent of the old method.
Time twenty minutes.

Child	%	Number of Examples
1	100	12
2	95	12
3	90	12
4	90	12
5	85	12
6	85	12
7	80	12
8	80	12
9	80	12
10	80	12
11	75	12
12	75	12
13	70	12
14	70	12
15	70	12
16	70	12
17	70	12
18	66	12
19	65	12
20	65	12
21	60	12

Arranged on the same basis.
New method - Time twenty minutes.
First group of examples.

Child	%	Number of Examples
1	96	25
2	89	29
3	89	29
4	89	28
5	89	29
6	89	23
7	89	22
8	76	25
9	69	23
10	66	24
11	76	25
12	73	23
13	89	26
14	63	22
15	78	28
16	78	28
17	89	21
18	90	22
19	73	23
20	76	21
21	73	19

Second group of examples.

Child	%	Number of Examples
1	95	20
2	88	25
3	74	27
4	86	23
5	87	24
6	76	24
7	84	19
8	89	19
9	75	16
10	68	19
11	80	25
12	85	21
13	81	22
14	80	20
15	63	19
16	86	22
17	94	17
18	76	17
19	68	16
20	90	20
21	74	19

Third group of examples.

Child	%	Number of Examples
1	87	24
2	75	36
3	89	28
4	86	29
5	83	30
6	85	21
7	76	19
8	95	22
9	66	18
10	75	29
11	77	22
12	64	28
13	75	29
14	61	18
15	60	28
16	87	32
17	94	17
18	95	22
19	95	21
20	46	19
21	77	27

The complete set counted in the experiment averaged.

Child	%	Number of Examples	Efficiency
1	92 2/3	69	63.5
2	84	90	70.6
3	82	84	68.88
4	87 1/2	80	70
5	86 1/3	83	71.38
6	83 1/3	68	56.44
7	83	60	52.44
8	86 2/3	66	56.76
9	70	57	39.90
10	69 2/3	72	49.68
11	77 2/3	72	55.44
12	74	72	53.28
13	81 2/3	77	62.31
14	68	60	40.88
15	67	75	50.25
16	83 2/3	82	18.06
17	92	55	50.50
18	85	61	51.85
19	78 1/3	60	46.8
20	70 2/3	60	42.
21	74 2/3	65	48.1

By the old method thirty-six examples would have been done.

Results of 6A test, 1915, and 6B test, 1914.
Eight of the children had a different teacher in 6B.

Child		6A 1915	6B 1914
1		70	90
2		100	88
3		80	90
4		90	80
5		80	88
6		80	90
7		80	88
8		90	100
9		90	90
10		90	98
11		70	70
12		60	80
13		70	90
14		70	50
15		70	90
16		100	100
17	One who can do mechanical work only.	40	88
18		100	Another School
19		60	78
20		90	80
21		80	70
	Average-	79	85

Average of the other 6A, 1915, 72.8%,- 17 in the class

Rearranged according to final percent of accuracy.

	Child		%	Number of Examples	
1.	1		92 2/3	69	
2.	17	Can only do mechanical examples.	92	55	An exceptional case.
3.	4		87 1/2	80	
4.	8		86 2/3	66	
5.	5		86 1/3	83	
6.	18		85	61	
7.	2		84	90	
8.	16		83 2/3	82	
9	6		83 1/3	68	
10.	7		83	60	
11.	3		82	84	
12.	13		81 2/3	77	
13.	19		78 1/3	60	
14.	11		77 2/3	72	
15.	21		74 2/3	65	
16.	12		74	72	
17.	20		70 2/3	60	
18.	9		70	57	
19.	10		69 2/3	72	
20.	14		68	60	
21.	15		67	75	

Mental Arithmetic, Halves, Quarters, Eights

Grade	Percent Correct	Time	Percent Passed
8A	95.5	4	100
8B	95.7	5	100
7A	94.8	6	100
7A	94.3	7	100
7B	93.4	7	100
7B	90.9	7½	90.6
6A	88.	3½	95.
6A	93.8	5	100
6B	90.5	7	100
5A	67.6	11	61.7
5A	89.1	10	100

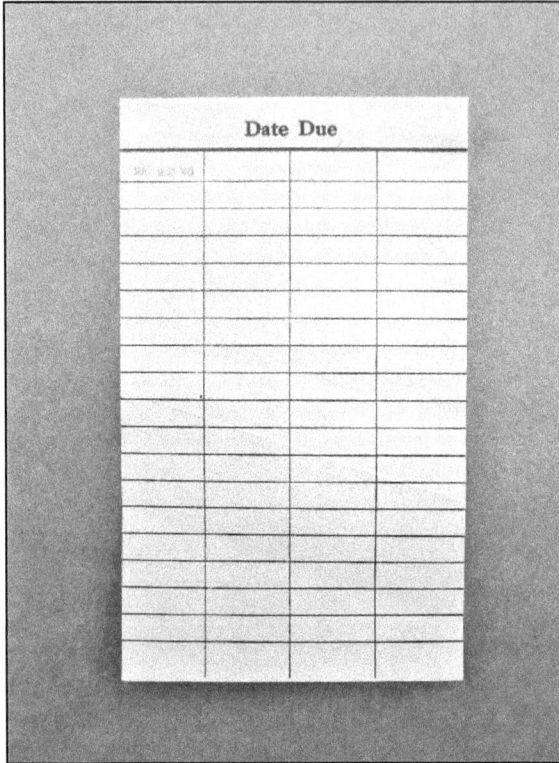

Dr. Gilbreth's dissertation was last checked out from a Brown University library 79 years ago, in early 1940. After that date it likely entered the Special Collections because Dr. Gilbreth had become quite famous in the United States and internationally.

Postscript

Dr. Gilbreth's Brown University doctoral dissertation fell into obscurity after its completion, presumably because the momentum established in earlier lines of work, such as motion and fatigue study, had to be carried forward in preference to her devoting time and effort to improving grade school education. Despite this, the dissertation remains an important work for historical reasons as well as practical reasons. In this work, Dr. Gilbreth demonstrates the broad applicability of Scientific Management to a field far removed manufacturing industries, yet very closely allied with it in terms of the need to educate and train both managers and workers. Dr. Gilbreth shows the need for improvement in teaching and points the way towards improvement by supplying concrete recommendations. But more than that, she, along with cooperating teachers, tested some of the recommended improvements in actual school settings. The results proved beneficial, of course, because the way work is typically done is by tradition, not by careful scientific study – observation, rational thought, and analysis.

Dr. Gilbreth's dissertation teaches many important things. We learn that we need to better understand the work that we do. We learn that all processes contain waste that must be eliminated so work can be made easier and the results better. We learn how the fundamental thinking of Scientific Management easily crosses boundaries, as do most of the methods developed in the manufacturing industries. We learn that when people are asked why they do what they do, in most cases, they do not know. It is the way they were shown or told to do the work, or how they observed others doing the work. This weak rationale does not support continuation of the old way of doing things. Rather, it provides the evidence that the work processes must be changed for the better. We learn that improvement must not be dictated by administrators; that stakeholders must be engaged in the process of understanding the work and in making improvement. We learn to respect the worker and their work.

We learn that many improvements are simple to make and can be implemented quickly. We learn much about time, how it is wasted, and how to use it more effectively. We learn how our motions, both physical and mental, are wasted, and how to become more efficient in our work. We learn that improvement can and must be achieved in ways that do not harm others. The benefits of improvement must accrue to those in direct and indirect proximity to the work.

We learn that teachers, like any worker, can easily make a lot of errors, most of which may seem inconsequential. The errors made are not because they are bad people or because they lack care or concern for their work or its impact on students. It is because they have been unable to see past "rule of thumb" and traditions that have seemed to work well enough in the past, and have difficulty seeing how these may be outdated and ineffective. It is because they have not been taught by someone to see things differently, or not led by someone who disapproves of the status quo and sees it as a barrier to needed progress.

We learn the positive outcomes of improvement and the perils of the status quo. We learn that we need to be open-minded and learn, and that the learning never stops. A teacher who thinks critically about their work and experiments with new methods – *continuously, for years* – is intrinsically motivated. It seems that such teachers are rare. Most teachers will require some type of extrinsic reward, or incentive, to participate in continuous improvement activities. Certain incentives that have been used successfully in industry might be applied to teachers in the schools. But even with incentives, participation will be low, and likely soon wither, if improvement work is forced upon people and made dull and uninteresting. Improvement work must be made fun, and usually includes the help of skilled facilitators. The creation of a "social spirit" matters greatly in the practice of progressive management.

Most of the teaching errors that Lillian Gilbreth observed in 1915 still happen today. That shows the devastating power of tradition. These errors will continue unless teachers and administrators commit themselves to improvement. Bad quality makes a lasting impression, whether it is a camera, automobile, manager, or teacher. As former students, we know this well because when asked who our best teachers were – whether in primary school, secondary school, or in higher education – we can cite only a few out of the many teachers we had in each level of our education. Typically, the numbers in higher education are 10 percent best teachers, 90 percent average, poor, or bad. These numbers must be reversed, and the goal should be 100 percent best and good teachers.

Finally, we must recognize that administration and teaching are connected to one another. Processes in one affect the other, and common processes cross the boundaries between administration and teaching. Administrative processes are like any other in that they contain massive amounts of waste. Therefore, focusing on eliminating waste in teaching is not enough. Administrators must also understand their work, the waste that exists, and make efforts to eliminate it. Administrators and teachers should cooperate so that together they can create better and more efficient schools.

☙

Contemporary Methods of Waste Elimination in Teaching

By Bob Emiliani, Ph.D.

Scientific Management has undergone much evolution since its inception in the late 1800s thanks to the efforts of countless dedicated leaders and individuals. Various changes and improvements were made to progressive management practice in the years prior to World War II. After World War II, large advances in its evolution were made by Toyota Motor Corporation, in what was later named the "Toyota Production System." But don't let the word "production" fool you because Toyota was developing its overall corporate management practice, not just its production practice. By the early 1970s it reached a state of development that was recognizable as a complete management system. Toyota's management system has continued to evolve since then, and it remains an important touchstone for other seeking to learn how to better lead and manage an organization. Importantly, Toyota continues to place great emphasis on education and training employees at all levels because developing people is how the company develops.

A rough translation of Toyota's production system was given the name "Lean production" in 1988, due to the system's ability to produce more while consuming less resources compared to other automakers. In 2007, the term "Lean production" fell out of favor and was replaced by term "Lean management" (see Note 1). While not an exact copy of Toyota's management system, Lean embodies some aspects of the thinking and some of its principles and practices. It is a useful proxy for Toyota's management system, which is somewhat complicated and difficult to understand in the absence of careful study and practice.

The elimination of waste remains a foundational objective in Toyota's management system, and of Lean management, as well as the elimination of "unevenness" and "unreasonableness." Over time, the importance of respecting people – workers and other key stakeholders inside and outside an organization – was strengthened thanks to Toyota – and likely due to the influence of Lillian Gilbreth's work in industrial psychology. It was only in 2007 that "Respect for people" finally started to become better and more widely understood in the practice of Lean management. This is important because without "respect for people," continuous improvement will languish or produce results that have little or no impact. Because "respect for people" enables continuous improvement, its absence usually results in only the appearance of continuous improvement.

Over the years, many organizations have adopted Lean management with varying degrees of success. Unfortunately, there has been more struggle than success, often because leaders want the great results that can come from continuous improvement, but without them having to make changes necessary to respect people (workers, in particular). The bigger impediment to success, we now know (Emiliani, 2018), is leaders' continued adherence to tradition; managing the company according to traditions, opinions, and "rule of thumb." The dissonance created by the simultaneous desire to change things and keep things the same, not surprisingly, leads to great difficulties. Despite this, many beneficial improvements can be made even in organizations whose leadership has no interest in Lean management. Usually, this means that one must do their improvement work in stealth mode or practice "Guerilla Lean." This describes my situation.

In the first university I worked at, the president and provost had a brief interest in Lean – sufficient to allow us to do some pioneering work. But, despite the good results, interest in Lean by top administrators quickly faded. In my current university, the current and past presidents have shown no interest in Lean. Nevertheless, I pushed forward with efforts to improve my teaching, to make the work less tedious, more interesting, more enjoyable, and to produce better student learning outcomes and knowledge retention for current or future practice on-the-job or in life.

Since 1999, I have been applying Lean principles and practices to improve teaching in both undergraduate and graduate courses (Emiliani, 2004, 2005) based upon what I had learned in industry about eliminating waste in processes. The many and varied types of teaching improvements made over the first 15 years have been documented in a small volume titled *Lean Teaching: A Guide to Becoming a Better Teacher* (Emiliani, 2015). This book, and the pages that follow, reflect contemporary thinking and methods of waste elimination in teaching. My initial objectives were to eliminate teaching errors, ambiguity, batching of assignments and evaluation, waste, unevenness, unreasonableness, and other problems that result in student and teacher dissatisfaction and poor learning outcomes. The principles and methods used included reducing the batch size of information, level-loading assignments, visual controls, 5S, standard work, just-in-time, continuous improvement, and respect for people. The results of these efforts have been consistently favorable in terms of course evaluations and student learning outcomes.

In recent years, I again became engaged in kaizen in manufacturing (see Note 2). These new experiences inspired me to apply what I had learned to my work. Specifically, to more closely mirror the types of improvements made during kaizen on the manufacturing shop floor to teaching. This represents an evolution in teaching method that builds upon the application and learning from teaching process improvements that were made from 1999 to 2015 (Emiliani, 2015). The new changes made to one graduate course, as a pilot study, included:

- Adoption of a hybrid course format, where half the classes are face-to-face and half are online
- The use of a learning management system (LMS) – basic functionality only
- Machine (LMS) evaluation of student assignments for 45 percent of the final grade
- Human evaluation only for those assignments that require human judgment
- No lecture
- Face-to-face classroom time used for students to make or create something that reflects one or more core learning objectives
- Establishing information "supermarkets" that house subject matter content
- Creating student pull for information (subject matter) from the supermarket
- Continue to reduce information batching, eliminate queues, and improve work and information flow

A principal objective was to further improve the teaching process by individualizing course content to student's interests, as well as improving student learning outcomes, and improving student satisfaction as measured by student course evaluations. These new concepts were put into practice in the 2015-2016 academic year (and in subsequent years with further improvements). Readers are cautioned to understand that the methods and results presented are a snapshot in time and not final. Improvements in teaching process are never-ending, mainly through trial-and-error. While this may seem to be an inefficient and circuitous route to improvement, it is a practical and creative method for revealing good or bad results quickly so that adjustments can be made promptly. It also helps avoid the problem of prejudging outcomes, which usually leads to inaction due to low perceived payoffs. The mindset is "just try it and see what happens."

Grading Inside the Process

Evaluation of students' work by the professor is typically performed outside of the learning process. Evaluation begins when all assignments have been received, thus creating a large batch that sits in queue until grading commences and the results subsequently communicated to students. Students strongly dislike gaps between assignment submittal and feedback from the teacher, and the delays disrupt the flow of learning. This is analogous to batch-and-queue processing in manufacturing (or service) work, where a batch of parts are inspected for conformance to quality specifications in a department located far from the value-creating manufacturing process. This results in delays between inspection and feedback to the operator. Organizations that practice Lean management do something different. They quickly evaluate work within the process, at each step along the way, the result of which is to "build in quality," thereby eliminating defects, delays in feedback, and smoothing the flow of work.

Because grading and assignment feedback, while necessary, are burdensome to professors, they typically prefer to reduce the number of graded assignments to the fewest possible – often just mid-term and final exam. Students dislike this because poor performance on one exam can have a significant impact on their final grade. Students would rather have more grading opportunities, each one worth fewer points. This creates a tension between professors' time and other professional interests and students' wants and educational needs.

A way to resolve this tension is to utilize the technology and functionality of computer-based learning management systems to create weekly assignments worth a few points each and which are automatically graded. This has the benefit of synchronizing the learning process and evaluation for a large portion of the final grade. But this begs a fundamental question: What type of assignments can be created and graded automatically inside the learning management system and what type of assignments should be created and graded by the teacher? And, what should be the proportion of automatic machine evaluation and human evaluation? The ratio of grading inside and outside the learning process will depend on the course and its learning objectives. Some proportion must be established to start, and then adjustments made later as the teacher receives feedback based on students' performance in the course and student feedback.

My current practice is to create assignments such that about half of the final grade is based on human evaluation of students' work. The assignments are designed in such a way so that they can be quickly evaluated the next day, and the results immediately communicated to students. The portion of the grade within the LMS, the small weekly assignments, are called "quick checks." The name is taken from the method used to build in quality in a manufacturing process using go/no-go gages. Right or wrong answers are machine-evaluated and graded, and the machine gives students feedback on their answers. The LMS eases some of the professors' burden of evaluating students' work while reserving their time for higher-value assessment of student work that requires the judgment and subject matter expertise of a professor.

Instant grading inside the learning process and rapid response to grading outside the learning process are consistent with Dr. Gilbreth's views on evaluating student work in both a timely and accurate manner and providing feedback to students.

Making Teaching a Pull System

Teaching is a "push" system, wherein faculty design courses with the information that they think students need to know. The subject matter is then pushed onto students through various types of interactions within and outside of the classroom. Figure 1 depicts the traditional approach, whereby the professor believes they possess the best solution to the problem of how best to teach students about a subject. The numbers 4 and 5 clearly indicate there can be only one answer or method for gaining knowledge about a subject, which includes traditional teaching methods such as lecture, mid-term and final exams, term papers, team projects, etc. Is this assumption correct?

$$4 + 5 = \boxed{}$$

Figure 1. Single solution concept (see Note 3).

The question is, can teaching be made more of a "pull" system, as is done in manufacturing (and service) businesses? Pull systems are a method of production where work is initiated by a demand signal from a customer, rather than the producer's forecast of customer demand. Forecasts are guesses, and therefore likely to be wrong in whole or part. Pull systems, based on actual customer demand information, have proven to be beneficial in terms of improving customer satisfaction by reducing the lead-time (wait time from order to delivery), improving quality, and customizing products or services to meet individual needs. From the producer's perspective, pull systems have benefits such as greater responsiveness to changes in customer demand and lower cost (due to less guessing).

In the context of teaching, students' pull subject matter from the professor and from the information that the professor has supplied to the learning management system, called a "supermarket." Pull (demand) for information is based on student's individual interests and needs. The method used in teaching to generate the signal for information is a worksheet in which students identify the answers that they seek from the course and the questions that they must ask in order to obtain the answers. The worksheet is shown in Figure 2.

Personalized Discovery and Learning

TM572 – Innovative Leadership

Name: _____
Date: _____

2. Questions I Must Ask	1. Answer I Want From TM572 for Work and/or For Life
Example of Question: "Who/What/Why/How.....?"	Example of Statement: "I want to know....."
• Up to 4 questions per box • Delete example questions below and think on your own	• No more than one Answer per box • Delete example answer below and think on your own
• What does a leader have to believe in to be an innovative leader? • How must a leader behave to be considered by followers as an innovative leader? • What are the competencies that an innovative leader must master?	• I want to know what constitutes innovative leadership.
• • • •	•
• • • •	•
	No more than one page.

Figure 2. "Seek Answers by Asking Questions" worksheet.

Students are given three weeks from the start of the semester to study and interact with the course materials in the LMS and identify the answers they seek and questions to ask. This assignment challenges students at the start of the course to think about what they want to get out of the course. They must ask themselves: "What are the answers that I need from this course to satisfy my interests or help me with my job?" "What useful answers can this course offer me?" "What questions do I need to ask?" The assignment is evaluated and graded by me, not by the LMS, because it informs me of important information about current interests and subject matter that will be added to, or deleted from, the course in future semesters. Students find this assignment both challenging and worthwhile, and they use it periodically during the semester for reflection. This method mirrors how people learn, which is by finding answers to questions that interest them. Answers are the final step in the process of learning, that is until new questions arise.

Figure 3 shows a "supermarket" containing a curated collection of different types of subject matter information that are placed into the LMS, including the professor, who also serves as an information resource to students. Students access this information on-demand, based upon the "Seek Answers by Asking Questions" worksheet and the learning objectives of the course. This differs from most courses which are over-contended and to which students must respond because it is pushed onto them by the teacher. The supermarket allows the student to think and decide what information is best suited for them, in addition to the content that the professor believes to be appropriate to achieve course learning objectives.

Figure 4 shows a diagram of the "pull" system. It begins on the right with the answers that students seek, which results questions. This, in turn, requires students to process information. But, before they can do that, they must obtain information from the supermarket.

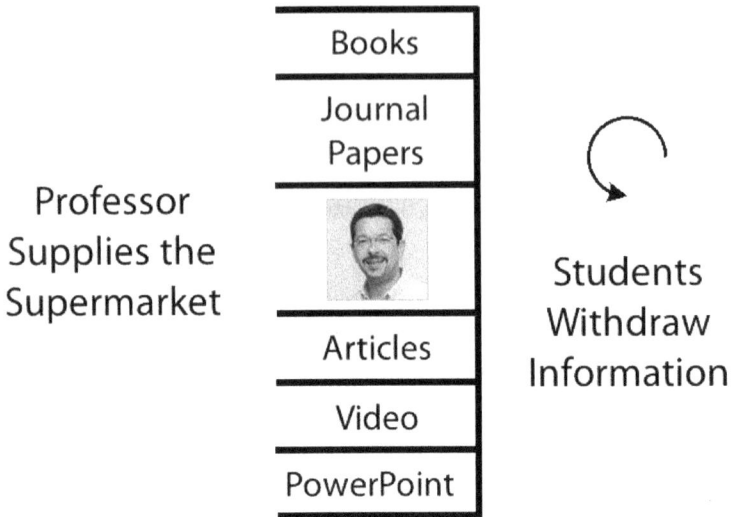

Figure 3. Contents of a course "supermarket."

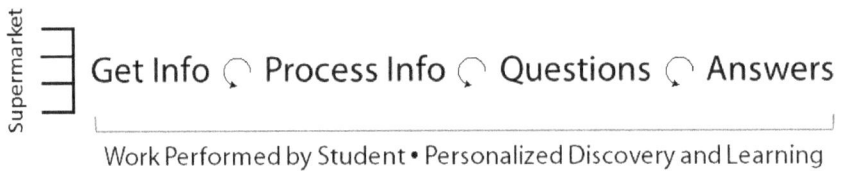

Figure 4. Pull system beginning with "Answers" that students
seek from the course (read from right to left).

Figure 5 shows the complete pull process, from right to left. It begins with an assignment that is graded by the professor, followed by automatic grading by the LMS inside the learning process, and concluded with another assignment graded by the professor. Other assignments requiring evaluation by the professor are interspersed throughout the semester. As noted previously, classroom time features hands-on activities where students must make or create something in relation to the course's learning outcomes.

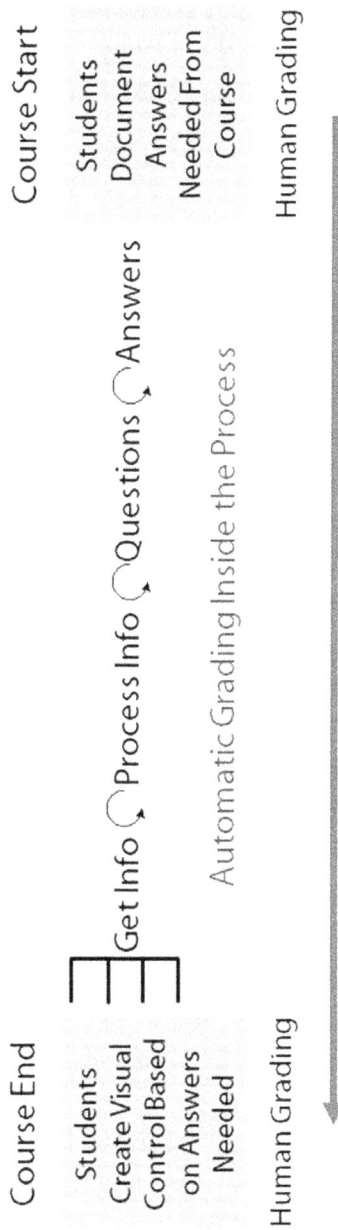

Figure 5. Overall view of pull system course design.

Figure 6 shows the concept that this new method strives to apply. The number 9 represents the primary course learning outcomes, which are specified by the professor in the syllabus, while the boxes represent infinitely different ways to achieve the learning objectives based on student's individual needs and interests.

$$\Box + \Box = 9$$

Figure 6. Infinite solutions concept (see Note 3).

The objective is for students to learn a few very important things that they will remember and apply, rather than many things that they will forget soon after the course is over. To help achieve this, students have a final assignment to create a one-page "visual control" of what they learned in the course in relation to the answers they were seeking and the questions that they asked. The purpose of the visual control, which is a combination of images and words, is to remind students of what they learned in the course and what they can apply in practice (Emiliani, 2015). At the end of the course, I also give students a visual control that I created which contains images and words that summarizes, from my perspective, the most important learnings that the course had to offer. Students are free to use their own visual control, a visual control created by other students, or the one given to them by the teacher. Students often post the visual control at home or in their workplace, which keeps them connected to the course for many years later – something that otherwise rarely occurs.

Recall that responding to the individual needs of was featured prominently in Dr. Gilbreth's dissertation. It was a key element of Scientific Management then and Lean management now. Making teaching a pull system helps achieve individualization of learning for students.

Observations and Commentary

Pull systems applied to teaching in higher education create new challenges with respect to student engagement and the amount of effort put forth to learn the subject matter. Students who are used to performing carefully-crafted tasks assigned by a professor face different intellectual demands that they likely have not faced in other graduate courses. It also challenges professors to put enough material into the supermarket to cover a board range of students' interests and needs, while simultaneously avoiding the temptation to create too large an inventory of information in the supermarket. Curation of information remains an ongoing challenge, as the supply of information to the supermarket must be continuously adjusted. Culling information that is no longer useful or which has been superseded with newer or better information is part of the curatorial challenge.

Learning management systems are helpful in establishing pull systems in teaching. However, learning management systems contain an abundance of features and functionality that are not particularly useful. They seemingly exist to enable professors to customize content on a student-by-student basis but may not be so effective in in doing so. The methods presented here, while early in development, show simpler ways to achieve customization to individual students' needs. The difference is that the student participates in the customization rather than the professor having to do it *a priori*, and by guessing what students want.

References

Emiliani, M.L. (2004), "Improving Business School Courses by Applying Lean Principles and Practices," *Quality Assurance in Education*, Vol. 12, No. 4, pp. 175-187

Emiliani, M.L. (2005), "Using Kaizen to Improve Graduate Business School Degree Programs," *Quality Assurance in Education*, Vol. 13, No. 1, pp. 37-52

Emiliani, B. (2008), *Practical Lean Leadership: A Strategic Leadership Guide for Executives*, The CLBM, LLC, Wethersfield, Connecticut, p. 10

Emiliani, B. (2015), *Lean University: A Guide to Renewal and Prosperity*, The CLBM, LLC, Wethersfield, Connecticut

Emiliani, B. (2015), *Lean Teaching: A Guide to Becoming a Better Teacher,* The CLBM, LLC, Wethersfield, Connecticut

Emiliani, B. (2018), *The Triumph of Classical Management Over Lean Management: How Tradition Prevails and What to Do About It*, Cubic, LLC, South Kingstown, RI

Toyota (2001), "The Toyota Way 2001," Toyota Motor Corporation, internal document, Toyota City, Japan, April

Notes

[1] Lean management is defined as: "A non-zero-sum principle-based management system focused on creating value for end-use customers and eliminating waste, unevenness, and unreasonableness using the scientific method" (Emiliani, 2008, p. 10).

[2] Kaizen is a Japanese word that means "change" (kai) "for the better" (zen). The context of change for the better is multilateral, meaning it must be non-zero-sum (win-win). Any change must be good for people within the process and for people upstream and downstream as well. To make an improvement at the expense of people or another process is not kaizen. Kaizen is often translated as "continuous improvement." This is one of two bedrock principles in Toyota management practice. The other is "respect for people" (Toyota, 2001), where people means stakeholders such as students, faculty and staff, payers, communities, industry, and others.

[3] Figures 1 and 6 are taken from a presentation titled (in Spanish): "El Toyota Way en Ventas y Mercadeo" ("The Toyota Way in Sales and Marketing"), 2007, by Toyota Global Knowledge Center http://slideplayer.es/slide/131475/ (accessed 22 September 2019), Slide No. 5, "¿Cuál escenario esta más identificado con el Toyota Way?" ("Which scenario is more identifiable with the Toyota Way?"). The equation $4 + 5 = \square$ symbolizes the existence of only one answer, while the equation $\square + \square = 9$ symbolizes the existence of infinite answers. In the context of higher education, this means there are infinite ways to achieve course learning objectives. Therefore, professors should never settle on one teaching method ($4 + 5 = \square$). Instead, they should continuously experiment with teaching methods, in trial-and-error fashion, to learn what works well and what does not work well at any given point in time ($\square + \square = 9$).

Authors

Lillian Evelyn Moller Gilbreth* (24 May 1878 – 2 January 1972) was an American psychologist, industrial engineer, consultant, educator, and early pioneer in applying psychology to time and motion studies. Gilbreth is considered to be the first industrial psychologist. She and her husband, Frank Bunker Gilbreth, were efficiency experts who contributed to the development of industrial engineering. The popular book *Cheaper by the Dozen* (1948), written by two of their children, Ernestine and Frank Jr., was later made into a feature film.

For more than forty years, Gilbreth's career combined psychology with the study of Scientific Management and industrial engineering. Gilbreth helped industrial engineers recognize the importance of the psychological dimensions of work. She was the first American engineer to create a synthesis of psychology and management – a concept she introduced at the Dartmouth College Conference on Scientific Management in 1911. In addition to jointly running Gilbreth Incorporated, their engineering consulting firm, Lillian and Frank wrote numerous books, papers, and trade magazine articles.

The Gilbreths believed that Scientific Management as formulated by Frederick Winslow Taylor was incomplete with respect to the human element on the shop floor and in management. The Gilbreths helped formulate a constructive critique of Taylorism that had the support of successful managers and academics. Their work grew to be very influential in the Unites States and internationally.

---

* This brief bio was taken from Wikipedia and edited to improve clarity and brevity (see https://en.wikipedia.org/wiki/Lillian_Moller_Gilbreth). Dr. Gilbreth's life and accomplishments have been extensively documented elsewhere.

M.L. "Bob" Emiliani is a professor in the School of Engineering, Science, and Technology at Connecticut State University in New Britain, Conn., where he teaches a course on leadership, a unique course that analyzes failures in management decision-making, as well as other courses.

Bob earned a Bachelor of Science degree in mechanical engineering from the University of Miami, a Master of Science degree in chemical engineering from the University of Rhode Island, and a Doctor of Philosophy degree in Engineering from Brown University.

He worked in the consumer products and aerospace industries for 15 years, beginning as a materials engineer. He has held management positions in engineering, manufacturing, and supply chain management at Pratt & Whitney. Bob joined academia in September 1999. While in academia, he developed the Lean teaching pedagogy and led activities to continuously improve master's degree programs.

Emiliani has authored or co-authored 20 books, four book chapters, and more than 45 peer-reviewed papers. He has received six awards for his writing.

Please visit bobemiliani.com and speedleadership.com

The John Hay Library on Prospect Street in
Providence, Rhode Island.